Effective Policing?

Effective Policing?

Implementation in Theory and Practice

Stuart Kirby
Lecturer in Criminology, Lancaster University, UK

palgrave
macmillan

First published 2013 by
PALGRAVE MACMILLAN

Palgrave Macmillan in the UK is an imprint of Macmillan Publishers Limited, registered in England, company number 785998, of Houndmills, Basingstoke, Hampshire RG21 6XS.

Palgrave Macmillan in the US is a division of St Martin's Press LLC, 175 Fifth Avenue, New York, NY 10010.

Palgrave Macmillan is the global academic imprint of the above companies and has companies and representatives throughout the world.

Palgrave® and Macmillan® are registered trademarks in the United States, the United Kingdom, Europe and other countries.

ISBN 978–1–137–02678–1

This book is printed on paper suitable for recycling and made from fully managed and sustained forest sources. Logging, pulping and manufacturing processes are expected to conform to the environmental regulations of the country of origin.

A catalogue record for this book is available from the British Library.

A catalog record for this book is available from the Library of Congress.

Typeset by MPS Limited, Chennai, India.

For my girls – Ann, Hannah and Kate

Contents

List of Tables

Preface

During 2010, I was present at a police HQ in the south-east of England when Sir Ronnie Flanagan (in his role as Chief HMIC) visited to present commendations. Addressing the group, he opened with a quote from Theodore Roosevelt:

> It is not the critic who counts: not the man who points out how the strong man stumbles or where the doer of deeds could have done better. The credit belongs to the man who is actually in the arena, whose face is marred by dust and sweat and blood, who strives valiantly, who errs and comes up short again and again, because there is no effort without error or shortcoming, but who knows the great enthusiasms, the great devotions, who spends himself for a worthy cause; who, at the best, knows, in the end, the triumph of high achievement, and who, at the worst, if he fails, at least fails while daring greatly, so that his place shall never be with those cold and timid souls who knew neither victory nor defeat.

The quote serves as a useful reminder that policing is a *hands-on* profession, and suffers the vagaries of any task that involves human interaction. However, it had special resonance for the police officers in the audience, who understood how challenging their work could be. They knew how spontaneous decisions, made in ambiguous circumstances, were later open to criticism by those who had the benefit of hindsight and who were unaware of the rapidly changing environment police officers operated within. This is not to suggest accountability should be avoided. As an institution the police is an extensive, powerful and costly institution to operate, and mismanagement can have significant ramifications. As Sir Ronnie Flanagan (2008: 4) said himself, 'policing is far too important to be left to the police alone'.

What the police officers listening to Sir Ronnie Flanagan would argue is that the layperson often only observes the final outcome of police activity, devoid of any explanation as to why it occurred. This book attempts to fill this gap and to provide a more thorough explanation of why some police activity is effective and some ineffective, at both organizational and operational levels. Two themes will emerge; the first is that the policing environment is complex. The second highlights the gulf between theories and practice in operational policing, highlighting the importance of implementation. Unfortunately, implementation is a relatively neglected area in both police practice and the academic literature although the concept is not new. The term 'praxis' (derived from the Greek word *Praxeis*) can be traced back to philosophers as influential as Aristotle, Kant and Marx, who used it to explore how theory is transformed into practice within a rapidly changing world (Seng, 1998). As individuals, we know from personal experience the effort and skill invested in bridging the gap between what we want to achieve and actually achieving it, and history is littered with individuals who were more accomplished at theory rather than practice. For example, Jean-Jacques Rousseau's (1712–78) writings on politics, nature and the value of marriage influenced many societies. Yet in reality, he lived unmarried with his servant in crowded Paris for 23 years and gave his children up for adoption (Garner et al., 2012).

Of course as citizens we may feel we already know a lot about the police. Kleinig (1996: 11) reminds us that 'As long as human societies have existed, the police function has been needed. Social co-ordination and harmony have never flourished without some form of executive authority'. It is also true that now, more than ever, the public are bombarded with information concerning the police via fictional television drama, 'fly on the wall' documentaries, select committees and news reports. The police are therefore quickly identified in generic terms as wearing a uniform with some level of insignia, carrying some means of personal protection, driving around in highly visible vehicles to provide 24-hour protection and dealing authoritatively with incidents. However, as Bittner (1974: 17) cleverly observed, 'the police are the best known but least understood of public institutions'. Indeed when this superficial level of analysis is stripped back, there is a general lack of understanding as to what they actually do and why they do it in a particular way.

Why would this book, sitting alongside so many other books on the subject of policing, add fresh insight? It is at this point I need to break cover and reveal my methodology. For 30 years I was a UK police officer, dividing my service between uniform and detective work and retiring at the rank of Detective Chief Superintendent. During my policing service I sat on national committees, worked with many police officers from other UK forces and also met (and sometimes worked alongside) officers from Europe, North America, Australia, United Arab Emirates and China. Since becoming a university lecturer in 2007 I have continued to concentrate on the subject of the police, having been able to research the subject extensively and communicate with 'policing' academics from all over the world. To ensure my views remained current when writing this book, I also conducted numerous formal interviews with senior police officers, community safety leaders and academics from the UK, USA, Australia and the Netherlands (see Acknowledgements). All examples and quotes in the book are authentic and have been chosen because they are representative of general situations and opinions of a much wider group of police officers.

Hopefully, the book can be read and interpreted at a number of levels. For students of policing it provides an overview of many theories and arguments surrounding contemporary policing, with a special focus on 'implementation'. For practitioners it shows how a more careful adherence to an evidence-based approach could improve the effectiveness and efficiency of any police agency. The six chapters (and conclusion) provide a wide base for these discussions. Chapter 1 deconstructs the police operational environment to show what a complex arena this can be. Chapter 2 focuses on the fundamental building blocks for any effective law enforcement agency: leadership, resource and performance management, operational policing models and the relationship with the public. Chapters 3 to 6 deal with 'the business of policing' covering such subjects as the reduction and investigation of crime, critical incidents (criminal use of firearms and serious public disorder), organized crime and terrorism. The conclusion considers the question of police effectiveness before going on to consider the significance of implementation failure. It argues this area of policing deserves a much higher profile from academics and practitioners, as increased performance in this area would deliver significant improvements to the effectiveness and efficiency of the police service.

Acknowledgements

There were many people who assisted with this book. Unfortunately space (and my memory) will not allow me to thank everyone. My particular thanks to Ian McPherson, Michael Barton and Nick Tilley who, as well as assisting me with this book, have helped develop my views on policing over many years. More generally my gratitude goes to the police officers, academics and practitioners associated with the POP Center, USA, and to Louise Porter and Jeanine Nas who enthusiastically arranged interviews for me. Finally, a thank you to all those listed below who gave up their valuable time to provide interviews (listed in alphabetical order).

Chief Constable Mike Barton (Durham, UK)
Deputy Superintendent Nora Baston (Boston, USA)
Mr Alan Beckley (Charles Sturt University, Manly, AUS)
Commissaris Jan Biemolt (National Programme Board, Chiefs of Police, NL)
Commissaris Rick de Boer (Twente, NL)
Commander Bob Broadhurst (Metropolitan Police, UK)
Professor Simon Bronnett (Griffith University, Brisbane, AUS)
Chief Constable Mike Cunningham (Staffordshire, UK)
Ms Janet Evans (Australian Crime Commission, AUS)
Commissaris Ann Marie Feije (District Commander, Haarlem, NL)
Chief Constable Steve Finnigan (Lancashire, UK)
Detective Chief Superintendent Graham Gardner (Serious Organised Crime Agency, UK)
Assistant Chief Constable Jerry Graham (Cumbria, UK)
Police Sergeant Neil Henson (Metropolitan Police Service, UK)
Dr Victoria Herrington (Australian Institute for Police Management, AUS)
Chief Constable Bernard Lawson (Cumbria, UK)
Mr David Mallaby (University of Central Lancashire, UK)
Mr Adrian McAllister (CEO Police Ombudsman, Police Service of Northern Ireland (PSNI))
Ms Karen McCluskey (Co-director, Scottish Violence Reduction Unit)
Mr Ian McPherson (partner at KPMG, former Assistant Commissioner, Metropolitan Police Service)
Mr Jan ter Mors (National Intelligence Model Programme Manager, NL)

Dr Jan Nap (Consultant for the Police Academy, NL)
Ms Jeanine Nas (Senior Advisor, Police Business Improvement, NL)
Sir Denis O'Connor (Former Chief, HMIC)
Commissaris Peter van Os (Deputy Director of knowledge and research, National Police Academy, NL)
Dr Louise Porter (Griffith University, Brisbane, AUS)
Professor Tim Prenzler (Griffith University, Brisbane, AUS)
Assistant Chief Constable Andy Rhodes (Lancashire, UK)
Chief Superintendent Mark Roberts (Greater Manchester Police, UK)
Inspector Jason Saunders (Queensland Police, AUS)
Commissaris Ab Spaan (National Programme for Business Improvement, NL)
Chief Constable Sara Thornton (Thames Valley, UK)
Professor Nick Tilley (University College London, UK)
Mr Michael Tonge (Cumbria University, former Chief Constable, Gwent Police, UK)
Ms Julie Wartell (Consultant crime analyst, USA)
Deputy Chief Constable Chris Weigh (Lancashire, UK)

1

'There Are Police and There Are Police': Exploring the Complexity of the Police Operating Framework

Introduction

> In moving between police forces in England and Wales, it is most striking that whilst they are all essentially engaged in the provision of the same service, they all feel very different in terms of their attitude and culture. That difference is not just between the large urban forces and smaller rural forces, each force has its own distinct cultural identity. This culture and attitude not only affects the way staff in each force relate to each other, it also affects the way in which they deal with the public they serve.
>
> Chief Officer, UK police

Addressing delegates at a recent conference on policing, Professor Herman Goldstein (2012) used the phrase 'there are police, and there are police'. This cryptic phrase highlights the diversity found within policing, whether across different countries, different police agencies or even within a single agency. How can this level of diversity exist? Mawby (1999) argues police agencies can be differentiated at an international level on the grounds of legitimacy, function and structure. The British police, for example, obtain their legitimacy on the basis of public consent, which separates them from other agencies that rely on the support of a government dictatorship. Secondly, in Britain the services (or function) provided by the police are operationally independent of the government, and range in scope from tackling organized crime to advising on neighbourhood disputes. This may differ from other countries that either restrict the service they offer or expand on them to include such matters as border control or the collection of taxes. Finally, the British police adhere to a local structure, whereas other countries (such as Japan) favour a national structure. Of course there are many variations; for example, although the USA has implemented a local approach, it in fact has 12,766 local police agencies, 3,067 sheriff's departments and 1,481 special jurisdiction agencies, creating greater co-ordination problems than that of the UK (Mastrofski & Willis, 2010).

Unfortunately, Mawby's useful analysis only takes us so far and does not explain why some police agencies may differ within the same country. For example, some are shown to be more susceptible to allegations of corruption or the unlawful use of Force, whilst others appear more effective in reducing crime and improving public confidence. This variation can even be seen within individual police agencies, with some departments or units favouring a specific strategy, utilizing specialist squads more frequently, or using technology and specialist equipment more effectively. This chapter seeks to explore the reasons behind this diversity and to explain how it impacts upon effectiveness. To do so it constructs a simple framework showing how a variety of external and internal factors can affect policing, dependent on the context. Furthermore, because numerous permutations can be generated within this framework, it is able to explain why diversity in purpose, style and effectiveness can be observed across and within police agencies. It also explains why the implementation of policing initiatives can be driven off course. The reader will notice that themes highlighted in this chapter will be constantly repeated throughout this book, as different facets of policing are discussed.

Section 1: External factors that influence the effectiveness of the police

The police as an institution reflect society; whilst external influences have always affected the police, this section will show how these changes are now occurring more rapidly and with greater intensity. In specific terms, this section will list five external factors that combine to make contemporary society an increasingly challenging environment to police.

(a) Late modernity and the contemporary policing environment – keeping pace with change

At a macro level, political, economic, social, technological, environmental and legal changes are constantly occurring in society. These influences affect how the police are perceived, how they are organized and how they operate. However, it is only when perceived from a distance that the full impact of this evolution can be understood. Commentators such as Garland (2001), Lea (2002) and Young (2007) argue that following a relatively stable period between the 18th century and the 1970s, society started to alter with increased speed. This latter period, variably referred to as *post, late* or *liquid modernity, late capitalism* or the *risk society* became synonymous with globalization, privatization, capitalism and the improved mobility of people, goods and information across international borders (Young, 2007). Whereas the accumulation of wealth was able to support continuity and social cohesion in the 19th century, this was unfortunately no longer the case in the latter part of the 20th century (Lea, 2002). Instead, developments such as individualism, consumerism, mobility and the move from manufacturing to a service/information-based economy all conspired to fragment society.

These high-level changes have affected society in many ways, including the way society perceives and delivers crime control. Garner (2001) argues that the period of late modernity has been characterized by a continued sense of crisis, coupled with a view that the public can and should be protected at all times. This has led to rational and systematic responses to quantify and counteract risk, which have ultimately served to reduce individual discretion and increase the level of control on the population (Moss, 2009). Garner (2001) describes the emergence of a 'new punitiveness', as populist demands for more retribution and less rehabilitation are answered. Indeed, in recent years, prison levels have increased throughout much of the world (whilst crime has been reducing), and this is particularly true of the USA, where, at its height, 1 in 34 of the US population were, at any one time, either in prison, on probation or parole (Young, 1997), a situation that has now started to ease as the financial cost becomes prohibitive in times of increased austerity.

Other changes, such as increased mobility, have also led to new policing demands. Whereas in 1950, Britons travelled an average of five miles a day, this figure has now increased to 30 miles, with the next generation expected to travel 60 miles per day (Moynah & Worsley, 2000). Urry (2007: 4) reveals that in 1950 there were 25 million arrivals at international airports, whilst in 2010, that figure is in the range of 1 billion. This movement has created an increasingly congested, urbanized, multi-cultural population that has led to numerous policing demands. One of these has been increased community polarization on grounds of affluence and race, leading in turn to increased community tension and protest. Furthermore, the advent of low-cost air travel has transformed the pattern of drug trafficking, people trafficking and counterfeiting, whilst virtual networks have increased the level of e-crime, such as pornography and fraud. Other commentators have illustrated the impact of increased consumerism. At a general level, personal choice has become increasingly important, leading to more sophisticated consumers who expect the police to provide tailored responses akin to those observed in the private sector (i.e. improved response times and enhanced customer service). At an operational level, the regeneration of towns and cities has led to a 24-hour society where consumers benefit from increased retail opportunities and a vibrant night-time economy, which again has increased and fragmented the demand profile for policing.

As society evolves, policing must adapt to its challenges. Adherence to local models of policing in Britain (and other parts of the world) means that individual police forces respond in different ways, with different levels of professionalism and different degrees of responsiveness. However, as the next element illustrates, it is no longer just the police who respond to these challenges.

(b) Partnership and plural policing

When evaluating the effectiveness of the police we should remind ourselves that the police as an institution are only one element of policing. In fact, 'policing' refers to the general process of preventing and detecting crime, and maintaining order, which many agencies or individuals engage in. This resonates with one of Peel's principles, upon which the Metropolitan Police was formed in 1829:

> The police, at all times, should maintain a relationship with the public that gives reality to the historic tradition that the police are the public and the public are the police; the police being only members of the public who are paid to give full-time attention to duties which are incumbent upon every citizen in the interests of community welfare and existence.
>
> (Lentz & Chaires, 2007)

Partnership working is described as a 'co-operative relationship between two or more organizations (that are otherwise independent) to achieve a common goal or outcome' (Berry et al., 2011:13). Community safety problems are often complex, and responsibilities for such issues often lie with a number of different organizations. Indeed Goldstein (1990) argued that the police cannot ultimately be effective in reducing crime and disorder, as they lack the tools with which to solve the underlying causes of the problems that confront them. For example, persistent offenders may require assistance from health services to control their drug or alcohol problem, or they may require employment/housing services to help establish some stability in their lifestyle. This means the police can play a more effective role in sustainable crime and disorder reduction when they act in partnership with other statutory, business or voluntary partners. However, the process of working in partnership with others is not simple. The Audit Commission (1998) set out the following key ingredients of good partnership working:

- Clear shared objectives
- Realistic plans and timetable for reaching objectives
- Commitment from partners to acknowledge the community safety partnership work when undertaking mainstream activities
- Deciding a framework of responsibility and accountability
- High levels of trust between partners
- Realistic ways of measuring partnership achievements

The police as an institution have a long history of working in partnership with other individuals and agencies, and this approach has had mixed success. As studies show, multi-agency partnership increases implementation challenges. For example, even in Britain where the Crime & Disorder Act 1998 sets out the statutory requirements for public sector agencies to work together, numerous multi-agency inspections have shown that partners may inadvertently work towards different objectives, whilst leadership becomes ambiguous, and information sharing can be limited (Audit Commission, 1998; Home Office, 2007).

Notwithstanding these challenges, the importance of partnership has been promoted as an effective means of doing business. This is especially true as more commercial agencies have become associated with policing, often referred to as the 'mixed economy' or 'pluralization' of policing. Garland (2001) argues that this change has occurred through 'responsibilization', whereby the state continues to play an important regulatory role (steering) but transfers the responsibility for personal security onto the citizen (rowing). Within this context four issues are pertinent. First, there has been an increased sense of public insecurity causing citizens to supplement public policing with private services. Second, the increase of consumerism has meant that there are now large areas of private space and property to be protected (e.g. shopping malls). Third, the public police are often viewed as overpriced and are only used for a minority of the tasks they are trained to deliver, whilst routine tasks can easily be performed by a less expensive workforce (Johnston, 1992). Finally, globalization has enabled many international corporations to amass significant power and resources, allowing them to dictate personal security measures and standards across international boundaries. The result of these four factors is that many countries have passed on critical functions (i.e. surveillance, security and immigration control), to private companies, whilst extra security services have been commissioned for the benefit and reassurance of the private consumer.

Loader (2000) summarizes the multi-faceted nature of this mixed economy by outlining five dimensions of plural policing:

I. Policing *by* government (traditional public-funded police forces, i.e. NYPD, Metropolitan Police Service)
II. Policing *through* government: those activities co-ordinated and funded by the government but delivered by agencies other than the police service (local government-funded street wardens and anti-social behaviour officers)
III. Policing *above* government (transnational police agencies such as Interpol, Europol, United Nations)
IV. Policing *beyond* government: activities funded and delivered privately by citizens and corporations (i.e. private security – guarding stadiums and shopping malls)
V. Policing *below* government: voluntary and community activities (such as neighbourhood watch and community support groups)

Perhaps the largest transformation has been in the private security industry, which has expanded dramatically since the mid-1980s. A recent examination of private security companies (PSCs) across 70 countries established that PSC personnel outnumber public police by 1.8:1, which if extrapolated would mean there are approximately 255 million PSC staff across the world (Small Arms Survey, 2011). Other studies have shown that specific companies are gaining a considerable foothold in this field – for example G4S is reported to employ 530,000 staff in 115 countries (Abrahamsen & Williams, 2009: 2). These numbers vary greatly according to geography, with the public police remaining in the majority for 56% of the surveyed countries. This includes Europe, and in particular the UK, with studies reporting a proportion of 0.9:1. However, countries that show the public police to be in the minority include India (5:1), South Africa (2.6:1), USA (2.3:1), Australia (2.2:1), China (1.9:1) and the Russian Federation (1.3:1).

Although private policing generates significant benefits, there are also concerns surrounding its expansion. First of all, if a private security firm fails to deliver contracted services, then the public sector are asked to intervene, a situation observed when G4S announced their inability to deliver sufficient security staff immediately before the London Olympics in 2012. Secondly, private security agencies practise less oversight and accountability in comparison to the public police. Finally, there are also concerns surrounding social justice, due to the possibility of people being refused admittance to general commercial areas based on their appearance and background. In summary, it appears the police are no longer the monopolistic guardian of public security, as a combination of police, wardens, private security staff and citizens all assist in this task. It is therefore important, before judging the effectiveness of the public police, to establish where their responsibility and accountability actually starts and finishes.

(c) The role of the police and how they are measured

Though in most industries statistics can be monitored in order to track levels of efficiency and achievement, it is difficult to judge the effectiveness of the police without knowing their purpose or role. For example, we know the effectiveness of a car manufacturing company, as annual reports reveal the level of their inputs (staff numbers and operational costs), outputs (number of manufactured cars and car parts) and outcomes (profits and share-price). However, the simple question 'What are the Police for' has been subject to intense debate for many years. The British police originated in 1829 with aims of preventing crime, the protection of life and property, and the preservation of public tranquillity. In 2007, the British Home Secretary (John Reid) added the 'detection of crime' and 'bringing offenders to justice' onto this list, leading to the first ever UK National Policing Plan (later called the Community Safety Plan 2008–11), which had the following priorities:

- Reduce crime and focus on more serious violence, serious acquisitive crime, alcohol-related crime and disorder, and antisocial behaviour
- Increase public confidence and satisfaction with the police
- Work in partnership to deliver a more effective, transparent and responsive Criminal Justice System
- Work jointly to tackle serious and organized crime and to provide other protective services
- Work with and through local communities to disrupt, deter and respond to terrorism and violent extremism

- Make the best use of resources to achieve efficiency and productivity improvements

These priorities (a mix of inputs, outputs and outcomes) identify the diversity of police work and will probably be replicated in many places across the world. Bittner (1970) argues that two critical issues differentiate the police from other organizations: the fact that they have large numbers of staff constantly available to deal with any situation and their ability to use legitimate force when appropriate. These factors mean that the police can be viewed as the agency of last resort, capable of responding to most situations. Newburn and Reiner (2007) state that the police deliver a diverse range of services that includes reassuring the public, peacekeeping, state security, order maintenance, crime investigation and crime reduction. However, these services are constantly increasing as society evolves and generates new demands, such as social media, environmental disaster, concern about sex offenders and the threat of terrorism. Wright (2002) argues that the police have responded by becoming more specialized and fragmented, no longer operating within Peel's vision as an omni-competent group of officers dealing with the simple aims of crime prevention and public tranquillity. In essence a more disjointed model exists, as the police deal with a myriad of objectives.

Attempts to rationalize and simplify police services have proved difficult due to ambiguity surrounding the police mission. In 1995 when the British government inquired as to which services could be outsourced, the analysis concluded there was 'little scope for the police service ... to withdraw completely from large areas of current police work' (Posen, 1995: 5). However, the call by some political and police leaders to simplify the mission by focusing on crime fighting continues (May, 2010a), even though studies consistently show crime to be a small proportion of the police role. A Home Office study in 1982 found that only 18% of citizen calls resulted in a crime report, a finding supported by the BCS 1998 (Mirrlees-Black et al. 1998). Even more recently, Cheshire police found just 9% of their citizen calls led to a recorded crime (Caulkin, 2011), a finding replicated by the Dutch police in Haarlem (Nas, 2012). These studies have recently been contradicted by Her Majesty's Inspectorate of Constabulary HMIC (2012b) who, using much wider parameters, argued that 80% of calls *potentially* relate to crime. For instance, calls relating to antisocial behaviour, missing children and injury from road collisions were all interpreted in this vein (although they almost never result in a recorded crime). Indeed this has been confirmed by the UK Home Secretary, who said,

> I think for too long, too many people have seen crime as a strict Home Office definition of recorded crime. When I talk about fighting crime, I do not mean a narrow category of activity. Cutting crime means catching criminals but it also means preventing crime. And preventing crime means intervening early in domestic disputes to prevent escalation, it means supporting the vulnerable person who could become a victim of crime, it means tackling anti-social behaviour, it means providing effective public order policing.
>
> (Teresa May, 2012)

Whatever the definition new recruits soon find out that most policing requests are mundane and complicated, with no obvious solution – therefore discretion, rather than clear rules and the use of enforcement, lies at the heart of what they do. Of course this ambiguity presents difficulty when judging police effectiveness. If the assessor can't define the exact role, how can performance be judged? Furthermore, is it fair to judge the police on one particular objective (i.e. crime) if they are expected to invest resources into a myriad of other services (e.g. road safety)? Finally, in practice, the leaders of individual law enforcement agencies may favour and emphasize different elements of their work, again generating differences between organizations. This conundrum is further exacerbated by the increasing influence of stakeholders.

(d) The emergence of stakeholders: Politics, the media and other influences

The term 'stakeholders' emerged in the management literature of the 1980s, with Freeman (1984: 46) defining it as 'any group or individual who can affect or is affected by the achievement of the organization's objectives'. In policing, like other public sector organizations, stakeholders are varied and can disagree between themselves. They exert influence not only on what the police should do but also on how they do it; for example, the ethics surrounding the delivery of police services is seen as a critical factor. In an era of risk management and continuous improvement, the police are subjected to more invasive stakeholder scrutiny than at any time in their history; indeed a recent survey showed that the British police are answerable to 17 statutory or government-related oversight agencies (HMIC, 2010c). In addition to this, police chiefs also meet with a variety of local stakeholders (e.g. church leaders, business people and landowners) who will attempt to influence them in a particular way. However, during the research for this book, police officers across the world consistently highlighted two forms of stakeholders that were making the environment much more complex to operate within: politicians and the media.

Politicians

The government (politicians), in many countries, can be viewed as the biggest stakeholder in relation to the police. The concept of crime is *socially influenced* and *politically constructed*, as the government determine not only which acts are criminal but also who should be defined as criminal. They influence how crime is identified, control the resources that tackle it, establish (or influence) policing priorities and formulate the legislation that the police are required to enforce. Of course this makes legislation inconsistent across different parts of the world, with some countries banning the drinking of alcohol, though allowing child brides (and vice versa). Furthermore, often the perception of crime changes over time, as society adapts to new experiences.

This relationship forges an undeniable link between politics and law and order. In the UK prior to 1970 there was little difference between the two main political parties, who agreed on a 'liberal progressive' ideology, supporting community-based, rehabilitative policies (Downes & Morgan, 1994). However, in the 1979 election, the Conservative Party used 'the fight against crime' as a major policy theme in their decisive election win. This was followed by the 1997 Labour Party whose iconic election slogan, 'tough on crime, tough on the causes of crime', also became associated with a successful campaign. Since then the rhetoric of *toughness* and *zero tolerance* has become endemic in politics, drawing the police into a period in which criminalization has increased (i.e. the use of anti-social behaviour orders (ASBOs), increased use of fixed penalty notices, police powers and criminal legislation). Stan Cohen (1985: 41–43) explains this process as 'net widening'; in using the analogy of fishing, he asks that we consider the entrance to the deviancy control system as a gigantic fishing net. In this case, deviants are the fish, whilst the size, reach and operation of this net dictates what and how much is caught. Using this analogy, Cohen and others argue that the net has widened and the mesh thinned, resulting in greater quantities and varieties of fish (offenders) being trapped. This is certainly true of the UK; Prime et al. (2001) have shown that a third of men aged 46 years (or over) have at least one conviction for a standard list offence. Similarly, even though crime has been falling, there has been an increase in the prison population in much of the developed world (in England and Wales it has increased from 45,600 in 1988 to 86,048 by June 2012 (Davies et al., 2005: 379; Ministry of Justice, 2012).

Of course politicians can also influence policing by more subtle means. Deciding where to target grants, instigate public inquiries or focus organizational reform (i.e. the recent introduction of Police and Crime Commissioners in Britain or the move to a National Police Force in the Netherlands) will all influence the police in particular directions. Similarly, this influence can also be extended to local politicians who view law and order through their own particular lens. Indeed it appears apparent that politics will continue to impact upon policing for some considerable time.

Media

The way the media has transformed into a major stakeholder is also worthy of mention. Chibnall (1977) generated a classic checklist of what makes a good media story, which included:

- Immediacy (news is highly perishable)
- Dramatic
- Personal (it focuses on individuals)
- It can be simplified (often described in dichotomies – good/bad, soft/hard)
- It provides titillation
- It is conventional (follows well-used scenarios, i.e. rogue cop, tragic victim)
- It uses structured access (experts are asked to comment)
- It has a novelty factor

Leishman and Mason (2003) point out that these issues have intensified as the media has grown and become more competitive, leading to the police–media relationship becoming increasingly symbiotic. Whilst the media rely on the police for information, they know that sympathetic reports on the police may increase public confidence, whereas highlighting individual or organizational incompetence will have the reverse effect. As such, Leishman and Mason (2003) point out that the police have become more proactive with the media, investing heavily to ensure that their staff perform more effectively in an information-driven world. Of course this relationship is taking place in an increasingly complex environment. An increase in mobile communication has allowed individuals to instantly capture news (in photographic, video and audio format) and to broadcast these images across the world through various social networking sites. Although a proactive media increases the transparency and accountability of the police, concerns have emerged surrounding the way certain journalists and police officers handle information. The UK-based Leverson inquiry shone a spotlight on the multifarious nature of this relationship, which culminated in criminal charges and resignation of some of those involved. However, as we will see throughout this book, the media continue to be a significant influence on the police.

The emergence of the expert critic

Before closing this section, a brief mention should be given to the 'critical expert' who has grown in significance in recent years. Government oversight bodies (i.e. HMIC, Independent Police Complaints Agency, National Police Improvement Agency), as well as the media, rely on professional critics to analyse, interpret and provide recommendations. Although experts are used legitimately and often facilitate improved standards, their interpretation of events can be influenced by a number of factors. First, there is a bias towards criticism; a review bereft of recommendations is of limited value, and a media report without reproach isn't particularly newsworthy. Second, any individual who makes a judgement on another can be affected by the fundamental attribution error (Jones, 1979; Nisbett & Ross, 1980). In this process the actors (in this context the police) are more likely to explain their behaviour on external or situational factors (e.g. the offender was unpredictable), whilst the observer (expert critic) is more likely to explain it through the internal or dispositional factors of those they observe (e.g. the police hadn't prepared sufficiently). As the observer is not privy to all the elements affecting the actor, they may exhibit less understanding as to why the outcome occurred. Further, critics will often use the best possible response (rather than a satisfactory one) as their baseline, often providing opinion without concern for other existing demands. Finally, critics have the benefit of reflection and hindsight, allowing them to give a considered view – a luxury not always enjoyed by the police. Indeed during this research many senior and experienced officers despaired at some of the critics, with one making the point, 'if it was so easy why didn't they do it that way when they were an operational officer'.

(e) The operational environment and the conscious opponent

The final external element that differentiates police agencies is the operational policing environment; here we will focus on two elements: the geographic community and the conscious opponent. It is clear to see that communities aren't generated equally. Just as crime does not occur randomly, many communities can be differentiated on factors such as deprivation, education, employment and population density. Often, urban areas that suffer the most deprivation are also associated with the most crime, although the greatest problems can be concentrated in particular hot-spots (Reece-Smith & Kirby, 2013; Hirschfield et al., 1995). Early studies in Chicago argued that there were socio-structural and cultural conditions to communities, which produced a neighbourhood effect (Shaw & Mackay, 1942; Bottoms, 2012: 451). Extending this principle Rosenbaum et al. (1986) and Sampson (2006) developed the theory of *collective efficacy*, defined as 'the institutional ability to achieve what a group or community collectively wishes to achieve' (Bottoms, 2012: 453). This incorporates two points: first, the willingness of citizens to intervene for the community benefit (i.e. challenging children caught spraying graffiti) and, second, the level of cohesion and trust amongst that specific community that supports pro-social activity (Sampson & Raudenbush, 1999: 612). In this way, residents with a strong sense of cohesion and who would be willing to challenge individuals engaging in specific crimes could be seen to incorporate a high level of collective efficacy and play an important role in the socialization of other residents (especially children). These neighbourhoods are associated with lower levels of crime and disorder, and presumably the residents that occupy them would be more willing to assist the police.

The second point focuses more on individuals, specifically those who oppose the police. Sparrow (2008) in his discussion of risk in regulatory organizations points out the academic literature that focuses on the natural, biological or man-made threats that emerge from technical systems, fails to explore the impact made by conscious opponents (i.e. enemies or criminals). A conscious opponent is different to other threats, as he or she can withdraw when initially obstructed, only to return at a later stage more educated and emboldened, armed with a new approach to circumnavigate defences. Ekblom (2003) has previously highlighted this adaptive behaviour, explaining that offenders and law enforcement personnel are in an *arms race* constantly looking for ways to outdo each other. This concept will be returned to later when the book discusses criminal offenders; however, at present it is sufficient to acknowledge it as a variable that fails to challenge many other organizations. In summary, different police forces will police varied operational environments, including communities, families and individuals who can be viewed on a continuum between supportive and antagonistic, and who will have an impact on their ability to deliver their services.

Section summary

In summary this section has shown that a variety of external factors influence the police. These emanate from the extensive challenges caused by the pace of change in society to the more specific requirements requested by stakeholders or members of the community. What they each have in common is that they require the police agency to change the way they work in a strategic or tactical way. Due to the localized and individual nature of policing, the response to these challenges can differ. However, there are also internal factors that conspire to differentiate police agencies and police practitioners, and it is to the attention of these that the chapter now turns.

Section 2: Internal factors that influence the effectiveness of the police

This section will continue to describe the factors that differentiate police organizations and that therefore influence police effectiveness. This section will focus on internal influences, which the police have more control of.

(f) The police organizational culture and the use of discretion

Organizational (also referred to as occupational) culture is defined as the 'basic assumptions and beliefs that are shared by members of an organization, that operate unconsciously, and define in a basic taken-for-granted way, an organization's view of itself and its environment' (Schein, 1992: 6). It is a phenomenon observed across many professional institutions. Shappell and Weigmann (2004), for example, found that nearly 50% of all US Navy/Marine Corps flight accidents in the late 1990s were associated with safety rule violations, a factor observed much less in the United States Air Force, who had a culture of zero tolerance regarding this behaviour.

Organizational culture has been a major area of research in policing since Banton (1964) highlighted differences between urban and rural officers, and Skolnick (1966) described how officers developed a working personality to accommodate the frustrations of the Criminal Justice System. Wilson (1968) also established that organizational culture could vary between US police forces, based upon departmental policy choices as well as varying social and political contexts. Since then numerous commentators have researched this theme, including Reiner (1992: 109), who defined *police culture* as the 'values, norms, perspectives and craft rules, which informs police conduct'. Reiner (2000) later set out seven core components of street cop culture:

1. Wider mission: officers see themselves engaged in a wider purpose, with the most exciting areas (enforcement) being the most prized.
2. Suspicion: a mental outlook generated through the type of work police officers conduct.
3. Isolation/solidarity: which is generated both by shift work and the type of work they do.
4. Conservatism: police officers tend to inhabit a morally conservative world and are generally resistant to change.
5. Machismo: the institution is often reported as sexist and male dominated.
6. Racial prejudice: often reported as problematic behaviour.
7. Pragmatic: police officers exhibit a 'can do' mentality.

There are many examples to show how officers adhere to the informal values of their police environment, even when these are in conflict with the formal values of their organization. The most serious ramification of this phenomenon is corruption; indeed the Fitzgerald inquiry (1989: 307), examining police corruption in the Australian Queensland Police, commented, 'Much of the focus of concern in this inquiry, and in this report, has been upon the structural, organizational and cultural malaises of the Police Force.' In fact, Newburn (2007: 625) argues the 'rotten apple' theory has all but been discredited, pointing out that corruption has been a distinct aspect of organizational culture research. He makes a number of general observations, including the following:

- Police corruption is pervasive, continuing and not bounded by rank.
- The boundary between 'corrupt' and 'non-corrupt' activities is difficult to define, primarily because it is an ethical problem.
- The causes of corruption include factors intrinsic to police work, with the nature of police organizations and their 'culture' facilitating such opportunities.
- Some areas of policing (e.g. vice and drugs) are more prone to corruption than others.

Neyroud and Beckley (2001) extend this analysis by explaining that corruption has many forms and can change over time. They suggest that the move towards *intelligence-led* policing and *crime fighting* can lead to officers becoming more aware of illegal activity, thereby increasing their frustration at the system's inability to deliver justice. This has generated the potential for *noble cause corruption*, where officers attempt to circumnavigate a flawed system to convict more offenders. In this endeavour, covert tactics such as surveillance, undercover officers and the use of informants have led to various forms of unethical practice (i.e. entrapment).

Organizational culture has long been associated with a variety of unethical behaviour, including racism, sexism and homophobia (Rowe, 2008). As policing is traditionally an insular institution dominated by white males, concern has often been raised regarding the equality of policing and its legitimacy across minority communities. This insularity coupled with the level of discretion available to police officers makes it vulnerable to bias, specifically in the abuse or withdrawal of specific powers. For example, sexist officers may be less enthusiastic to arrest male domestic violence offenders or empathize with a female victim, whilst a white officer may disproportionally stop and search individuals from a minority ethnic background. Further organizational culture can also transfer into internal decision-making, with sexism or racism affecting the internal progression of female/minority officers (for example, it wasn't until 1977 when the first UK female Chief Constable was appointed, and 2004 when the first UK Chief Constable from a minority ethnic background was appointed). However, the ramifications of organizational culture and discretion can be seen in wider policing environments. For example, studies have shown that police officers will modify their approach to speeding motorists according to their personal characteristics and behaviour when stopped (Engel & Calnon, 2004; Schafer & Mastrofski, 2005). Waddington (1999) is one of the few commentators who talks positively about police culture; he argues that as policing can often be dangerous and confrontational, distinct values emerge as a coping mechanism. Rather than being deviant it works as a release mechanism and rarely materializes as unprofessional behaviour. Similarly, Chan (1997) argues that police culture should not be viewed as a universal and static phenomenon, as the police continue to change in relation to ongoing political, legal and organizational context.

In summary, police organizational culture emerges in different forms at different times. The phenomenon is particularly relevant when explaining police effectiveness as well as the diversity between and within police agencies. In a recent UK study, Westmarland (2013: 9) highlighted the improvements in ethical behaviour, pointing out, 'police officers have a strong and unfailing moral compass' when it comes to actions and beliefs; showing many officers would report colleagues 'misdemeanours'. However, the study also illustrated that whilst officers were very likely to report a colleague for dishonesty, only 68% thought they would report someone for the unlawful use of force. The impact of a small minority of unethical officers can have a disproportionate effect on police reputation, and it appears this problem is enduring. Between 2008 and 2011, the Independent Police Complaints Commission (IPCC) revealed that police forces in England and Wales recorded 8,542 allegations of corruption. During that period, 87 officers faced internal misconduct hearings, and a further 18 were prosecuted in the courts, of which 13 were found guilty (*The Guardian*, 24 May 2012). Those sanctioned included a mix of line and senior officers (including Chief Officers); therefore it appears organizational culture will continue to feature prominently in police research. Critical to the delivery of a positive organizational culture is the role of police leaders.

(g) The police leader

Police leadership is widely observed to be one of the most important factors (if not the most important factor) when delivering effective policing services. Flanagan (2008: 72) states, 'In any sector, where people form the core of a business leadership is key; ensuring that the "central nervous system" of our forces is operating to the best of its potential is vital. To complement this we also need to enable and support our frontline officers to act autonomously where appropriate, making sound decisions and feeling responsible for those decisions.' This sentiment was supported by Southgate (1983: 58) who after working for an extended period with a UK police force concluded, 'Some human relations problems result not from the inadequacies of individuals, but from the rules, procedures and structures within which they have to work.'

The academic literature is saturated with studies related to police leadership, and it may be useful to visit some of the main points prior to examining the concept in practice. Leadership is defined as a process involving influence within a group context, which involves the attainment of a goal or goals (Northouse, 2007). Bennis and Townsend (1995) differentiate between leadership and management, asserting that the former involves 'doing the right things' as opposed to management which involves 'doing things right'. Clearly both are needed, as political and police leaders need to focus on both correct priorities and on delivering services in an efficient and effective manner. Although there are many theories explaining effective leadership characteristics, many of these can be understood as a dichotomy contrasting *charismatic* leaders (those who form a vision for the way forward and energize others to implement it) with *instrumental* or *transactional* leaders (who concentrate more on improving existing systems and activity) (Kets de Vries, 1994). These views have some similarity with Kirton's (1989) description of *innovation* versus *adaption* leaders, which focuses on the level of creativity possessed by the leader. Adaptors work within existing norms and use a transactional style to improve efficiency within the existing policy framework, whilst innovators look for new opportunities and solutions by breaking away from the status quo (Burnes, 2000; Kreitner et al., 2002). Studies show that meaningful police reform often requires a transformational rather than a transactional leader, coupled with innovation – a quality often associated with charismatic leadership behaviour (Kotter, 2007). However, Peters and Waterman (1982: 287) argue the most effective strategic leaders are those able to master both approaches – being able to see the bigger picture, whilst also being able to grasp operational detail. These leaders can be both strategic and action orientated, maintain credibility through significant change, and communicate in ways that can be understood by front line staff. Indeed Whitfield et al. (2008: 218) argue that leaders need to provide functional and directive leadership, ensuring correct planning, organization and communication as well as supportive leadership in the form of accessibility, inspiration, empathy and appreciation. Similarly, commentators such as Kantner et al. (1992) highlight the importance of both 'bold strokes' (key strategic decisions that make an immediate but short-term impact) and 'long marches' (less impact but nevertheless required to sustain organizational change). Finally, Kotter (1990) argues that whatever their approach, leaders should demonstrate consistency between words and deeds.

The studies show that police leadership is complex, and it becomes more challenging as society becomes increasingly fragmented and expectations rise. As Drew highlights, 'The performance of police has come under increasing scrutiny in the previous few decades. The expectations placed on police organizations and their employees, driven by the goals pursuing optimal effectiveness and efficiency, have shifted along with the demands for significant programmatic, technological, administrative and strategic innovation' (Drew, 2012: 110). Unfortunately the quality of police leadership appears to generate constant concern. As Vick (2000: 4) reported, 'The overarching criticism of police leadership is its perceived failure to lead and adapt to change.' Indeed Thatcher became so concerned about police leadership that she talked of bringing direct entrants to the police from other industries (Savage, 2007; Golding & Savage, 2008), a view that persists and is being actively pursued in many quarters today. In summary, the complexity of the external and internal environment requires excellent police leadership to deliver effective policing. However, as with all human behaviour, the quality of police leadership appears varied.

(h) Choosing the correct intervention: Knowledge of 'what works'

Even when a competent, well-trained and experienced officer is in place, effectiveness is not guaranteed. Ideally those involved in policing (including political and police leaders as well as police practitioners) are able to choose the most appropriate intervention to deal with the circumstances before them. Fortunately, knowledge surrounding 'what works in policing' is becoming more extensive in both quality and quantity, as scholars, research institutes and professional associations continue their work. The argument for using evidence-based practice to support appropriate policy and practice is a strong one. It can make policing more effective and efficient as well as reduce the potential for unintended negative consequences to occur (iatrogenic effects). However, as with all these sections, there are complications in establishing what works, as not all evidence is created equally and relies significantly on the design of the evaluation programme to filter out bias. Later chapters will explore in more detail the use of academic research in highlighting appropriate interventions. However all evidence based approaches require a practitioner to implement it.

(i) The police practitioner – competence, knowledge and motivation

As the police practitioner is on the delivery end of the implementation process, it seems reasonable to suggest that if they are effectively directed by political and police leaders in delivering specific, measurable, achievable, relevant and time-bound objectives, then these aims should be achieved. However, a number of factors complicate this view.

The first issue is whether the police organization employs the most appropriate people to do the work. Although there appears to be no specific police personality, British research has reported officers as being more conservative, extraverted, tough minded and resistant to change when compared to the general population (Cook, 1977; Colman & Gorman, 1982). Although the recruitment process is often competency based, and involves written, medical and psychological tests, together with a background check and oral interview, this process has not reliably predicted job performance (Falkenberg et al., 1991). Indeed, 'many researchers would agree that current selection methods are based on eliminating the unfavourable candidates rather than finding recruits with specific positive qualities' (Sanders, 2008: 129).

Likewise, once officers are selected they need to be trained. Again, considerable academic literature surrounds the subject of police training, with many studies unable to prove that strong academy performance (training school) is indicative of strong field (operational) performance (Burkhart, 1980; Topp & Kardashi, 1986). Indeed the relevance of classroom training in preparing individuals for their role has often been questioned, especially when the influence of organizational culture is considered. In a recent study of UK patrol officers, it was reported, 'Training was focused on procedures and legal use of powers rather than becoming an effective crime fighter. The emphasis is on removing risk, rather than proactive interventions. Some evidence based knowledge is taught, but there is little evidence that it is being applied on the ground' (HMIC, 2012a: 2).

Once employed, it generally appears difficult to dismiss officers, predominantly because of the difficulty in defining ineffectiveness as well as an apparent inability of supervisors to assess accurately. Fyffe (1999) argued that whilst evaluation tools have gone beyond counting arrests and enforcement tickets, recognizing an effective officer remains difficult due to the complex nature of the role. In a more recent study, Sanders (2008) reviewed 96 American police officers from eight non-urban police agencies, and discovered that supervisor ratings were generally overinflated. The study also found absenteeism, citizen complaints and personality traits to be of little use in identifying good or bad police officers, establishing that age and attitude were in fact the best predictors of job performance. It emerged that very young inexperienced officers, together with much older officers, appeared less valued by supervisors and senior officers, whilst a cynical work attitude was also negatively associated with job performance. Mastrofski (1981) has encouraged citizen evaluations to be used when assessing police officer performance, whilst Falkenberg et al. (1991) have supported the use of peer ratings.

It is also important to highlight the craft involved in operational policing. Even when officers are motivated and well-intentioned, decision-making can often go awry as a result of naturally occurring cognitive processes. Alison and Crego (2008) accept that both context and individual characteristics are important, highlighting that quickly moving events rarely allow time for officers to gather sufficient information for optimal decision-making. Grieve (2008: xxvi) adds that in complex, rapidly changing circumstances officers are unable to follow an instruction manual, and rather have to deal with shifting objectives within time and resource limitations. This process is often exacerbated by information overload and is fused with subconscious prejudice and bias. Of course the more complex the incident, the more people and variables are present to complicate the process. However, on a more positive note, it is clear there are many exceptional officers who achieve outstanding results. We have already mentioned police leaders, and during this research many examples were revealed of operational officers who appeared to outperform their peers on criteria such as the arrest of offenders or receiving more commendations or letters of appreciation. Deconstructing practitioner characteristics to establish what makes individuals exceptional has so far proved impossible. However, a similar process has recently begun to distinguish what makes a good soldier in conflict situations. The research has suggested that effective soldiers are those who are able to listen, make sense of the situation more effectively, and hence respond accordingly. It may be that police research can follow a similar path in the future.

Section summary

It is interesting to note that Shane (2010) previously associated the internal workings of police organizations with a greater source of stress for officers than the external operational environment. Indeed, this section has shown there to be a significant number of internal factors that can influence the delivery of policing services, thereby forging differences between and within police agencies. The next section will explain what happens when these external and internal factors co-occur in particular contexts.

Section 3: The importance of context

Sections 1 and 2 have outlined the external and internal factors that can influence the effectiveness of the police; however, one further element plays an important role – the context.

Again, it is useful to consider some of the research relating to aviation accidents when attempting to understand the concept of implementation failure in police practice. This research has discovered that between 70% and 80% of aviation disasters can be associated with human error; however, the critical finding is that the error often emanates from a chain of events (Reason, 1990; Weigmann & Shappell, 2003). In fact, the research argues there are four major categories of human failure in aircraft accidents, all interdependent of one another. The chain commences with the wider organizational influences that determine the general operating environment. This general environment is then affected by the ability of the supervisor to manage his or her operating environment. Dependent on how these two concepts inter-relate, the potential preconditions for an unsafe act to occur may or may not occur. If it does, the performance of the practitioner (pilot), at that particular time, then becomes critical. These four categories are supplemented by a further 19 causal subcategories to produce a process model known as the Human Factors Analysis and Classification System (HFACS) framework (Wiegmann & Shappell, 2003), which is shown in greater detail below:

- *Organizational influences*: Resource management, organizational climate, organizational process
- *Unsafe supervision*: Inadequate supervision, planned inappropriate operation, failure to correct problem, supervisory violation
- *Preconditions for unsafe acts*: Environmental factors (physical/technological), condition of operators (adverse mental, psychological, physical state), personnel factors (crew resource management, personal readiness)
- *Unsafe acts*: Errors (decision, skill based, perceptual errors), violations (routine, exceptional)

Although policing is clearly different to air travel, the central principle is transferable. This means that in the context of policing, a particular implementation failure can often be associated with a chain of events preceding it. For example, a review into the death of Ian Tomlinson at the London G20 protest crucially discovered the police officer to have used an inappropriate level of force. However, the chain of events underpinning this particular tragedy actually started many years earlier, as it was revealed that the officer had previously resigned from another police force whilst under investigation for a similar allegation. Of course, had the officer not been allowed to re-join the police, the incident in London would have been avoided. The decision to re-hire him was criticized by the IPCC (*The Telegraph*, 19 July 2012), and the British government has now put plans in place to prevent this scenario occurring in the future.

Throughout this book, we will see this phenomenon re-occurring. The effectiveness or ineffectiveness of policing, specifically the implementation of the final intervention, is influenced by a series of interrelated systems, processes, actions and individuals. The complex nature of this process can be understood by using the framework explained in this chapter, and will be further illustrated in subsequent chapters. It will explore how strong leaders, when in a positive organizational culture and supportive community, can make effective use of scientific developments to achieve outstanding results in relation to homicide investigation. Conversely, examples can be given of sophisticated conscious opponents, who are more likely to go undetected because they are met by poorly led, demotivated and incompetent officers, working alongside ineffective partner agencies, within an apathetic organizational culture.

Conclusion

At the start of this chapter it was pointed out that the standard of policing could differ across countries as well as between and within police agencies. The chapter provides a framework to show how external and internal influences conspire together and generate a complex operational environment for the police to work within. When coupled with a particular context, these issues can build a chain of events, which either assists or hinders the successful implementation of police actions. The process can be summarized as follows:

Stage 1 (external influences) dictates the external operating environment, which the police are relatively powerless to change, as follows:

- The advent of late modernity has affected the macro environment, which encompasses consumerism, increased mobility and the management of risk. These and other factors create both opportunities and challenges for the police, which they need to adapt to with increased speed and flexibility.
- An increasingly complex environment makes it important to tackle policing problems in partnership with others. Increased pluralism is generating a more fragmented policing environment, where responsibility and accountability between agencies is more difficult to define.
- There is ambiguity surrounding the police role, making it difficult to establish a baseline on which to judge effectiveness.
- More powerful stakeholders have emerged who are able to influence and change the behaviour of the police. This is exacerbated by oversight agencies, who influence policing in more invasive ways, at times leading to unintended consequences.

- Communities differ in levels of crime and collective efficacy. This, coupled with the emergence of more sophisticated *conscious opponents*, presents increasingly innovative challenges that require new policing approaches.

Stage 2 (internal factors) influence how effective the police can be in the operational environment they construct for themselves, notably:

- An organizational culture sometimes prioritizes informal values ahead of the more formal rules of the organization, which can impact on the effective delivery of policing. A positive organizational culture improves effectiveness whilst a negative culture counteracts it.
- There are different approaches and levels of competence in relation to police leadership, which has a significant impact on effectiveness.
- There are different levels of competence in relation to police practitioners, which impacts on effectiveness.
- Although there is greater knowledge as to 'what works in policing', this information is not always implemented for a variety of reasons.

Stage 3 (context) describes the environment in which external and internal factors converge. In this way, the delivery of effective or ineffective policing is not due to one individual or group, but is influenced by a much wider series of events. The interplay between these influences can generate many permutations, which can also explain the diversity of policing between and within police agencies. As we progress through the chapters of this book, the themes described in this chapter will constantly emerge.

2 The Fundamental Building Blocks of Police Effectiveness

> The day starts at 6 am when I reach for my Blackberry and check my e-mails. I get to the office and review overnight occurrences in London – murder, abduction, an off duty officer arrested, and a politician voicing concern about a closing police station. From 8 am. I start a relentless schedule of meetings that dominates my day. Delivering territorial policing across London now shares equal space with the challenge of finding a 20% budget reduction and dealing with the associated fall-out that comes with organisational change. Throughout the day, events conspire to blow me off course, as I'm regularly interrupted by enquiries mainly from politicians, the police authority or the media asking me about the Mets position on a variety of issues. The news that one of our officers is stabbed makes me drop everything and I hurry to the scene and then onto the hospital to confirm all needs are being catered for. With everything in place, including an agreed press statement, I quickly get changed and go on to an evening charity event, one of many good causes the Met are asked to support. As I walk in I consider the cancelled meetings and wonder how can they be rescheduled as the week is already accounted for. I know we'll manage ... we always do.
>
> (Chief Officer, UK Police)

Introduction

This chapter is divided into three sections and will look at the fundamental elements that underpin effective policing. The first section explores strategic leadership issues encompassing the police mission, use of resources and performance management. The second section examines the police–public relationship, while the final section explores different policing models designed to facilitate the reduction of crime and disorder. Critical to all these sections is the importance of political and police leadership as well as the ability to transform theories into practice.

In commencing this chapter, it should be highlighted that policing relies upon a symbiotic relationship between political and police leaders to be effective. The government decide upon the priorities for policing, and establish different mechanisms to ensure this takes place (i.e. legislation, policy, funding and oversight frameworks). The process then relies on the expertise of Police Chiefs to operationalize this political direction by generating priorities and policy for their staff, apportioning resources and accountability and finally developing their own performance oversight process to establish the impact they are achieving. Though politicians and police chiefs ultimately have to rely upon each other, their relationship generates tensions in practice. For example, the government may be critical of Chief Police Officers in their inability to implement good practice, whereas Chief Officers may complain as to the lack of funding or level of political interference. Difficulties occur not in terms of *what* should be done, but *how* they should be done.

Two recent UK examples provide further detail in terms of how this tension can manifest itself in the implementation of policing. The first example surrounds the number of sworn police officers employed by British Police agencies. Flanagan (2008) argued that only 10% of existing staff in British agencies actually needed to be sworn officers, which if corrected, would allow Chief Constables to stretch their existing budgets through the employment of less-expensive (non-sworn) staff to deliver many policing functions. However, political leaders, who previously announced that police numbers would not be reduced during their tenure, blocked this approach. As such, police and politicians become embroiled in defining what constitutes *front-line officers*, rather than focusing on the outcome these officers are able to achieve. The second example surrounds a structural debate concerning the optimal size and number of British Police forces. At present there are 43 police forces across England and Wales, each functioning independently, which means they often carry individual infrastructure costs (i.e. recruitment, selection, estates and financial services). HMIC (2009b) argue that between 15 and 30% savings could be achieved by agencies cooperating and sharing these services; however, collaboration has proved difficult to implement. The Association of Chief Police Officers (ACPO) has previously stated that they would rather achieve these savings by amalgamating a number of police forces together, which would also provide added resilience when dealing with the threat from organized crime and when policing large events (i.e. protest, serial homicide investigations). Unfortunately, ACPO's advice is contrary to a political objective that wants locally elected Police and Crime Commissioners (PCCs) included within the policing structure to improve accountability. To do this, they need to maintain the current number of Police Forces, hence preventing the current structure from changing.

Given all of these examples, there is general agreement between political and police leaders about what should be done, whether this is in relation to reducing costs or maintaining a local and effective police service. Nonetheless, tensions and problems emanate from how this is achieved. As this chapter will show, implementation issues such as these are constantly occurring and often detract from the ability to deliver optimum policing practice. Many of these scenarios can be tracked back to leadership issues, as examples in this chapter will illustrate.

Section 1: Strategic leadership – mission, resources, performance management and unintended consequences

It is universally accepted that effective leadership is critical to the process of organizational change and effective performance (Silvestri, 2007; Dobby et al., 2004). Home Office and ACPO guidance continually states that leadership starts with Police Chiefs and permeates through the organization to reach the front line. However, police studies will often overlook the integral role political leaders have within the wider police environment. This next section will look at their role, and how it affects direction, resources and oversight.

The mission

The effectiveness of any organization, including the police, is underpinned by its awareness of what it exists to do. Unless that strategic direction is clear, it cannot determine the best structure in which to operate, or the type of skills its staff will require. The opening chapter has explained that a level of ambiguity exists regarding the police mission. Different political leaders across the world have placed different emphasis on whether they see the police predominantly as crime fighters, or whether they should embrace a wider social role. This diversity is illustrated by the following Home Secretaries that represented the previous three UK governments:

'The main job of the police is to catch criminals' (Michael Howard, 1993: Home Secretary 1993–97)

'To build a safe, just and tolerant society in which the rights and responsibilities of individuals, families and communities are properly balanced'. (Home Office statement of purpose1997: Home Secretary Jack Straw, 1997–2001)

'I couldn't be clearer about your mission: it isn't a thirty-point plan; it is to cut crime. No more, and no less' (Teresa May, 2010: Current Home Secretary).

This fluctuation in approach drips down into individual police forces. As HMIC (2010a: 2), point out, 'Forces all use different mission statements and these vary even across Departments within a Force'. More recently, in July 2011, the police leaders of England & Wales agreed a Statement of Mission and Values (ACPO, 2012), defined as follows:

> The mission of the police is to make communities safer by upholding the law fairly and firmly; preventing crime and antisocial behaviour; keeping the peace; protecting and reassuring communities; investigating crime and bringing offenders to justice.
>
> We will act with integrity, compassion, courtesy and patience, showing neither fear nor favour in what we do. We will be sensitive to the needs and dignity of victims and demonstrate respect for the human rights of all.
>
> We will use discretion, professional judgment and common sense to guide us and will be accountable for our decisions and actions. We will respond to well-founded criticism with a willingness to learn and change.
>
> We will work with communities and partners, listening to their views, building their trust and confidence, making every effort to understand and meet their needs.
>
> We will not be distracted from our mission through fear of being criticised. In identifying and managing risk, we will seek to achieve successful outcomes and to reduce the risk of harm to individuals and communities.

> In the face of violence we will be professional, calm and restrained and will apply only that force which is necessary to accomplish our lawful duty.
>
> Our commitment is to deliver a service that we, and those we serve can be proud of, and which keeps our communities safe.

This mission is expansive although it does not emphasize any particular element. Unsurprisingly, it catered for all the views of senior police officers interviewed for this book. They were in general agreement as to their purpose, seeing their role as predominantly protecting and serving citizens, as well as facilitating a safer society. None saw the role of the police primarily as crime fighters, with many citing extraneous issues such as traffic safety and assisting vulnerable people, as being important. However, the Police Chiefs placed different emphasis on different features of the mission statement and articulated different views on how the mission should be achieved. At one end of the continuum were Chief Officers (who I refer to as crime warriors), who wanted to concentrate their efforts on enforcement. At the other end of this continuum, there were those (who I refer to as proactive partners) who saw a much wider role for the police in relation to prevention and the protection of vulnerability. Of course there are arguments for each path, with the former promoting an unambiguous focus on the traditional police role, supported by improvements in tactics and equipment. Conversely, those in the other camp argued that enforcement-based interventions are too late, as they merely deal with the problem when it breaks down. As one Chief Officer said, 'It is an ineffective use of resources to continually pick people up at the bottom of the cliff; it is far better to intervene at the top of the cliff and stop them falling off in the first place'.

The differences in these approaches are fundamental. Preventative approaches can be delivered at primary (general community level), secondary (focusing on those individuals and locations who are predicted to be at greater risk) and tertiary levels (dealing with prolific offenders). Obviously, there is a significant distinction between those Police Forces who invest heavily in enforcement teams, and those who support diversionary schemes for young people in deprived areas; the utility of which will be further discussed in Chapter 3. Ultimately, whatever the strengths and weaknesses of these approaches, the police mission and how to achieve it remain ambiguous and will vary across police areas. Depending on whose study you believe (and how you define crime), 20% or less, of police activity results in a crime report, and in the UK, this is reflected by the fact that crime prevention is only 1 of

190 modules an officer will receive during their initial training (HMIC, 2012a: 2). Nevertheless, most police activity fits within a wider framework of *reducing harm* using a variety of approaches. The central question surrounds the breadth of responsibility the police should accept in the reduction of this harm, and to what level their approach embraces prevention, rather than enforcement. There are different views on this, and O'Connor in his valedictory speech as Her Majesties Chief Inspector of Constabulary highlighted this ambiguity. He explained how a group of police officers he was shadowing in London apologized for dealing with a number of domestic incidents, saying, 'We will deal with some real police work soon', even though they had effectively intervened and reduced the opportunity for harm. As O'Connor argues, preventative work is the essence of policing, though it is too often demeaned and seen as peripheral by the officers delivering it.

The question arises as to whether the police mission should be further clarified? Yet, arguments against this approach in the UK highlight that policing is constantly evolving, and that it would therefore take too long to invoke a Royal Commission to ponder these issues. Further, it is thought the cost of an inquiry would not provide value for money, especially as Chief Officers are agreed on their general purpose. In contrast, more clarification on the police mission would allow for a much clearer understanding of this purpose, and confirm the best way to deliver it, as well as providing greater fairness in terms of judging whether the police were effective. At present, there is no wider debate on how the police identifies, prioritizes or reduces vulnerability. In essence, throughout the UK and further afield, the presence of mission statements are ultimately not enough to drive police activity, therefore different levels of emphasis are constantly being generated in relation to the implementation of services.

Resourcing

Once the strategic direction of a police agency is determined, then sufficient resources are needed to achieve it. Data provided by the United Nations indicate that police agencies are inconsistently resourced across the world (Eurostat, 2009); for example, England and Wales employ the highest level of civilian staff, though with 260 police officers per 100,000 population, they are below the European average of 338 police officers (European Sourcebook of Crime and Criminal Justice Statistics, 2010:113). Nonetheless, when assessing police spend against GDP, it appears the British consume a higher proportion than virtually any other Western democratic country, and about 20% more than the USA

(HMIC, 2009). On the other hand, England and Wales has proportionately more officers than Japan (199 per 100,000), but dramatically less than Afghanistan (401 officers per 100,000). The level of local taxation further affects this inconsistency, meaning that the cost of policing is determined by political or historical factors, rather than by identifying what is needed and then establishing the cost.

This approach to resourcing creates a dilemma for governments who want to know what is to gain by spending more on policing, or what is to lose by investing less. In recent years, financial growth, coupled with increased concern about security, has provided many police agencies across the world with increased manpower and resources. This is true of Britain, as between 1994/95 and 2008/09, spending on the police in England and Wales doubled (from £6.45 billion to £13.7 billion). Indeed, since 1969, overall staff numbers increased by over 124,000 (51,000 sworn officers, 57,000 police staff and 16,000 Police and Community Support Officers (HMIC 2010b:5). Unfortunately, there appears no simple correlation between the level of resources and improved performance, especially in relation to the reduction of crime (Machin & Marie, 2011; Cameron, 1988). In fact, some have shown that additional resources can lead to increased police productivity, thereby increasing the disclosure and reporting of crime (Levitt, 1977). More recently, a number of studies have thrown further light on this association. Bradford (2011), reviewing 13 studies in this area, argues that up until the mid-1990s there appeared to be no evidence that the rise, or fall, of officer numbers could affect the level of crime. However, since that time, methodology has improved and the number of studies has increased. Although a direct causal link cannot be shown, there is evidence to show 'the potential of an effect of police numbers on crime' (ibid.:9). This is particularly true of property crime, whereby a 10% increase in officers seemingly leads to a 3% reduction, and vice versa. However, evidence for an effect on violent crime is weaker, and at times contradictory. Even more recently, Chalfin and McCrary (2012), looking at US cities, estimate that for every dollar spent on the police, $1.60 is saved in reduced victimization costs.

There is no doubt crime has fallen, and this appears to have occurred across the industrialized world. The British Crime Survey shows that between 1995 and 2007, violent crime decreased by 49% and house burglary by 58% (Hoare, 2009:21). There were also significant declines in most of Europe (van Dijk et al., 2007), as well as the USA, Canada, Australia, Japan and others (Farrell et al., 2008:22). There seem to be many explanations for the reduction of crime, with a reduction of atmospheric lead (caused through the change to unleaded petrol) being the most recent (Monbiot, 2012). Other explanations have related to changes in demographics, use of prison, gun and weapon control, teenage pregnancy and abortion, and the economy. However, many of these theories fail to explain the uniform reduction across all countries, making the *security hypothesis* appear most probable (Clarke & Newman, 2006; Farrell et al., 2008). This theory suggests that a significant level of crime is opportunistic, and that increased security – especially in relation to manufactured vehicles – has therefore reduced crime. Although this may explain the most significant drops in crime across the world, there is also considerable evidence to suggest that police officers can serve to curtail potential law breaking by their visible presence. Similarly, when used proactively with evidence-based approaches, they can make a significant impact on specific community problems (described further in Section 3 of this chapter).

This analysis explains crime reduction at both macro and micro level, clarifying why crime can fall in the UK (and other countries) despite police numbers reducing, and also why crime levels can differ between specific localities. It also demonstrates that conditions on which the government release funding, together with the way police leaders use resources, are extremely important to the reduction of crime and disorder; in essence, it is not just the level of resources but also how they are used that determines effectiveness. Unfortunately, studies are not complimentary when commenting upon resource management by the police. HMIC (2010) estimated that if the current system was redesigned, police availability in England and Wales could remain constant, whilst 12% of the budget could be withdrawn. Criticizing the deployment of officers in the UK, HMIC (2010: 3) stated, 'On average only 11% of total police strength are visible and available to the general public at any one time; and in our sample, more police were available on a Monday morning than on a Friday night. There is scope to improve this by more closely matching shift patterns to demands and through measures such as police patrolling on their own rather than in pairs'. In summary, although there have been significant strides forward in using police resources more efficiently, major opportunities still remain. This links to the next section that concerns performance management.

Improving police performance: New Public Management

Although good practice dictates that governments will devolve as much responsibility as they can, they still want to maintain some level of control. This conundrum has been assisted by the separation of *steering* and *rowing* in the delivery of services. The government steer by providing policy direction and budget, whilst the rowing (or implementation) is the responsibility of the police (Golding & Savage, 2008).

The approach, referred to as New Public Management (NPM), emerged in the UK during the era of Prime Minister Margaret Thatcher, where ironically between 1979 and the early 1990s, a 90% increase in the police budget was associated with a doubling of the crime rate (Garland, 2001). NPM attempted to instill private sector management into the public sector (Savage, 2007) by promoting the view that further investment was conditional on the ability to show, 'where possible [by] quantifiable output and performance measures' that objectives were being met (Weatheritt, 1986:26). This approach had a significant impact on the way policing was delivered, with officers warning at the time, 'The philosophy of economy, efficiency and effectiveness is forcing police managers to concentrate their resources upon the quantifiable aspects of police work to the exclusion of the traditional service role of British Policing' (Joint Consultative Committee, 1990:27).

From then on, various UK politicians continued to influence the police mission and the performance management framework reacted accordingly. The new Blair government in 1997, introduced a more sophisticated, balanced score card approach to match the wider police mission of the time. This was called the Policing Performance Assessment Framework (PPAF), and it subsumed both national and local priorities within six domains. The 'resource' (inputs) domain was connected to the higher level domain of citizen focus through four other domains: reducing crime, investigating crime, promoting public safety, and providing assistance. It was hoped that these contained all the standards necessary to monitor the delivery of a consistent first class service (Barton & Barton, 2011). Two further performance review processes supported PPAF. The first was the traditional inspection process by HMIC, known as the 'baseline assessment', where police forces and Basic Command Units (BCUs) could be reviewed individually and against other police areas sharing 'similar' characteristics. This was supplemented during 2003/04 by a software program (iQuanta), which publicly published a variety of management information online, allowing a much clearer connection between resources and performance. However, in 2008 the performance framework changed again as PPAF was replaced by APACS (Assessments of Policing and Community Safety). This allegedly simplified the process and integrated police performance with community safety partners, as well as including qualitative measures of confidence and satisfaction (Barton & Barton, 2011).

Whilst not replicated to the same extent in other countries, the principle of monitoring key performance indicators and setting targets has been followed widely. However, it is only when collating these separate demands that the level of scrutiny can be understood. During 2002, I analysed the demands for my own Constabulary, which revealed that the following information was provided to the Home Office:

- 55 indicators relating to crime and disorder, complete with contextual explanations (provided every 3 months).
- 35 varied indicators to the Home Office (i.e. criminal use of firearms) (provided every 3 months).
- Frequency counts on all crime class categories (approximately 100 in the UK) from each Police Division and local government area, plus nine crime detection indicators (provided monthly).
- 19 indicators, relating to Road Traffic Collisions (provided monthly).
- Robbery statistics provided from each Police Division in relation to a specific national initiative on street crime (weekly).

The following were also provided for internal agency monitoring:

- 23 Community and Race Relations indicators to lay advisors and internal audience (provided every 3 months).
- 19 support indicators (provided monthly).

This monitoring of performance information was also taking place within a culture of inspection and improvement, as a total 17 organizations made regulatory demands on the police (HMIC, 2010). During 2003/04, my own Constabulary had been subjected to two Force Inspections, two Police Division inspections (and re-inspections) and a number of thematic inspections. The recommendations from these were supplemented by national reviews on specific aspects of policing, and new legislation (i.e. Freedom of Information Act, Health and Safety Act and Human Rights Act), which all created significant resource issues. In fact, my own Constabulary collated a database of these demands, of which 663 discrete elements were included in the annual policing plans. Shortly after these plans were accepted, 36 additional demands were added from further national reports (*Death of Victoria Climbié*, *Training Matters* and *Diversity Matters*). In fact some of these demands, such as those highlighted in the Criminal Justice System Reform plan, contained over 200 lower level recommendations. One such example was to co-ordinate a force-wide purge on outstanding arrest warrants – a major task requiring weeks of work.

In summary, although the NPM framework improved levels of accountability within policing (which became associated with reductions in levels of crime and disorder), this level of monitoring also caused unintended consequences, which will now be explained.

The unintended consequences of New Public Management – system failure and bureaucracy

The unintended consequences of public sector targets have been explained by a number of commentators (Pekkanen & Neimi, 2012; Seddon, 2008) and can be observed throughout this book. As one British Police Chief said in interview, 'Once I set a target I have to consider what mechanisms I should put in place to prevent the perverse behaviour that can accompany it'. As an explanation he disclosed two examples shown below.

Example 1

'Consider you own an expensive carbon frame racing cycle. You keep the bike in your secure garage and wake up to find it has been stolen. What is the response from the police? Well that depends – if the garage is attached to your house it would be recorded as a 'burglary in a dwelling' and would be aligned to a police detection target. You would receive the premium service – fingerprints, DNA testing and a detective to take charge of the case. However if your garage was not attached to your house this would be a burglary other than a dwelling and as such the details may only be recorded and filed. The loss to the victim is the same, but the response from the police is completely different'.

Example 2

'A man phoned in to say he had a spare tyre stolen from his lorry whilst he had parked it overnight. The man did not expect any investigation as he realized the police had no chance of catching the culprit because the property wasn't identifiable. He wanted a crime number to prove to his employer, and the insurance company, that the matter had been reported to the police. However because there was a target to reduce theft from motor vehicles the caller was interrogated as to where he had been, and exactly where he last saw his spare wheel. The caller was forced to admit there was a possibility it had been taken when he parked his lorry in another county. As such the officer receiving the call did not register the crime against the Force statistics and there is no doubt the victim (who had his wheel stolen somewhere), was left extremely disgruntled by the experience'.

Seddon (2008) is scathing in his attack on NPM and argues this to be the reason why such a significant level of investment in public services has not been associated with a similar level of improvement. He asserts that every public service has been burdened by specifications, regulations and targets, which actually make performance worse. Similarly, he argues that inspections show, 'cheating is not an exception – it is ubiquitous and systematic' (ibid.:10), suggesting that the emphasis of NPM is to deal with people quickly rather than effectively. Summarizing his view, Seddon (ibid.:42) argues:

- Designs for service are based on opinion, not knowledge. Plausible ideas are promulgated without any evidence as to their efficacy.
- Targets do not represent the reality of a service from the customer point of view.
- Targets drive people to use their ingenuity to meet the target, not improve performance.
- The regime seeks questionable evidence to support its point of view (pilots are destined to succeed).

According to Seddon, the regime generates significant waste and cost, specifically: the cost of people writing specifications, the cost of inspection, the costs of preparing for inspection, the costs of the specification being wrong and the cost of demoralization.

Yet, there is further evidence to suggest NPM has created unintended consequences. In Britain during August 2001, the Home Office, in their aim to increase productivity, asked the firm *PA Consulting* to establish what the average patrol officer did during their tour of duty. Examining 378 police officer diaries across seven police agencies in England and Wales, they discovered that police officers spent nearly as much time in their police station (43.1%) as outside it. In fact, for 5 hours a day in any one shift, 50% of the available officers were in the station (including local neighbourhood beat officers). The time spent in the police station was explained as designation to paper work and processing offenders (PA Consulting, 2001). This level of bureaucracy horrified politicians, and consistent with the times, a working group was formed to review and respond to the crisis. As such a *policing bureaucracy task force* was initiated under the control of Sir David O'Dowd (the Chief HMIC), which later made 52 recommendations to reduce bureaucracy. Between 2002 and 2007 a flurry of activity ensued, aided by bureaucracy champions from each British police force. The impact of this effort was revealed in 2008 when Sir Ronnie Flanagan (Chief HMIC), conducting a fundamental review on policing, made 59 recommendations – many of which related to bureaucracy. Indeed, such was the similarity of the two reviews that many argued little had been achieved. In 2008, the government took the bold step of asking a previous critic of government policy, Jan Berry (the recently retired chair of the British Police Federation), to work on the anti-bureaucracy brief. Although acknowledging policing required some level of paperwork, Berry was extremely critical of the extent it had risen. At the time of her review, a single target of 'increasing public confidence' had been prioritized, although many other performance indicators remained, from a variety of other plans (i.e. Public Service Agreements, Local Service Agreements, Local Policing plan, The Policing pledge, APACS, Local Criminal Justice Board plans and different government initiatives) (Berry, 2009:30). Jan Berry faced a considerable challenge in reducing bureaucracy, illustrated by this quote from HMIC (2010a: 3), who set out the scale of the task in England and Wales,

> In seeking to reduce every risk to the public and possibility of error, all police officers' work has increasingly become controlled by rules of good practice or guidance. In 2009 alone 2,600 pages of guidance were issued to police officers setting out how their work should be done; and there are now 100 processes in the criminal justice system, requiring 40 interventions by police officers, staff and specialists. The cost to policing is estimated at £2.2 billion per year. A further effect has been to draw resources into investigation, intelligence and other specialist functions, away from the public: the number of sworn officers working in these areas increased by 3000 over the previous four years, while the number working in the community declined by 1,400.

They go on to explain that this drift towards specialization, combined with other working practices, such as the desire of operational officers to work variable shifts (working longer, but fewer days) led to a lack of visibility, with some officers only working 171 days of the year.

Berry's position as the government's 'independent reducing bureaucracy advocate' came to an end in October 2010 with her fourth and final report. Berry (2010:1) stated that, 'listening to hundreds of front-line officers, you can count on one hand those who report an overall reduction in bureaucratic demand, with old bureaucracy quickly replaced by new demands for data and information'. She goes on to say that 'one third of effort is either over-engineered, duplicated or adds no additional value' (ibid.:2), a level of bureaucracy which is unaffordable in the present financial climate. Unfortunately, it was also revealed that Berry, although critical of the bureaucracy like O'Dowd, had made little impact in changing it. Her recommendations were ambiguous, with insufficient detail as to how they should be implemented. For example, she asked all forces to 'engage with a systems approach built around understanding demand, designing quality systems, leadership, empowerment of staff, flow (end-to-end systems), measurement, and continuous improvement' as well as suggesting that 'a public debate should be held to consider the optimum structure for efficient and effective policing'. Wide-ranging strategic statements cannot drive change; it relies on clear and specific understanding of what should be done and how it can be achieved. Unfortunately, these statements were exacerbated by anti-bureaucracy initiatives that were not thought through and poorly implemented. For example, Berry pointed out that the Home Office had invested £80 million in providing mobile data units to front line officers; however, the claims that they could save 30 minutes per officer per shift had not been proven.

Section summary

Although it is widely accepted that the definition of the police mission, the management of resources and the oversight of police delivery are all important, this section shows the difficulty of delivering these elements in practice. Specifically, clarity is required as to the importance of prevention in the police role; and it is also apparent that significant improvements can be made to resource management. However, it was the approach to performance management that created the most startling impact.

Although it should be applauded the British government wants to ensure police resources are used effectively and efficiently it appears

NPM, with its bundle of performance indicators and targets clearly created unintended consequences. The lists of targets created a number of issues. First, too many objectives create ambiguity in terms of what is important. McChesney et al. (2012:6) refer to this as the 'whirlwind', where the energy required to maintain a daily work schedule makes it difficult to prioritize particular initiatives, or separate the urgent from the important. Secondly, the examples given illustrated that by ignoring the fundamental cause of the problem (in this case the culture of control), the symptoms (bureaucracy) cannot be eradicated. As was seen in the anti-bureaucracy initiative, the eradication of a monitoring form or performance indicator, was often shortly followed by another to take its place.

More recently HMIC (2010a:18) have argued, 'The police need a new touchstone on risk management where they are only judged against the most probable risks that arise routinely, that they can reasonably be expected to deal with'. HMIC (2010a) also argued for a simplification in crime recording, more flexibility in deployment, a reduction in demands through health and safety legislation, and a change in government oversight. However, the danger of these reports is that they merely serve to add to the daily *whirlwind*. They will be added to the numerous other lists of recommendations and priorities emerging from other stakeholders. Like Berry's report, this rhetoric will be meaningless unless leaders analyse the issues in detail and drive forward the most important recommendations. Fortunately, the implications of NPM have slowly been recognized and the current UK government has signaled its intention to replace *bureaucratic accountability* with *democratic accountability*, specifically by reducing central targets. However, an early attempt in the way crime detections will be monitored and recorded has not been encouraging. Although 86% of the 65 organizations consulted supported the recommendation to change the term sanction detections to crime outcomes and allow community resolution to deal with low level offending (including restorative justice) 66% were unsure or disagreed that it would reduce bureaucracy, and 68% were not convinced it would reduce the financial burden. Also, ironically, during this research it appeared that many were finding it difficult to stop monitoring performance indicators, as it left a vacuum that could not be filled by anything else. Time will tell whether performance information and bureaucracy can be reduced in an environment where citizens expect greater transparency, whilst governments demand quick results and value for money. Whatever the result though, the British NPM experiment serves as a useful case study to other countries considering the same route.

Section 2: The police–citizen relationship

Disciplines as diverse as surgery to sales have discovered that interpersonal relationships are related to effectiveness. For example, Levinson and Chameton (1999) established that good communication in primary care settings actually improves patient satisfaction and compliance, as well as psychological and physical outcomes. Similarly, Levinson et al. (1997), found that educating patients about what to expect, checking understanding, being friendly and spending more time using better methods of interaction, was associated with fewer malpractice claims. Conversely, Ambady et al. (2002) established that specific conversation and tone (projecting higher dominance and lower concern) could be associated with increased risk of malpractice claims. Unsurprisingly, the importance of good public relationships is also at the core of effective police work in democratic countries. Since 1829, with the formation of the 'new police' in England, Peel wanted to distance his officers from the army who were associated with the brutal submission of disorder. Police officers were dressed in 'quiet' uniforms, armed only with rattle and baton for their protection. Peel's views were expanded by Rowan, one of the first commissioners, who wrote:

> ... he will be civil and obliging to all people of every rank and class. He must be particularly cautious not to interfere idly or unnecessarily in order to make a display of his authority; when required to act he will do so with decision and boldness; on all occasions he may expect to receive the fullest support in the proper exercise of his authority. He must remember that there is no qualification so indispensable to a police officer as a perfect command of temper, never suffering himself to be moved in the slightest degree by any language or threats that may be used; if he does his duty in a quiet and determined manner, such conduct will probably excite the well disposed of the bystanders to assist him, if he requires them.
>
> (Ascoli, 1979:86)

This focus on interpersonal relationships was constantly reinforced, with the first Commissioners demanding officers to be civil to all people, whatever their class, 'as any man who acts otherwise cannot be allowed to remain in the Force' (Reith, 1956:142). It was clear these warnings were carried out, as by 1834, only 562 of the 2,800 original officers remained (Elmsley, 1991). The Commissioners emphasized the importance of positive police–citizen relationships because they realized a democratic nation can only be policed with the consent of the public, and for that to occur the police institution must be perceived as legitimate. Critchley (1973:163) warns, 'If ever, unhappily, confidence in the police were to be withdrawn on any significant scale, it will be evident ... that the nation might have to accept a tougher more authoritarian institution, in which, the traditional concept of *service* gradually gave way to that of *force*'. The importance of police–public interactions has become even clearer with new research, predominantly from the US, UK and Australia. Referred to as the Procedural Justice Model (Tyler, 2004; Tyler & Huo, 2002; Tyler & Fagan, 2008), it argues that police can obtain trust and legitimacy in the eyes of the public, if they follow a number of simple principles:

- They are friendly and approachable
- They treat people with respect
- They show fairness in their decision making
- They take time to explain their decision making
- They should appear neutral and provide the citizen with an opportunity to present their view.

The impact of these principles has been extremely encouraging. Myhill and Beak (2008) found that treating people fairly and with respect is associated with higher public confidence levels, thus enhancing police legitimacy. The effects of positive encounters are obviously important in general patrol, but as the approach encourages respect for the law and fosters social responsibility, it also benefits the reduction and detection of crime. Surveys showed individuals were more likely to help police tackle crime in their neighbourhood if they perceive the police to be legitimate (Tyler & Fagan, 2008). Positive encounters can encourage the public to report victimization, act as witnesses, and provide intelligence as well as engage in crime prevention activities (Reisig & Lloyd, 2009). Similarly, those receiving a negative experience were less willing to cooperate with investigations, less likely to report crime and more likely to behave defensively when approached (Sced, 2004:6). Taken together, these findings are important for two reasons. First, they create a positive environment, where the public receive a better service and the police enjoy more cooperation and less conflict. Secondly, it presents an inexpensive and effective method of instilling a crime prevention ethos (Myhill & Quinton, 2011). This is because the police rely greatly on the public to provide information (Burrows et al., 2005, showed that 42% of those crimes detected emanates from victim and witness information). Also, this approach has been seen to increase *collective efficacy* at a community level (Sampson et al., 1997). This is where residents feel more confident in challenging disorderly behaviour, and create a sense of informal control that reduces the number of individuals who are willing to engage in crime. There are many good examples of this approach and one can be observed in Boston, US, where a Boston Neighbourhood Policing Programme has been running for the past 6 years. Rather than continually responding with crisis management, the police have embedded street crime teams in hot-spot areas to generate long-standing and mutually respectful relationships. In this way, more accountability is demanded from both the police and the citizens who live and work in the area. The approach has not only reduced crime and antisocial behaviour but has also increased the number of positive relationships in the area (Braga & Baston, 2012).

To summarize, implementing a procedural justice model can make police work 'easier and more effective' (Skogan, 1998:183; 2006:118) as it appears police legitimacy is the most critical factor when establishing public cooperation. Once achieved, it appears more of an incentive to adhere to lawful behaviour than the deterrent affect of being caught and punished (Myhill & Quinton, 2011). Indeed, individuals are more likely to accept even unfavourable decisions from authority figures, providing they are treated properly and see the process as fair.

This approach results in citizens deferring to the police because they want to, not because they feel obliged to; in fact 'bedside manner' appears more important to victims than the actual outcome (Skogan, 1998:187). Studies have also found that procedural justice holds across all ethnic groups, albeit different groups have different views on how they are treated (MacCoun, 2005). Indeed, Tyler et al. (2010:368) found that American-Muslim citizens were more willing to report terror-related risks if they viewed the police as legitimate.

The current state of public/police interactions

The British Crime Survey (BCS) suggests that the percentage of public-initiated contacts with the police has declined over the last 25 years. During 1981, a total of 43% of the population had initiated contact with the police (mainly to ask directions); however, by 2005/06, this had declined to 39% (Bradford et al., 2009). A random survey of 3,710 individuals commissioned by the Independent Police Complaints Commission (IPCC) (2012) established that 20% of these people had experienced some contact with the police over the past 12 months, down from the norm of 27–28% found in previous surveys. This finding may be influenced by cultural factors, for example, Sced (2004:1) estimated that more Australians (50%) had direct contact with the police each year.

Numerous studies have described the outcome of those interactions. Whereas the Crime Survey for England and Wales (2011/12) reported that 62% of the population felt the police to be doing a good job, the IPCC (2012) found that 76% of their random sample was satisfied following their contact with the police. Similarly, studies in the UK illustrate that 85% of the public feel that police would treat them with respect (Myhill & Quinton, 2011). Sced (2004) reports data from the 2002/03 Australian national survey of community satisfaction with policing, which shows that 82% were satisfied or very satisfied with the police. Of course, interactions differ in type: whilst the vast majority of public-initiated contacts were 'consumer contacts', the vast majority of police-initiated contacts could be viewed as 'adversarial contacts'. Sced (2004) divided his Australian sample into 67% non-targeted (random) contacts; 12%, where a citizen required police assistance (neutral); 10%, where the outcome was likely to be arrest (negative); and a further 10% of miscellaneous contacts. Higher dissatisfaction was associated with neutral and negative contacts, with officer demeanour cited as the main reason for levels of satisfaction.

Not all groups have the same view of the police. Although the BCS shows public perceptions of police fairness to have stayed relatively stable since 2005 (between 82 and 85%), this reduces to between 63 and 67% when asked whether the police would treat everyone fairly, regardless of who they were. Furthermore, 27% of those from black and minority ethnic groups expect the police to treat them worse than other races compared with 6% of white people (Reza & Magill, 2006:27). Wake et al. (2007:7) argued that the 'highly disengaged' – predominantly young men, black and Asian individuals, together with people from the traveller community – felt that 'their relationship with police was almost exclusively antagonistic', and stated they were unfairly stereotyped and targeted as troublemakers. Unfortunately, these opinions are not just formed from personal experience, but are acquired from friends, family and other contacts. Research in the USA suggests that negative encounters with police have greater impact on levels of satisfaction than positive ones, as more weight (between 4 and 14 times) is given to negative rather than positive experiences (Skogan, 2005). As Skogan (2006:99) argues, 'At its worst, the police may get essentially no credit for delivering professional service while bad experiences can deeply influence people's views of their performance and even legitimacy'. Confidence in the police is greater in those who had not 'witnessed crime or antisocial behaviour, who felt safe walking alone after dark in their neighbourhood and had University levels of education' (Myhill & Beak, 2008:8). Indeed, those who had no recent contact with the police were more likely to feel the police were doing a good job (Allen et al., 2006:3).

Gaining an overview of how many people complain about the police is obviously reliant on reporting procedures. The IPCC (2011), publicizing information in England and Wales for 2010/11, showed that complaints did not fall randomly, but were concentrated disproportionately across specific forces and officers. It also discovered that whilst there had been a 100% increase in complaints between 2002/03 and 2009/10, there had been a 4% reduction the following year, leaving an average ratio of 225 complaints per 1,000 officers, of which 11% were upheld. Five categories account for 69% of all complaints, as can be seen below:

- Other neglect or failure in duty (27%)
- Incivility, impoliteness and intolerance (18%)
- Other assault (12%)
- Oppressive conduct or harassment (7%)
- Unlawful or necessary detention (5%).

These categories reinforce the fact that people are less satisfied in the police when they are treated poorly, in line with the findings of the Procedural Justice Model.

Can the police follow a procedural justice model?

Although police–public encounters are generally positive, evidence shows that there is some scope for improvement. It seems obvious that if police knew how to participate in more effective interactions with the public, then they would modify their behaviour accordingly. However, history shows us that this philosophy (referred to in the UK as a *citizen focused* or *quality of service approach*) is not straightforward to implement. This view is reinforced by Loftus (2010) who argues that a procedural justice approach relies on culture change, which is difficult to achieve given the persistence of the enduring *cop culture*. The first tension relates to rank, and file officers seeing crime fighting as 'real' police work, with softer elements – such as community policing and customer service – as less important. McLean and Hillier (2011) also found that whilst police officers stated high visibility was the key to effectiveness, the act of interacting positively with the public was not. Therefore, even if political and police leaders emphasized the importance of procedural justice, it is unclear how well it would be implemented.

With these tensions existing, it is the role of leaders to ensure that the necessary approach is implemented effectively. Flanagan (2008:72), referring to citizen focused policing argued. '... meeting these changing demands will require strong and effective leadership from all those involved in policing – from the Home Secretary and Chief Officers, right through to sergeants and individual officers'. Unfortunately, a recent study suggests that senior political and police leadership has varied in its level of support for this approach for many years. Fisher (2012) provides an illuminating account of attempts to implement a citizen-focused approach in the UK between the formulation of Peel's new police in 1829, through the premierships of Thatcher and Blair, and finishing with the tenure of Teresa May as Home Secretary in 2012. Fisher states that three factors are required to achieve a citizen-focused approach: political will, police leadership and performance management. In tracking these historical periods, he felt that the tenure of Peel was compromised by the lack of performance management. Although the police considered a citizen-focused approach critical in restoring confidence during the Thatcher reign, political will forced them to prioritize crime fighting. Fisher highlights the Tony Blair period as one in which a political imperative and a performance management regime were in place; however, a mixed response from senior police leaders across Britain meant that implementation effort did not match the rhetoric. In essence, although a citizen-focused approach has been seen as a critical element of policing since 1829, it has been sporadically and inadequately implemented.

Section summary

In summary, this section has shown that the relationship between the police and the public is an enduring principle in which to deliver effective policing. Although satisfaction with police services appears relatively high in the countries discussed here, there are clear opportunities for these to be improved. However, implementing approaches to improve police-citizen relationships have not proved easy to achieve.

The implications of studies surrounding procedural justice should be considered when generating operational approaches. For example, placing targets or quotas on officers for certain procedures (such as stop/search) can encourage blanket behaviour, which is seen as unfair. Similarly, saturating hot-spots with highly visible police officers may deliver short-term crime reduction, but can also create anxiety and produce less sustainable reductions in crime than community problem-solving approaches (Taylor et al., 2010). A further example is provided by Myhill and Quinton (2011) who, citing Hansard show that between the years 2000 and 2005, UK traffic camera sites increased from 1,935 to 5,371 (a rise of 184%), with prosecutions rising from 768,100 to 2,001,700, a 150% increase (Fiti et al., 2008). A rough calculation reveals that approximately 5% of the UK population is issued with a speeding ticket every year – a wholesale approach that has caused widespread public concern. As such, there appears a long-standing tension between reducing crime/road collisions and enhancing police–public relationships. This is an issue that will be further explored in the next section.

Section 3: Implementing a policing model

Introduction

Much is spoken about the level of individual discretion displayed by patrol officers; although discretion is also available to police chiefs who favour particular methods and approaches. Senior police officers interviewed for this book admitted that individual bias makes it difficult to standardize national approaches, as police chiefs frequently argue that their jurisdiction is distinct from others. One of the areas in which Chief Officer discretion becomes evident is in the choice of policing models, as all police agencies will have implicit or explicit operational strategies that guide their day-to-day activity. This section will explore the main approaches and evaluate their strengths and weaknesses. All of the models described here are proactive approaches and can be differentiated from one another as to their level of internal or external orientation. The more externally focused models (Community Policing, Problem Oriented Policing and Reassurance Policing), emphasize citizen choice and use a partnership approach more frequently to generate solutions. Conversely, the internally focused models (Intelligence Led Policing, Zero Tolerance and Compstat), in practice rely more heavily on the use of police statistics to direct police resources, and use enforcement as their preferred response. Before these different models are explored, the default model for policing will first be described.

The professional policing model

Perhaps the most common strategy, still persisting in many countries today, is the professional policing model – also known as the 'traditional' or 'crime fighting' model. In essence, it is synonymous with a reactive approach based on a strict hierarchical command and control system that deals with demands from the public on an incident-by-incident basis. Put simply, the police wait for public contact; they then record, visit and deal with the incident, before moving on to the next call. The strengths of the model are that the citizen is at the centre of the process, there is clear accountability, the approach is simple to implement, and that it is consistent with the organizational culture of the police. However, reactive models are slow to respond to political or citizen-led priorities, and ultimately fail to show value for money. As Weisburd et al. (1988:31) concluded, 'Whatever the historical achievements of the bureaucratic, military model of organization, its shortcomings are increasingly evident to scholars and police administrators, who argue that the demands of contemporary urban society undermine the assumptions upon which traditional police structures were built'.

From the 1970s onwards, studies started to expand the knowledge surrounding policing. The Kansas City Preventative Patrol experiment in 1972, led by George Kelling, monitored the impact of police patrol in three different modes over a 12-month period: reactive (where the police visited only after receiving a call from the public), proactive (where they spent significantly longer in the area) and a control area (where they spent their normal patrolling time). The study found that there was no significant difference in the level of crime, police response time (or satisfaction levels), citizens' fear of crime or citizens' attitude towards police services across the area. The study argued that uncommitted police time (60% in the experiment) could be more valuably used for duties other than routine patrol, with no adverse impact on public safety. Indeed, they recommended that deployment should be more proactive based around specific crime prevention or service goals. This thinking led to numerous proactive policing approaches that have since proliferated as technology has come to enable better data management and more effective communication. Although this section outlines the six most prevalent models, it is important to note that there are many adaptations (e.g. evidence-based policing, predictive policing, smart policing, systems policing, total policing).

Community policing

In the 1960s and 1970s, the advent of a faster paced, more mobile society negatively affected the relationship between the police and the public. From this emerged Community Policing, which is perhaps the oldest, most common, and most durable of all proactive policing models, seen extensively in North America, Europe and Asia (particularly Japan, where the Koban system is well documented). Chief Constable John Alderson (UK) argued in the 1970s that in a period of rising crime, traditional 'authoritarian' policing was no longer fit for purpose in a plural 'libertarian society' (Alderson, 1977, 1979). However, the clamour for community policing accelerated following the UK and US urban city riots in the 1980s, when disorder was often ignited by an event or rumour associated with police heavy handedness. As Tilley (2003:315) explains, Community Policing emerged in a bid to reclaim the trust of all sections of the Community. Specifically, he argued that policing is done *with* and *for* the community rather than being viewed as policing *of* the community. The approach prioritizes community-generated problems in an attempt to improve the quality of life for its citizens, and by the year 2000, over 90% of US police agencies reported that they engaged in Community Policing (Chappel, 2007).

Skogan and Hartnett (1997:5, 6), highlight the characteristics of Community Policing as incorporating such things as organizational decentralization; two-way communication between police and public; a commitment to respond to citizens' demands, problems and priorities; and an ability to assist neighbourhoods to solve their own community problems. Specifically, these principles can result in '... opening small neighbourhood substations, conducting surveys to measure community satisfaction, organising meetings and crime prevention seminars, publishing newsletters, forming neighbourhood watch programmes, establishing advisory panels, organising youth activities, conducting drug education projects and media campaigns, patrolling on horses and bicycles, and working with municipal agencies to enforce health and safety regulations'.

Although there are obvious benefits to this approach, many critics came forward to voice their concerns. Ambiguity surrounded the practical implementation of Community Policing, with police chiefs interpreting the concept in different ways. Other criticisms came from front line officers who saw the approach as idealized, promoting a softer form of policing that could be exploited by violent and persistent offenders. Certainly within the UK, this approach was viewed as a less robust style of policing, with community consultation required prior to any significant police operation being implemented. It was generally felt by commentators that police subculture was the single greatest impediment to successful implementation of these policing reforms (Chappel, 2007). On top of this, there were other implementation concerns; it became problematic to define what a 'community' was, as well as identify those individuals who were representative of it. In this way, mature, white, middle class individuals, who rarely required the services of the police, often became community representatives. All of these elements conspired to make it difficult to evaluate Community Policing.

> I've never seen any police department that doesn't say they do some level of community policing, but this can be implemented so badly. A police officer driving into a neighbourhood, and waiting for a member of the public to knock on their car window, isn't my idea of community policing.
>
> (Senior police officer, USA)

Problem-oriented policing

From the 1980s onwards, theoretical understanding of policing improved significantly, and during this time problem-oriented policing (POP) emerged, devised by a Wisconsin-based Professor, Herman Goldstein. Goldstein (1979, 1990) was concerned that the police had become too internally focused, losing sight of their mission, which was to solve community problems. In this, he argued that police officers too often respond to the symptoms, rather than fixing the underlying causes. His views can be summarized as follows:

- Police work comprises a wide array of problems that threaten public safety and security, not an endless string of isolated incidents and criminal cases.
- The police function is broader than merely enforcing the law. Enforcing the law is only one means to achieve a range of police objectives; it is not the objective itself.
- Line-level personnel have tremendous insight into the nature, causes and handling of these problems and should be closely consulted in developing improved responses to them.
- Understanding how police should respond to problems requires more than merely knowing what conduct is unlawful; it requires understanding the varying interests at stake, as they relate to how police handle the problems.
- How police respond to problems entails the exercise of considerable professional discretion.
- Better choices about how police should respond to problems can be made through careful, open deliberation, and be informed by rigorous analysis of the problems.

(Scott & Kirby, 2012:4)

Problem-oriented approaches aim to deliver sustainable solutions to predictable and re-occurring incidents by providing innovative responses through careful analysis of why they occur. Eck and Spelman (1987) provided a four-step process to implement POP, known by its mnemonic SARA. The first stage involves Scanning (identifying the recurring problem), followed by Analysis (establishing why the problem occurs at that particular location and time, involving those particular offenders and victims). This is followed by Response (implementing an appropriate intervention to prevent the crime or other incident occurring), and finally Assessment (evaluating the impact of the intervention). As this approach has evolved, it has been embraced by a strand of Criminology referred to as Crime Science. This has developed a series of theories, the most notable being Routine Activity Theory and Rational Choice Theory, that concentrate on blocking crime opportunities and examples will be provided in later chapters.

In theory, POP is an enduring model, which is well used across the world. In an English survey undertaken during 2000, almost all police forces stated that they engaged in this model to some level. Similarly in the US the POP center (popcenter.org), have generated and collated a large body of knowledge that uses this approach in diverse areas of operational policing. Unfortunately, numerous studies suggest that few police agencies have been able to embed it as common practice across their organization. The Lancashire Constabulary is highlighted as being one of the most successful in this approach (Goldstein, 2005) and can be distinguished from other forces by the level of project management they used to develop the supporting infrastructure, supplemented by the proactive support of three consecutive Chief Constables over a 15-year period.

There are considerable benefits of POP. As a means of policing, it is popular with citizens and politicians alike, for not only does it provide sustainable solutions to community problems but it also engages communities and partners in the process. Further, POP also stands out as the only model systematically evaluated as effective. Weisburd et al. (2010), in reviewing 5,500 articles, found 10 methodologically rigorous evaluations using meta-analysis techniques, to conclude that POP had a statistically significant impact on crime and disorder.

However, although POP is conceptually simple, it is notoriously difficult to implement. Weisburd et al. (2010) corroborated this by showing that only 1 out of the 10 initiatives (reported earlier) did not suffer from any implementation problems. Tilley (2010) highlights a number of reasons for what he sees as the chronic implementation issues plaguing successful POP initiatives, specifically: the lack of understanding behind the SARA process; failure to implement the intervention properly; and a lack of appropriate evaluation. Indeed, a particularly illuminating study conducted by HMIC (1998) asked police forces to supply their best examples of problem solving. On further examination, they discovered evidence of a problem in only 67% instances; 27% had been analysed correctly; 20% used a response that could be aligned to the analysis; and only 7% had been evaluated. When the same methodology was used in 2000, the level of successfully implemented initiatives had risen to 24% (HMIC, 2000). Chappel (2007:510) laments that rather than implementing POP in Goldstein's proposed form, many officers 'have redefined problem solving into a simplistic pro-activity which includes little more than stopping bicyclists and other vehicles to look for more serious violations e.g. drugs'. Studies (Bullock et al., 2006; Scott & Kirby, 2012) show that a number of reasons exist for poor implementation, as follows:

- The imperative to respond to emergencies and routine incidents overwhelms the need to adopt a problem-oriented way of working.
- The response to problems focuses on enforcement and detection rather than prevention.
- Police executives and/or police supervisors provide inadequate leadership and organizational support for problem solving.
- POP champions are too soon replaced by those less committed to the approach.
- Line personnel become cynical about reform movements and do not engage in them.
- Line personnel fail to understand or accept POP as constituting real police work.
- Responsibility for problem solving is delegated solely to line officers with inadequate management support.
- Police lack the understanding and ability to work effectively with non-police partners.
- Extraneous political turmoil distracts the organization from properly developing POP.

As Scott (2010:136) argues, POP should be viewed as 'a process theory about how police should seek to be effective, rather than a substantive theory about policing methods to reduce crime and disorder'. According to Scott, the approach provides the process and principles for a more efficient method of delivering effective policing, particularly compared with other policing models.

Reassurance policing

Our final citizen-focused model emerged in the UK. The research headed by Dr Martin Innes (now Professor) highlighted that the public did not believe crime was reducing. (Duffy et al., 2007). This is a finding that has been replicated in Australia, where only 3% of those surveyed were aware that crime rates had reduced (Roberts & Indermaur, 2009). Innes and Fielding (2002) argued that this was due to members of the public being surrounded by tangible symptoms of criminality (i.e. damaged public telephones, graffiti and burnt out vehicles), which, although never recorded in official statistics, had a disproportionate impact on their perception of safety. These were labelled 'signal crimes' and related to incidents that had a disproportionate effect on those perceiving them, causing them to reconfigure their beliefs and/or actions in some way. Extending their argument, Innes and Fielding (2002) stated that the signal crimes were exacerbated by other 'triggers for fear', understood as troubling background noise, such as fly-tipping, or the remnants of broken glass on the street. Innes insists that by accurately identifying and addressing these signals, improved levels of public confidence could be achieved. These *signals* could be combated by partnership activity coupled with the implementation of *comfort factors*, in the form of visible authority figures or the engagement of citizen groups (i.e. Neighbourhood Watch).

This knowledge provided the foundation for the National Restoring Reassurance Project, as implemented in eight British Police Forces, which utilized operational responses previously found successful in the Chicago Alternative Policing System. Regular community meetings were held with police and other partners to identify and prioritize local problems, supplemented by the deployment of identifiable neighbourhood officers. Further partners consistently met to systematically deal with these issues, and residents were informed of progress. Also critical was the strict national and local project management system used to implement the approach, supplemented by independent academic support to provide baseline and evaluation data. The pilot not only raised public confidence but also reduced crime across the trial areas (Tuffin et al., 2006); although the impact was less pronounced when implemented nationally (in the form of Neighbourhood Policing Programme).

Intelligence-led policing

Whilst police forces in the USA and UK were experimenting with POP, another game changer was starting to take shape, as prompted by the

UK Audit Commission (1993). The commission pointed out that the previous decade had experienced a significant increase in calls for service, a 74% increase in recorded crime, a 9% reduction in the detection rate and only a 6% increase in police officers. They were extremely critical of the fact that policing resources were deployed randomly with little account taken of place, time or problem. They argued that three changes were required:

1. Develop integrated crime strategies that clarified roles and responsibilities (i.e. Detectives, patrol, administration).
2. Make the best use of resources (i.e. reduce duplication).
3. Target the offender rather than reacting to crime incidents.

This generated a response that later became known as intelligence-led policing. As Tilley (2008:146) explains,

> Intelligence-led policing aims to reduce crime through the informed direction of enforcement agencies. Information is collected from a variety of sources, to produce 'intelligence'. This is then used to direct the activities of enforcement agencies in ways that enable them to disrupt, disable or undermine criminal behavior.

As intelligence-led approaches started to improve the deployment of police officers, the British government became agitated that good practice in one particular area was not implemented in another. Increased pressure was therefore placed on individual police forces to become consistent in using good practice, and the first process to be agreed upon was the National Intelligence Model (NIM). The model was described by National Criminal Intelligence Service (2000:11) as one that 'involves identifying and limiting the activities of volume criminals and dangerous offenders, controlling disorder and tackling the many problems that adversely affect community safety and quality of life. The specific outcomes required are improved community safety, reduced crime rates and the control of criminality and disorder'.

The NIM guidance is extensive; however, to distil the main points it dictates that police forces adhere to a number of consistent processes to engender a consistent way of working. First, it distinguishes between different levels of policing: Level 1 relates to local policing (police divisions or command unit level); Level 2 relates to cross-border issues (requiring collaboration between divisions in the same force area or neighbouring police forces); whilst Level 3 encompasses offenders and problems at a national/international level. Second, the model provides consistency in how information and intelligence should be gathered, establishing nine standardized intelligence reports:

- Crime pattern analysis
- Network analysis
- Criminal business profile
- Market profiles
- Subject profile analysis
- Risk analysis
- Demographic/social trends analysis
- Operational assessment
- Results analysis

Third, it sets out a process whereby priorities are set (described as the strategic or tactical assessment) and subsequently tackled. Important to the delivery of the response are the 'Tasking and Coordinating Groups', who are responsible for devising strategy and tactics to target offenders, locations or types of crime/incident. The groups have three basic responses: the development of further intelligence, an enforcement response (i.e. arrest, search warrant) or a preventative-based response (utilizing disruption or situational crime prevention).

There are many strengths to this model, which has been described as '... the pre-eminent intelligence model internationally' (Jones & Newburn, 2007), and it has been adopted or adapted in a variety of other countries including the US, Australia, New Zealand, Abu Dhabi and parts of Europe. The positive elements of the model are that it follows a systematic process as decisions are formed on the basis of evaluated information. Similarly, the process emphasizes effective delivery and evaluation. However, in practice, the approach is dependent on both the collector of intelligence and the quality of the Police Commanders. Cope (2004) conducted a piece of qualitative research with two police forces in the UK, concluding that officers lacked sufficient understanding of crime analysis and crime intelligence, and neglected this approach during the planning of operations. There were also other significant criticisms. The first related to bureaucracy, as attempts to implement consistency and accountability generated 213 pages of guidance and nine volumes of supporting documents (totaling 816 pages). This has lead to some of the most important guiding principles being hidden within the detail of the advice. Chainey (2012), for example, recently illustrated how 'hypothesis testing', an approach where analysts generate and test theories of why the crime was occurring, could improve police effectiveness. However, this advice was already provided within the NIM guidance, and had been distributed to each UK police headquarters, although rarely implemented in the way Chainey recommended. A second criticism was that the approach generated too many specialists that often remained invisible to the public whilst they analysed data, engaged in surveillance or dealt with informants. In summary, Harfield and Harfield (2008) conclude that 'A decade into the era of intelligence led policing there is enough evidence in various forms to suggest that the police service has not yet fully embraced the intelligence profession'. In fact, Evans and Kebbell (2012:81) argue that this evolves into a *vicious* intelligence cycle. At the start of the process, intelligence staff are poorly selected, leading to weak intelligence products. This means the intelligence requirements aren't met, and that commanders consequently have less faith in the intelligence model. This causes them to invest fewer resources in the selection of quality staff, and so the negative process continues. As with POP, 'Police agencies frequently lack the skills for effective evaluation and fear that what they have done may not withstand scrutiny' (Evans & Kebbell, 2012:84).

Finally, perhaps the most significant weakness of an intelligence-led approach is that responses (in practice) are over-reliant on arrest and enforcement. Ratcliffe (2008) graphically illustrates the inefficiency of an enforcement-based approach, using general crime data from the BCS and UK police crime records. Using a hypothetical sample of 1,000 crimes, he shows how only 410 (41%) would be reported to the police, 287 (28.7%) subsequently recorded, 75 (7.5%) offenders detected, 37 (3.7%) receive criminal charges, 21 (2.1%) proceed to the court, 15 (1.5%) found guilty and only 4 (0.4%) would receive a custodial sentence. He continues that even if a further 10% were prosecuted, this would merely raise the incarceration rate by 0.4%, whilst consuming significantly more resources.

Zero tolerance

The use of an intelligence-led, targeted approach was extended with the evolution of zero-tolerance policing in New York. By the late 1980s, the city was in trouble due to a severe economic depression, a crack epidemic and a significant rise of crime – specifically serious violent crime. Time Magazine referred to it as the 'rotting of the big apple' (Newburn, 2007:620). The incumbent (Mayor Dinkins) tackled the problem by recruiting more police officers, and although crime started to fall, the intervention was not swift enough to change public perception; as such Rudolph Giuliani was elected during 1993 on a quality of life and crime manifesto. The new Mayor recruited Bill Bratton as Chief of Police. Bratton had previously worked with George Kelling, co-writer (with James Q. Wilson) of the 'Broken windows' article, who argued that if small incivilities and physical deterioration were allowed to take hold, more serious social disorder would follow.

Zero-tolerance policing emerged as a 'style of policing associated with the assertive policing of minor crime and disorder', as a means of 'taking back the streets' and preventing and reducing the level of more serious crimes (Mawby, 2008:292). It was supported by an enormous increase in police officers (7k between 1990 and 1995), and the key elements of the approach were as follows:

- Vigorous law enforcement of minor crime and disorder offences
- Use of civil remedies, i.e. harassment, eviction
- Enhanced accountability (COMPSTAT)
- Conspicuous use of media.

Although the media, rather than the police, generated the term 'zero-tolerance policing', it was undoubtedly associated with a significant reduction in crime. Between 1994 and 2001, crime in New York reduced overall by 57%, murder by 66% and shootings by 75%. By 2002, the level of 580 murders was the lowest in the city for 40 years (Mawby & Wright, 2008). Yet the approach had mixed reviews. Like Community Policing, it was subject to different interpretations, in fact Bratton referred to it simply as a tough form of community policing (Dennis, 1997). Although not clearly defined, it was synonymous with a simple, unambiguous and morally strong approach to policing. The approach was generally popular with police officers and politicians alike, with the British Prime Minister, in the immediate aftermath of the 2011 UK riots, telling the police to take a zero-tolerance approach to street crime. Despite this, critics stated that it disproportionately targeted the disadvantaged, with the *no compromise* approach becoming associated with rule bending and unethical police behaviour. Innes (1999) reports of increased complaints and civil litigation, which was disproportionate compared with increased officer numbers. Others argued that the zero-tolerance approach was not the main causal factor in the reduction of crime, citing the increased police numbers, the diminishing crack-cocaine epidemic (Bowling, 1999), and the incarceration policy of the US (Karmen, 2004).

Compstat

There are those who would argue the Compstat approach is an accountability system rather than a model of policing as its principles are closely aligned with all intelligence-led approaches (and was a specific element of the New York zero-tolerance initiative). However, such has been its continued prominence that it deserves specific comment. Compstat (shorthand for computerized statistics) is a police management tool based on four elements: accurate and timely information (often displayed in computerized crime data, crime analysis and crime mapping), selection of the most appropriate tactics, the rapid deployment of police resources to the locations where crime patterns exist and devolved decision making with associated police commander accountability (Willis & Mastrofski, 2012). Compstat was seen to be playing a critical role in the enhanced effectiveness and efficiency of policing, especially across the USA. It became associated with a forthright management approach that could be brutal to police commanders; in fact it was reported that more than two thirds of the police departments' 76 precinct commanders were replaced within the first year of operation (Henry, 2003:1).

The Compstat approach has been evaluated in detail. Moore and Braga (2003) examined six US police departments and also researched other Compstat assessments before highlighting a number of benefits. These included: the performance measures being aligned with operational units providing clear accountability; the performance measures being simple, reliably measured and continuous, matching stakeholder expectations; meetings being held frequently enough to maintain the attention of Commanders, who understood that the process affected their current and future promotion prospects; and that the reviews were public, allowing transparency regarding a manager's performance. However, there were also deficiencies. The approach did not engage with softer issues, such as the fear of crime or quality of service; similarly, it didn't examine resource management and showed little consideration for sustainable long-term problem-solving initiatives.

It was also discovered that Compstat was implemented very differently across police agencies. The departments associated with a high degree of change made more intensive use of performance management than those who delivered lesser change, and most steered away from using external oversight. In a further study, Willis and Mastrofski (2012:82) said, 'The strategies used most often were location-directed patrols, crackdowns and traffic enforcement, involving police using their traditional law enforcement powers'. In describing the strategies used by his department's Compstat approach, a respondent said, 'enforcement is the hammer and everything looks like the nail'. Further, although cited as a potential Compstat response, *problem solving* was rarely observed in practice. In fact researchers concluded by lamenting the lack of reform the process had actually delivered, saying that, 'Given these findings we conclude that Compstat had reinforced, not mitigated, traditional police approaches' (ibid.:82).

Section summary

In summary, although this section has not provided an exhaustive account of policing models, it nevertheless covers the main themes and illuminates a number of issues. Lum et al. (2011) is able to provide an overview by summarizing the findings from the National Research Council (NRC, 2004). This analysis established that the standard reactive policing model has not been effective in reducing crime; some of the community policing strategies have been effective in reducing crime and disorder (as well as the fear of crime), while others haven't. Police approaches that concentrate on particular crimes, places and offenders are more effective (especially hot-spot policing); and out of the assessed models problem-oriented policing was found to be effective.

What is concerning is that there exists a constant stream of approaches associated with policing since the 1970s, which have consumed significant resources to enable their implementation; further, there have been few evaluations to identify the most effective approach. Constantly changing approaches by police leaders is counterproductive, as it leads to *innovation fatigue* in practitioners and diverts attention towards internal organizational change, rather than externally on operational outcome.

Although the proactive policing models differ on how much they are affected by citizen priorities or driven by recorded crime figures, they share similar principles. Clear identification of the problems to be addressed, together with an ability to prioritize and analyze the reasons why they occur is crucial. This needs to be followed by appropriate and timely interventions that are evidence based. Finally, some level of evaluation is needed to assess the effectiveness of the intervention and to determine whether it delivers value for money. Although the studies show positive and negative elements associated with each model, the major concern relates to their implementation. As Evans and Kebbell (2012:88) stated, 'There can be little debate over the view that modern policing should be 'intelligence led'. However, available evidence suggests that best practice – such as the UK NIM – have been adopted more at the level of rhetoric and policy than in the structure and everyday practices of police organizations'. It also appears that leadership and police organizational culture have a significant impact on which police models are chosen and how they are implemented. Whilst enforcement is done well, preventative action is less ably implemented, and evaluation is missing in the majority of cases – factors which ultimately lead to less sustainable results. Moore (1990) suggests that some approaches, such as zero tolerance, are easier to implement as they are more in line with traditional police values than a community-oriented approach. Whatever the chosen model, it is important that police chiefs are committed to their approach for a sustained period of time, in order to drive implementation forward. This enables the police agency to commit its staff to the approach and develop expertise around it. Further, the organization needs to provide the infrastructure and tools required by staff to engage in the approach effectively. In essence, the theory regarding policing models is in place, it is rather the implementation that needs to be developed.

Conclusion

This chapter has discussed some of the fundamental strategic building blocks underpinning the delivery of policing. During the interviews conducted prior to writing this book, it was startling to hear that a large number of practitioners and academics cite Peel in relation to the principles of policing. It is clear that views of Peel in 1829 left a legacy, which continues to affect policing across the world. His ideas in relation to the police mission provide a rare clarity, as does his views concerning the relationship with the public (referred to here as the procedural justice model). In fact, it could be argued that the principles of policing have remained relatively constant, whilst the environment in which they are implemented is constantly shifting.

This chapter explored the issues of mission, resource management, relationship with the public and proactive policing models. It is unlikely that any political or police leader, or member of the public, would disagree that these are important issues underpinning the effectiveness of policing. However, what we have seen here are clear differences in the way they are approached, together with an abundance of challenges surrounding their implementation. This diversity of approach supports the finding in the preceding chapter that policing differs both across and within agencies.

Of course when reviewing the issues in this chapter, it should be remembered that the police are judged to be effective compared with numerous benchmarks. In Britain, as with many countries, crime has reduced; 62% of the population feel they are doing a good job and 65%

trust them to tell the truth (21% for journalists and 18% for politicians – Ipsos Mori, 2013). However, without wanting to rehearse the arguments again, there are obvious opportunities where the police can enhance their performance. First, there remains ambiguity in relation to the police mission, especially in relation to their approach to prevention; one can only think of the benefits that could be achieved if police forces were to act together in this endeavour. Secondly, there is considerable scope to improve the effectiveness of resource management. Third, whilst performance management is important, inappropriate implementation can bring unintended consequences. Fourth, although research shows why positive relations with the public are important and how this can be improved, studies question whether the police can implement this change. Finally, in terms of proactive police models, some leaders want more emphasis on enforcement, whilst others recognize the benefit from a wider service provision. Further, despite it being known how these models should be best implemented, there are many examples in which they are executed unsuccessfully.

By considering these elements together, other lessons are apparent. Implementation is clearly an important issue; indeed, if each of these areas had been executed more efficiently, there would be a significant improvement in police effectiveness. Imagine a police service that has the unconditional support of the public, that systematically reduces crime and community problems through an effective and efficient policing model, and that is able to establish what works through its performance management system. In the short term, one cannot escape from the waste of effort that goes into failed implementation. The Policing environment is a busy one, not just externally but internally, as the organizational setting is constantly bombarded with requirements to change from external and internal influences. As McChesney et al. (2012) stated this creates a whirlwind where it is difficult to separate the urgent from the important. In this chapter, we saw the constant methodological changes to oversight systems that increased bureaucracy and resulted in more officers being withdrawn into administration duties. We have also seen how police chiefs engage with different policing models and initiatives that are constantly breaking down and are rarely evaluated to establish whether they work. As Moore says, 'One cannot learn much about whether a particular operational approach worked or not unless one can measure what the police did to ensure that the operational approach was actually implemented'. Evidence suggests that political and police leaders should place more focus on implementation to ensure a more effective and efficient use of resources.

3
Reducing Crime

Introduction

An earlier chapter described how certain politicians and police officers viewed the police as crime fighters; indeed, many nations associate police effectiveness with the level of crime. This chapter will focus on the ability of the police to reduce crime and will be divided into three sections. The first section will examine the reliability of official crime statistics as an instrument to compare police performance. The second section will expand on good practice and present a staged process that shows how the police can facilitate the reduction of crime and disorder incidents. The final section will concentrate upon implementation failure in the crime reduction process, examining the reasons why police officers often find it difficult to bridge the gap between theory and practice.

Section 1: The level of crime: A baseline on which to judge effectiveness?

> As a Divisional Commander I was asked to attend a local public meeting by my MP [Member of Parliament] to discuss crime issues. The meeting was held in a school in the centre of a large housing estate and was well attended. I had all my crime statistics with me and was in a confident mood as they showed crime had been reducing in the area. However after being introduced it was clear those present didn't believe me. I continually tried to tell them the area was safe and crime was reducing but they weren't reassured. After a while a woman raised her hand and the MP asked her for the question, 'Divisional Commander', she said, 'If it is so safe in this area, why

> would you have a Constable outside, guarding your car'. I learnt a valuable lesson – police recorded statistics do not tell the whole story
> (Senior Officer, UK Police)

As crime is viewed as a critical measure of police effectiveness, it is important to establish the reliability of the indicator before judging the performance of the police. Indeed, as globalization increases, there is a debate as to whether police agencies across different countries can be compared on crime levels. For example, between 1994 and 2012, recorded crime in the US fell by about 40% compared with approximately 60% in the UK (HMIC 2012a). Is it fair to judge the merits of the police between these countries on these statistics?

Foucault (1977) points out that crime exists as a central issue for contemporary society, and as a result it is primarily the government (rather than an independent body), who ultimately control its identification, collation and dissemination. Britain has a sophisticated crime recording process that emanates from two different sources: the Crime Survey of England and Wales [previously known as the British Crime Survey (BCS)] and Police Recorded Crime (PRC). The Crime Survey, first published in 1983, is an annual victim survey, based upon telephone interviews. It asks a representative sample of the population (46,000 people) about their experience and attitude to crime over the previous 12 months. The other approach (PRC) publishes crimes that have been recorded by the police. To engender consistency in this process, the government publish the 'Home Office Counting Rules (2009/10)', that designates 1,495 'notifiable offences', and also provides advice for the police on how to record crime information. The strength of the Crime Survey is that it provides a victim-centered account, which lessens its likelihood of being manipulated by recording practices. The disadvantages are that it lacks detail, concentrates on household crime, avoids those crimes committed on more vulnerable groups (i.e. the homeless) and suffers problems relating to the respondent's ability to interpret questions and recall events. In contrast, Police Recorded Crime comes from a much larger sample (potentially anyone within the population) and provides detail as to when, where and how the crime has been committed, which in turn provides detailed analysis to direct crime reduction activity. The disadvantages of PRC are that it is affected by changes to legislation and recording practice, and suffers different interpretations on how the rules should be implemented.

As could be expected, the two approaches demonstrate different levels of crime. Whilst the Crime Survey estimates (from their representative sample) that 9.6 million crimes were committed in England and Wales during 2010/11, the police recorded 4.2 million crimes during this period. The systems overlap on approximately three quarters of the crime categories, and the Crime Survey shows victims report crime levels three to four times higher than illustrated by PRC; going some way to provide an idea of the hidden level of crime (Maguire, 2012). However, the two processes should be understood as complementing each other and are now published in one document, 'Crime in England and Wales'.

Even with such an extensive process many incidents aren't recorded, for example, professional or *white collar crime* is rarely reported or recorded by the police. Furthermore, in England and Wales during 2011, approximately 1.15 million minor convictions were delivered in magistrates' court (summary court); 49,000 Fixed Penalty Notices were handed out for Disorder (PNDs); and about 10 million traffic and parking notices distributed, none of which were recorded as crimes. Neither are the many incidents of antisocial behavior, dealt with by the police, which cause significant distress in the community (HMIC, 2010).

There are also concerns about police recording practice, and these can vary depending upon the country concerned. During 2000, HMIC led a thematic review across England and Wales into crime recording practices and found widespread and varying interpretation of the rules. In essence, a significant proportion of offences were either wrongly classified or not recorded at all, culminating in an error rate of between 15 and 65%, and an average non-recording rate of 24%. The most common issues proved to be failure to record a crime, or recording a crime within a less serious category – behaviour that was often stimulated by pressure to meet crime reduction targets. In 2002, attempts to eradicate these failures heralded the introduction of the National Crime Recording Standard, together with a number of other recommendations. These required the police to use a lesser standard of proof when recording crime (from *beyond reasonable doubt* to the *balance of probabilities*). It also required legally binding crime recording protocols to be used; a Police Statistics Committee be formed; more information be provided within the Home Office crime return; all forces to monitor and inspect their crime recording process; and that all forces be re-inspected for compliance. These obligations caused all police forces to immediately divert more staff into back-office functions and increased the bureaucracy of the system exponentially to guarantee crime recording compliance. This change was thought to increase crime artificially by about 23% in the first year, and increase it for a number of years afterwards (Simmons & Dodd, 2003; Maguire, 2012). The argument to support the change was that crime levels could now be compared fairly between different British Police Forces. However, senior police officers I spoke to highlighted the unintended consequence that some officers had to be removed from public facing duties and placed into administrative roles.

The UK approach reveals a number of issues when using crime statistics to compare the performance of police agencies. First, as mentioned in the introductory chapter, politics is inextricably linked to law and order, which means legislation ultimately determines *who* and *what* is defined as *criminal*. Across the world, cultural diversity leads to different interpretations as to what is lawful and what isn't. For example, in Europe the age of criminal responsibility is either 12 or 14 years of age, whilst in England and Wales it is 10 years. Secondly, even accounting for this diversity, it is apparent that different countries count crime in different ways. For example, although the US use police recorded crime data (FBI Uniform Crime Reports) and victim surveys (National Crime Victimization Survey), their reporting procedure is less extensive and does not experience the same level of scrutiny as the UK (Lab, 2010). Similarly, other countries have a much more relaxed approach to the recording of crime, placing accuracy in further doubt. No matter how police agencies record crime, there is always likely to be attrition between the number of crimes occurring and the number captured in police records. Warner and Pierce (1993) argued that only 65% of all victim calls are officially recorded as a crime in the US. Further to this, Yu and Zhang (1999) have shown under-recording by Chinese police officers to be a significant issue, as only 20–30% of crimes were accurately recorded in the 1980s although this rose to 59% in 1990 following national changes.

Section summary

This section has illustrated that recorded crime categories and levels are affected by different political interventions. When coupled with national systems to identify and record crime, it appears unlikely that any country could publish a completely accurate inventory of crime, or that accurate comparisons could be made between countries. Although crime levels are more accurately assessed across police agencies within the same country, even this comparison is dubious depending on the levels of compliance to crime recording rules. Of course the question then arises that even if crime levels are accurate, how sure can one be that the police are effective in reducing crime?

Section 2: Reducing crime

> It should be understood at the outset, that the principal object to be attained is the 'prevention of crime'. To this great end every effort of the Police is to be directed..
>
> Draft instructions on establishing the Metropolitan Police Service.
> (Cited by HMIC, 2012:4)

Introduction

As was mentioned in the preceding chapter, when forming the Metropolitan Police in 1829, Peel placed great emphasis on the prevention of crime. However, later in the 20th century, there were a number of opinions that undermined this view. Martinson (1974) when reviewing the literature on rehabilitation between 1945 and 1967, cast doubt on the theory that rehabilitation reduced recidivism. This generated a pessimistic ideology that 'nothing works', as crime was considered the byproduct of structural issues such as poverty, unemployment and class, which only wider social justice could overturn. This attitude extended to policing. Clarke and Hough (1984), reviewing the preventative capability of London-based foot patrol officers, estimated they would only walk within 100 yards of a burglary taking place every 8 years (and would probably be unaware it was occurring). However, from the mid-1980s onwards, amidst the political, social and technological changes associated with late modernity, came a rethinking that the police (and other public sector agencies) could play a role in reducing crime. This philosophy came from the emergence of targeted community-based, crime prevention projects, that later became associated with more proactive policing models in the 1990s. As knowledge increased, further academic theories materialized, which could be corralled under the general heading of *Crime Science*. Laycock (2012:102) defined Crime Science as an outcome-focused discipline, aimed at the prevention, disruption or detection of crime using science in an ethically acceptable and design sensitive manner. Clarke (2004) distinguishes crime science from mainstream criminology on a number of criteria. In essence, whilst criminology looks at long-term social reform, crime science looks at more immediate crime reduction. Whilst criminology looks at the *why* of crime, crime scientists look at the *how*, and focus on the importance of criminal opportunity. Whilst criminology attempts to understand and explain crime, crime scientists attempt to equip community safety practitioners with the tools to reduce or prevent crime in operational settings. This approach of using scientifically validated studies to support police approaches is a key element of Sherman's evidence based policing approach. As he argued, 'Of all the ideas in policing, one stands out as the most powerful force for change: police practices should be based on scientific evidence about what works best' (Sherman, 1998:2). Sherman and others have cited the medical model as an effective means by which practitioners can develop their profession, specifically using scientific method, peer review and publication of their findings.

Evidence-based crime reduction interventions can be delivered at a number of levels. For example, primary responses focus at a wider community level, such as the planning of houses or roads (Newman, 1972), the design of products (Ekblom, 2005) or the use of CCTV. Secondary prevention techniques 'rely on efforts to identify potential offenders' locations or situations that have a higher likelihood for criminal activity' (Lab, 2010:170). Finally there is tertiary prevention, where the emphasis is on preventing prolific offenders from further harming society (Lab, 2010:274), an approach that mainly focuses on incarceration, rehabilitation and deterrence. The knowledge surrounding primary, secondary and tertiary approaches is constantly improving. Kennedy (2008:185) has outlined new approaches to deterrence, explaining how gang members have been diverted from violent behaviour. In one scenario, referred to as the 'crossed legs' strikes, he explains how partners of gang members withheld sexual activity until their men had disarmed. Kennedy argues that we should see deterrence as a dynamic process, where trial and error, as well as continued effort to prevent people tipping back, is needed. In the UK, the ACPO Children and Young People strategy provides a tiered approach to delivering services. Using the labels: core; targeted; specialist and priority services, the strategy outlines how the police tailor their approach from the general population to those in need of more acute services (ACPO, 2010).

There is a growing publication list in relation to what works (and what doesn't) for the benefit of both practitioner and academic. More recently, Lum et al. (2011) at the Center for Evidence-Based Crime Policy, George Mason University, has devised the Evidence-Based Policing Matrix to provide an overview of these approaches. Lum and colleagues have mapped 97 formally evaluated police studies across three dimensions of crime prevention. These are the nature of the target (individual, group, micro places, neighbourhood, jurisdiction, and nation-state), the extent to which the intervention is proactive or reactive and the level to which it is general or specific. The results provide a visual overview on the effectiveness of particular approaches in particular contexts.

They conclude, 'proactive, place based, and specific policing approaches appear much more promising in reducing crime that individual-based, reactive and general ones' (Lum et al., 2011:3).

A four-stage process to reduce crime and disorder

Chapter 2 described a number of proactive police models that are used to facilitate the systematic reduction of crime and disorder. This section will now extend this explanation by concentrating on individual crime reduction initiatives that fit within these frameworks. Again, there is a diversity of individual crime reduction models to choose from, and Table 3.1 shows a number of these options. The Problem Oriented Policing (POP) approach most commonly uses the four-stage SARA model (Scanning, Analysis, Response, Assessment), and although conceptually simple, some commentators have argued that it lacks the detail to handle complex initiatives. Others, such as Ekblom (2003) have devised alternative models, and his 5i's model emphasizes the importance of the implementation stage. Table 3.1 shows the UK National Intelligence

Table 3.1 The different decision stages of various operational models

	SARA	5i's	National Intelligence model	National Decision model
Identifying the problem	Scanning	Intelligence	Strategic and tactical assessment; control strategy	Gather information and intelligence
Understanding why the problem occurs	Analysis	(Intelligence)	Seven analytical products, i.e. problem profile, target profile	Assess threat and risk and develop a working strategy; consider powers and policy
Developing and implementing an effective intervention	Response	Intervention, implementation, involvement	Strategic and tactical tasking and co-ordinating groups	Identify options and contingencies, take action and review what happened
Assessing the impact	Assessment	Impact	Operational assessment, results analysis	Take action and review what happened

model in addition to the more recently introduced National Decision model. Each share similar characteristics, as they identify the problem, comprehend why the problem occurs, implement an effective intervention and finally assess the impact.

This section will now explore these four stages in more detail. The examples used in this section have been gleaned from good practice, established over the past 20 years, together with examples provided to the Tilley (UK) and Goldstein (International) problem solving awards.

Stage 1: Identifying the problem

When identifying the problem to be tackled, there are two important elements for the police to consider. The first is to identify and prioritize the wider problem category (i.e. burglary, domestic violence, drug-related problems). Once the overarching problem is accepted, an individual problem from that category can then be highlighted. This is best explained with an example. Imagine you are the police commander for a small town and your objective is to reduce crime. If you are based in the UK, you may be informed of a particular priority via national objectives or from the local Police and Crime Commissioner (PCC). However, in this instance there is no such steer and you are merely told to reduce crime; how do you choose which crime to focus upon? A tool that may assist is the 80/20 rule, also known as the *pareto principle*, named after Vilfredo Pareto, an Italian economist who discovered that 80% of the land was owned by 20% of the population. The basic principle established that most things in life are not distributed evenly, and it now exists as a rough guide to understand typical distributions across a variety of issues. In the crime context, it would predict a small number of crime categories are responsible for the greatest proportion of all crime (i.e. theft from cars); or that a small geographic area within the town (i.e. the commercial area) is responsible for a disproportionate level of theft (shoplifting during the day), and violence (during the evening surrounding licensed premises). This approach allows for the prioritization of specific crime categories on a quantitative basis; therefore, it may also be appropriate to use qualitative methods to ensure that *low volume – high impact* offences are not overlooked.

In practice, it is imperative that the strategic issue or objective is framed unambiguously. For example, specifying car crime is insufficient as it occurs in many different ways (i.e. carjacking, joy-riding, stealing radios and stripping for car parts). Similarly, it is insufficient to highlight the 'drugs' problem, as we know that a significant proportion of the population use legal drugs on a frequent basis. In this case, the problem could be framed more specifically as 'the sale of heroin in open drug markets' or 'illegal cannabis cultivation'.

Once an overarching crime category is chosen, the next element is to highlight a specific problem to be tackled. Again, the 80/20 rule can be used to establish where crime concentrates, as a number of theories show specific people, places, products and events to suffer repeat victimization. For example, locations such as terraced housing (made vulnerable due to access provided by the alleyway at the rear) or late night local convenience stores that have poor guardianship are often at heightened risk. It is also apparent that these repeat incidents of crime can be very durable, unless a significant intervention is made to ameliorate them. Braga and Baston (2012) point out that between 1980 and 2008, there were 7,359 shootings in Boston, US, and these were not distributed randomly. Their analysis showed that 89% of the Boston area did not experience any shooting, whilst 5% of the areas experienced 74% of the shootings – with these hotspots being present for over 30 years. Taken overall, studies show crimes concentrate around:

- Repeat offenders (i.e. 4% of offenders account for almost a third of offending, Hales et al., 2009).
- Repeat victims (i.e. 4% of victims suffer about 40% of crime – Bolling et al., 2003).
- Repeat locations [a US survey found 6.5% of convenience stores suffered 65% of robberies (Clarke & Eck, 2003); similarly certain licensed bars, petrol stations, schools and shops are also found to feature highly as risky facilities].
- Hot products (i.e. thieves are more likely to steal specific items, specifically if they are concealable, removable, available, valuable, enjoyable and disposable (Clarke, 1999). This explains why 'smart phones' account for the most frequently stolen item in the London street crime category).
- Specific events (i.e. football matches, protests).

By focusing on the small number of people, places, property or events that cause or suffer a disproportionate amount of crime, the police can deliver the most impact. As before, it is important to be specific when identifying the problem. For example, a robbery problem in a hot-spot area may in fact be two problems – theft from school children on the way home from school, and theft from those who use ATMs close to licensed premises late at night. Identifying both under the heading of *town centre robbery* creates difficulty, when the solutions to deal with each may be completely different. Lacking specificity is not just a trait of the police though, as this amusing example from aircraft engineers shows below. In essence, on finishing their journey, the flight staff leave a *gripe sheet,* highlighting any minor issue they wish the engineer to check. The ground staff deal with the issue and leave a note of confirmation. However, the ambiguity of the note left by the flight staff often exasperates the engineers, who respond with some unhelpful comments of their own:

PILOT:	'Left inside tyre almost needs replacing'
ENGINEER:	'Left inside tyre almost replaced'
PILOT:	'Something loosened in cockpit'
ENGINEER:	'Something tightened in the cockpit'
PILOT:	'Dead bugs on windshield'
ENGINEER:	'Live bugs on order'
PILOT:	'Evidence of leak on right main landing gear'
ENGINEER:	'Evidence removed'
PILOT:	'Friction locks cause throttle levers to stick'
ENGINEER:	'That's what they're there for'
PILOT:	'Number 3 engine missing'
ENGINEER:	'Number 3 engine found on wing after brief search'

Reference: DCL news editorial 9.9.03.

It is therefore important to describe the problem as accurately as possible. This should include:

- What is occurring and what is the cost
- Who it happens to
- Where it occurs
- When it occurs
- How it occurs

Note: Why it happens will be discussed at the next stage.

Having considered these issues, it is useful to show how they work in practice using an example. For ease, we will assume that the highest proportion of crime in the area we are concerned with involves theft from vehicles (the overarching problem). On further inspection, we find that one particular car park suffers a disproportionate amount of these thefts (the specific problem). Before the first stage is explored, one further operational tool will be mentioned. Ian McPherson, a previous Assistant Commissioner with the Metropolitan Police building upon

Eck's (2003) problem analysis triangle, devised the VOLT acronym to remind practitioners to consider the characteristics of the Victim, Offender, Location and Time, at each stage of the crime reduction process. This methodology will also be used when working through the car crime example:

> **Example: Stage 1 – Identifying the car crime problem**
>
> At Central pay and display car park, between 1st January and 31st March unknown offenders have smashed at least 24 car windows and stolen CD players and other items left on display. This has mainly occurred between 8 pm Thursday and 1 am Sunday. The total cost of property stolen is £5,900.

Stage 2: Understand why the problem is occurring

Now that the specific crime problem has been identified, the next stage is to understand why it is occurring at that particular place and time. In the SARA model, this would be known as the analysis stage. Criminological studies have previously defined the causes of crime through biological, psychological, sociological and cultural explanations. So, for example, a street robbery could be explained by: aberrant individuals (biological), who suffer distorted thinking patterns (psychological – specifically cognitive), who are socially deprived (sociological) or become involved in gang initiation rituals (cultural). Although this brief description is clearly inadequate to explain these approaches, the important point to be made is that each of these explanations requires long-term interventions that are outside the control of the police. As such, further theories were needed if the police and other Community Safety partners were to intervene to reduce crime.

Since the 1980s, a number of theories have emerged that emphasize the role of criminal opportunity in crime. For example, Paul and Patricia Brantingham used *Crime Pattern theory* to explain the way crime concentrates in geographical patterns. Crime clusters around the focal points in an offender's life, such as home, work and leisure areas (which they call nodes); as well as the routes between these locations (referred to as pathways). This explanation is conceptually similar to *Routine Activity Theory* (Cohen & Felson, 1979; Felson, 2002), which suggests crime emerges from the opportunities generated through the rhythms of every day life; so, for example, the prevalence of firearms in the US would explain why that country suffers proportionately more gun-related homicides than the UK. Felson and Clarke (1999:2) argue that our everyday movements, together with social and technological changes, constantly present crime opportunities that are highly specific and are concentrated in time and space. Continuing this theme, they argue that crime only occurs where a motivated offender comes together, in the same time and place, with a vulnerable victim, in the absence of a capable guardian (Cohen & Felson, 1979). Following this rationale, it can be predicted that a young person is more likely to be involved in a violent altercation at a taxi rank, close to licensed premises at 2.30 am on a Saturday morning, than an elderly male who (7 hours later and 200 yards further down the road) attends his place of worship. Consequently, most criminals offend in areas they frequent the most – which is why the majority of burglars commit offences close to home, often in socially deprived areas (Wiles & Costello, 2000).

This knowledge can assist the practitioner when analyzing the problem. Good practice dictates that a hypothesis should be established, explaining how opportunities enable crime to take place in that particular area and involving those particular individuals. In our car crime example, these issues are deconstructed across victim, offender, location and time variables.

Example: Stage 2 – Understanding the reasons behind the car crime problem

Victim:

Car park owner – there has been no investment in the car park. The pay and display ticket left in the window informs offenders how long a car will be left unattended.

Vehicle owners – leave items on display; they also leave windows and doors insecure.

Offender:

Uses the car park as a shortcut to walk into the town centre.

Uses the rubble from the rough ground in the car park to break the windows.

Location:

There are many access/exit points that provide easy access and escape routes.

There is no surveillance (formal or informal) providing the opportunity for detection.

Time:
The car park is unlit and it is difficult to see cars or individuals during the night time.

Stage 3: Developing and implementing an effective intervention

The next stage is to consider an intervention that is both operationally effective (in blocking the opportunities that facilitate the crime taking place) and is also feasible to implement. A number of academic theories support this approach at both a strategic and tactical level.

Oscar Newman (1972) in his theory of *Defensible space,* looked specifically at the design of buildings, arguing that crime rates were at their highest in places with little sense of ownership or territoriality, where anonymity existed due to a lack of surveillance, and where there existed a preponderance of accessible escape routes. According to Newman, it was important that environmental planning 'designed out' criminogenic features and 'designed in' defensiveness. In this way, housing should be designed to allow natural surveillance (for instance, the dining area at a fast food restaurant should look out towards the car park), and residential housing should have visible delineators of ownership, such as gateways.

A number of other commentators (Ekblom, 1995) argued that it was useful to devise prevention schemes by looking at the crime through the eyes of the offender. Cornish and Clarke (1986) based their Rational Choice Theory on the premise that offenders make rational decisions and consider the effort, risk and reward of their actions (albeit their decision may be flawed due to poor cognitive skills, lack of information or the effects of drugs or alcohol). Derek Cornish developed this approach with the notion of crime scripts. He states that when undertaking everyday lawful actions (such as going out for dinner), individuals make a series of decisions, which may include: choosing the restaurant, establishing the time to eat, the choice of seat and selection from the menu. According to Cornish, offenders do the same thing; that is, a robber decides upon the time, place, victim type and method of attack before committing the crime. Therefore, at each of these stages it is possible to block the opportunity for the action to occur. Extending this analysis, Cornish and Clarke (1986) proposed that if the personal cost of committing the crime outweighs the benefit of committing it, then the offender can be diverted. They argue that practitioners can support this process by considering interventions based on the following five approaches:

1. increase the effort required by the offender to commit the offence;
2. increase the risk of detection;
3. reduce the reward gained by the offender from the crime;
4. remove any excuse the offender may use to justify their actions; and
5. reduce the provocation that may surround the crime (this is a category often applied to disorder).

These five approaches can be subdivided into specific tactics. Table 3.2 provides examples of how they have been used to reduce various volume crime scenarios.

Returning to the car crime example, we can use the knowledge gleaned from these theories to generate specific interventions that systematically block the opportunities generated by the victim, offender, location and time.

Example: Stage 3 – The response to the car crime problem

Victim:

Persuade the owners to invest in the car park and *target harden* (increase effort).

Display notices to users about securing their car and putting property out of sight (reduce rewards).

Ask police officers or car park staff to place notices on such vehicles, pointing out they have left their vehicles inappropriately (remove excuses).

Offender:

Display notice, warning offenders that only car owners are allowed access to the car park, and that everyone else is trespassing (remove excuses).

Location:

Erect fence to limit access (increase effort).

Install barrier or other system to pay on exit (increase effort, reduce provocation).

Removal of rubble (increase effort).

Time:

Provide lighting during hours of darkness (increase risk of detection).

Table 3.2 Tactics to block the opportunity of crime, based upon Rational Choice Theory

	House burglary	Violence at football ground	Shoplifting
Increase the effort to commit the crime	Target harden the crime location by improving the security of doors and windows	Provide individuals with banning orders.	Leave personal bags at the front of the store
		Use bail conditions or civil orders to get specific offenders to report to police stations during specific games	
Increase the risk of detection	Use overt and covert property marking	Use confidential free phone numbers for other supporters to provide information	Use CCTV and store detectives to increase surveillance
Reduce the reward from crime	Remove coin-operated energy meters and replace with non-coin (token) system	Ban violent supporters from purchasing future tickets.	Tag items with security fixtures that are difficult to remove or spoil the item if illegally removed
		Withdraw season tickets from convicted supporters	
Reduce provocation	N/A	Have filter systems to segregate opposing supporters	Move expensive and portable items (i.e. razor blades and alcohol) away from access points
Remove the excuses	Use boundaries or signs to highlight areas of private ownership	Use notices and announcements to clarify a no tolerance approach to violence	Ask customers to select/use store basket

It is readily accepted that some of these interventions may be difficult to achieve. For example, the owner of the car park may not want to invest money into the facility, as it will detract from his/her profits. Scott (2007:389) provides examples of how the police can apply pressure on individuals to accept responsibility for crime problems. These range from mild persuasion (e.g. educating others regarding their responsibility) to the use of coercion (from naming and shaming to bringing a civil action). Facilitating ownership for crime problems is just one of the many challenges associated with the process of implementation, and this will be covered in more depth within the final section of this chapter.

Stage 4: Assessing the impact

The final stage of the crime reduction process is evaluation. There are many ways to assess the impact of intervention, and it is useful to establish the assessment criteria at the start of the project. This helps the practitioner maintain focus on what the initiative is trying to achieve, as well as avoiding *mission creep*, as more objectives are added. The following are examples of measures that can be used as assessment criteria:

- Total elimination of the problem
- Fewer incidents
- Less serious or harmful incidents
- A more efficient response to the problem (less cost)
- Reduction in the fear of crime
- Increased public satisfaction and confidence in the police.

These are outcome measures, and it may also be useful to consider some level of process evaluation, to establish whether the proposed intervention has been implemented as expected. Assessment of crime reduction methods can be established using qualitative and quantitative methods. Finch and Fafinski (2012) explain quantitative research as the gathering of numerical figures in order to produce data analysis in statistical formats. Numerical data is amenable to precise measurement, and can be argued to take a positivist and objective approach (Noaks & Wincup, 2009). Conversely, Patton (2002) explains qualitative data as a method of analyzing data from an observatory perspective, allowing a naturalistic approach to research. Patton supports the use of qualitative research, by arguing that the real world is subject to change, therefore allowing the researcher to acknowledge these changes in more descriptive ways. 'It is the means by which some form of explanation, understanding or interpretation of the people and situations under investigation is sought' (Finch & Farfinski, 2012:375). Qualitative approaches can include such techniques as questionnaires, interviews, focus groups and participant observation. As Jick (1979) suggests, qualitative and quantitative data, when used conjunctively within research, can in fact compliment one other, to give a stronger methodological design.

However, as this book has already shown, crime is a complex phenomenon and can lead to unintended consequences. Van Dijk (1994), in his explanation of Crime or Problem chains, pointed out that one crime can lead to another; that is, if someone steals a person's dustbin, he/she is more likely to steal another one in the future. Felson and Clarke (1999) extend this argument and point out that a single burglary can also involve precursor offences such as criminal damage, and may lead onto other crimes such as handling stolen goods or the fraudulent use of credit card. Similarly, as one crime unfolds another crime opportunity might appear; for example, an offender may have originally intended to commit a burglary but when finding himself alone with a vulnerable female he commits a rape. Therefore, when evaluating the impact of the intervention, it is also important to contemplate the possibility of displacement of crime, as described below:

- Spatial or territorial (crime moves to another area),
- Temporal (crime occurs at another time, i.e. from day to night),
- Tactical (more effective methods or tools used),
- Crime or functional (offenders move to other approaches, i.e. from car theft to car jacking),
- Target (offenders may move to less protected targets).

(Repetto, 1976; Barr & Pease, 1990; Guerette & Bowers, 2009)

It is now widely accepted that displacement occurs less frequently than initially thought, and that even when it does occur this is usually below the original level. There can also be positive displacement when an initiative leads to a 'diffusion of benefits', meaning that the planned initiative has a wider benefit than those initially intended. For example, the media publicity regarding an anti-burglary initiative on one housing complex may also deter offenders on the adjacent housing complex (Bowers & Johnson, 2003). Finally, it is important to remember that crime can be affected by time, be it hourly, daily weekly, monthly or seasonally. Summer evenings may result in more outdoor activity – associated with specific crimes, whilst Halloween brings an increase in anti-social behavior. It is therefore important to take the concept of time into the evaluation, and make sure that any assessment is carried out for a sufficiently long period, so as not to be affected by seasonal influences.

Section summary

Whereas crime reduction was initially thought to be outside the scope of police officers, studies now show the possibility for law enforcement agencies to make an impact when using evidence-led approaches. Many studies show that crime is linked to opportunity; for example, the theft of scrap metal or petrol is linked to powerful economic incentives such as market price (Sidebottom et al., 2011; Moffat & Fitzgerald, 2006). Similarly, the design and management of licensed bars can predict alcohol-related violence (Graham & Homer, 2008). A number of models exist to facilitate the crime reduction process, and these generally share four critical stages: identifying the problem, understanding why it occurs, identifying and implementing evidence-based responses and evaluating the impact. Although the rationale for this approach is straightforward, a number of commentators have pointed out that these approaches suffer a considerable amount of implementation failure, as the next section will show.

Section 3: Implementation failure in crime and disorder initiatives

Whilst many of the approaches discussed in this chapter are theoretically simple, their delivery can be complex. Hough (2006) argues that policymakers and managers have underestimated the complexity of the crime prevention process. Ekblom (2012:17) supports this finding by saying, 'It seems no kind of crime prevention programme or project, and no institutional setting, is immune from implementation failure'. Indeed, Ekblom questions the attempts by many practice-oriented academics, who have tried to simplify approaches to crime reduction, making them more accessible to practitioners. He concludes that much of this work has been over-simplified, to the detriment of crime reduction activity, and that it is only when the reality of this approach is understood that implementation will become more effective. Wandersman (2009) took the stance that policing often appears influenced by leaders who produce a high number of new initiatives. These are often accompanied by unrealistic expectations, as relatively small interventions are expected to affect complex and deep-rooted crime and disorder issues.

Rosenbaum (1986) previously raised concern regarding implementation failure when assessing American crime reduction initiatives. He specifically highlights three elements of implementation failure: theory failure (when an evidence-based approach is missing), implementation failure (where there is insufficient care taken in relation to the staff, resources and other factors necessary for the effective delivery of the project) and measurement failure (where there is an absence of evaluation or the evaluation is done poorly). These views have been endorsed by a number of commentators including Wandersman (2009), who argued that there are four keys to success in the delivery of interventions: theory, implementation, evaluation and resources. The remainder of this section will review these issues in more detail.

Theory failure

Wandersman (2009:2) explained this phenomenon when he stated that 'Theory failure occurs when a program is based on an invalid theory of operation, when the underlying idea or mechanism is unsound, when a strategy is inappropriate to meet a certain goal, or when there is an absence of a causal connection between intermediate and long term goals'.

At times, Police Commanders have been known to explain an increase or decrease in crime retrospectively. An unkind interpretation of these explanations would assume crime reduction to be caused by effective proactive policing tactics, whilst crime increase would be attributed to external situational matters. Such explanations lack scientific validity, as the hypothesis should be established before the intervention takes place. What is required is for the practitioner to first explain why the intervention should work, for if there is no theory underpinning the process, then experience shows it is likely to fail. Sherman (1995) supports this principle, and demonstrates that a reduction in crime can take place if police interventions are appropriate. Studies by Sherman reveal that an initiative only works successfully when a causal mechanism (something that could prevent the crime from taking place) is introduced in the correct contextual environment.

Pawson and Tilley (1997) and Tilley and Laycock (2002) highlight the importance of considering both mechanisms and context carefully, when deliberating how the planned response may work. Laycock (2005) provides a number of examples, one of which is Neighbourhood Watch. She explains that this approach could only be effective in reducing crime when the offender realizes a greater risk of detection is present. Laycock argues that whilst this mechanism might work successfully in a middle-class area with no resident offender population, she doubts the same outcome in a high crime low cost housing area, where few people would volunteer information to the police. Consider the role of mechanism and context in this list of crime reduction approaches provided by Sherman et al. (2002). The police initiatives that worked included:

- Increased directed patrols in hot spots;
- Proactive arrests of serious repeat offenders;
- Proactive drink driving arrests;
- Arrests of employed suspects for domestic violence.

The study also highlighted what didn't work:

- Neighbourhood watch;
- Arrests of some juveniles for minor offences;
- Arrests of unemployed domestic violence suspects;
- Drug market arrests;
- Community policing with no clear crime risk factor focus;
- Adding extra police with no specific assignment.

There are a number of interesting findings within these lists, particularly in the case of domestic violence, where an arrest appears to work in one context but not another. It may be that the threat of arrest to an unemployed individual has limited lifestyle impact; whereas to an employed individual, stigma amongst peers and the possibility of losing their job may be more distinct. Considering how mechanisms work in different given contexts is important, as it allows the practitioner to assess their potential effectiveness and provides a method by which to prioritize them.

Let us go back to the car crime example in the earlier section. The quote below shows an alternative approach, which culminated in a less sustainable solution to the crime. Although the process of identification and analysis followed good practice, the mechanism in relation to the response was not fully thought through.

> As a newly promoted Detective Inspector I am posted to a city area. My priority is to reduce crime and using the pareto principle I ascertain that the most frequent crime is the theft from vehicles. Using Crime Pattern theory I establish that particular crime is concentrated around three of the seven city centre car parks, and I highlight the most prevalent for action. At this stage I know the most likely time and place where the majority of car crime offences will occur. It now comes to the intervention. In hindsight I made a poor choice as I rely on enforcement. I set up observations and as the afternoon

goes on we arrest three offenders as they prepare to break into the cars. However all these offenders were released the following day and after a small lull in crime it was soon back to its normal level. (Senior Officer, UK Police)

Implementation failure

Fixen et al. (2005:5) defines implementation as a 'specified set of activities designed to put into practice an activity or program of known dimensions'; he goes on to say that 'implementation processes are purposeful and the activity or program being implemented is described in such a way that independent observers can detect its presence and strength'. Rosenbaum (1986) said that 'implementation failure occurs when the program theory is sound but not properly put in place'. Durlak and Du Pre (2008) extend this definition to include a scenario where the final delivery varies significantly from the original plan.

There are many reasons for implementation breakdown at this stage of the crime reduction process. Earlier sections have already referred to difficulties surrounding partnership initiatives or individuals not taking ownership of the problem. Hope and Murphy (1983) identified five main obstacles to implementation. These included unanticipated technical difficulties, inadequate supervision of implementation, failure to co-ordinate different agencies, competing priorities and unanticipated costs. Ekblom (2012:13) summarizes the reasons for implementation failure as 'pragmatic constraints' – including resource issues such as not obtaining sufficient information or finance to implement the initiative; as well as 'lack of generic enabling resources' that includes poor leadership and management and a lack of project management. Wandersman (2009) adds that any new intervention requires system support, specifically a supportive working environment (effective leadership) and sufficient capacity to implement the program, process or strategy. Conversely, system failure is often associated with limited funds, inadequate facilities and insufficient or inadequate (i.e. poorly trained) human resources to implement the programme with sufficient quality (Wandersman, 2005).

There are also cultural issues involved in the successful introduction of initiatives. Dalton et al. (2007) argued that it was important to use people who will be engaged in the participation of the project, to play a part in its design. This is because the individuals have particular knowledge that will contribute to the solution of the problem, the solution is more likely to be tailored to their needs and it will increase the feeling of involvement and reduce the risk of alienation. Some highlight that cultural issues inherent in the police organization may serve to obstruct creative and tailored problem-solving approaches. Indeed, Mastrofski (1988) asserts that bureaucracies will often generate hierarchies, rules and procedures to be used by inflexible organizations, whose employees are often unresponsive to those they serve. In this way, bureaucratic organizations can tend toward structural inertia (Willis & Mastrofski, 2004). Others have spoken of the resistance from groups of powerful police practitioners, whose careers and interests are threatened by the proposed change. Hope (1985) also came to the conclusion that the organizational context, in which these new initiatives are implemented, is a critical determinant of outcome.

Often, it is not about the process but about the detail and level of perseverance within it. The 2012 Goldstein award winner was the 'Strike Force Piccadilly' project, which was designed to tackle the problem of ATM ram raids in Sydney – then occurring at the level of one offence every three nights. Unfortunately, as there were 70 separate ATM alarm activations every night, and ram raiders were only taking 2 minutes to commit the offence, the traditional intervention of a rapid response task force did not work. However, when all the partners shared information to establish the best way forward, an analyst discovered that the ATMs had multiple alarms and that there was only one multiple alarm activation a night (which were less likely to be false alarms). Focusing efforts only on multiple activation alerts gave the police a one in three chance that they were responding to a crime in progress. Success quickly followed, and when coupled with target hardening approaches the offences reduced dramatically.

Read and Tilley (2000) also ask us to consider how compliance is facilitated within the specific interventions. They give an example of a junior football scheme in Skelmersdale, UK. The scheme could be considered successful, as complaints regarding antisocial behavior fell from 340 to 266 recorded complaints over a comparable school holiday period. The scheme targeted the diversionary activity at appropriate children and at relevant times; however, the innovative element of the project was the threat that league points could be deducted from any team whose player got into trouble with the police. This produced a system of informal control that operated beyond the football game.

During the research for this book, practitioners also highlighted the need for tenacity in implementing crime reduction initiatives. One highlighted that the reason the Proceeds of Crime Act was not as effective as it could be was because court orders to confiscate money were often not enforced. This can be extended to many contexts; for example, an alley-gating scheme won't work if people leave the gates insecure, or a deterrence scheme won't work if offending individuals aren't sanctioned. A further example surrounding a simple problem also highlights this issue:

> I looked at the PACT [community] priorities and found that litter surrounding the youth shelter in the local park had been consistently highlighted for years without being solved. I went down with a volunteer and picked up the litter. The problem was that local people had stamped bottle tops into the ground surrounding the area so it still looked untidy. What was needed was someone to go that extra mile, and that's what we did. We devised an instrument to dig these bottle tops out of the ground and immediately the area looked much better. All too often with longstanding initiatives people do the minimum and expect it to change. It needs relentless follow up. Reducing crime and disorder isn't about the process, it's about the delivery.
>
> (Chief Officer, UK Police)

Tilley (2009) sets out many reasons as to why a good idea in one area often fails when transferred into another. The most obvious reasons are that the factors of place, victim and offender characteristics are never exactly the same from one scenario to another. Similarly, those who are responsible for implementation also vary in levels of skill, experience, enthusiasm and resources compared with the original project. As Lab (2010:45) says, 'too often experimental design fails to consider the context within which a program of intervention operates. What this means is that the program may be successful in one location at one time while it is a dismal failure at another location or time ... there is a need for a thorough process evaluation to accompany the impact analysis'.

Evaluation or measurement failure

Wandersman et al. (2005a) argues that evaluation failure occurs if the assessment methodology is poorly designed, has an inappropriate comparison group or the design uses a measure which is insensitive to change. Further, Fetterman (1996) points out that in some cases, the subjects do not co-operate with the evaluation.

Ekblom (2012:13) provides an insight into police culture by recalling a Home Office publication that had a 'learning from mistakes' column, which had to be stopped after a year as police practitioners only submitted one entry. The wider point is that the police, as an institution, have an organizational culture whereby formal evaluation is rarely supported and (as such) initiatives are rarely seen to fail. The initiatives that are evaluated often lack a strong research design; control groups are lacking and extraneous variables aren't considered. Furthermore, many initiatives are *personality* rather than *evidence led* making them difficult to replicate.

In the last decade, there has been considerable debate as to the most appropriate method of evaluation – a debate prompted by academics engaged in the evidence-based policing approach. Sherman et al. (2007) and Sherman et al. (2002) reviewed over 600 crime prevention studies and graded these on five different levels of evaluation, which became known as the Maryland Scientific Methods Scale:

- Level 1: There is a correlation between program and measure of crime at one point in time (e.g. areas with CCTV have lower crime rates than areas without CCTV).
- Level 2: There are measures of crime before and after the program with no comparable control condition (e.g. crime decreased after CCTV was installed in an area).
- Level 3: There are measures of crime before and after the program in experimental and comparable control conditions (e.g. crime decreased after CCTV was installed in an experimental area, but there was no decrease in crime in a comparable control area).
- Level 4: There are measures of crime before and after the program in multiple experimental and control units, after controlling for the other variables that influence crime (e.g. victimization of premises under CCTV surveillance decreased compared with the victimization of control premises, after controlling for the features that influenced their victimization).
- Level 5: Random assignment and analysis of comparable units to program and comparison groups.

The authors stated that programmes could be judged as effective, as long as they were supported by two or more studies of high methodological quality (i.e. experiments and rigorous quasi experiments). In a seminal report prepared for US Congress, Sherman et al. (2007), concluded few programmes, judged as effective, used these rigorous evaluation criteria and argued it should be the future standard. Crime Scientists provide an opposing view, however. They point out that Level 5 is the gold standard, and although deemed acceptable practice in the experimental approach to hard sciences (i.e. chemistry), it is less suitable in crime reduction for a number of reasons (Ekblom, 2002; Laycock, 2012). First, they argue that the most appropriate evaluation method should be determined by the hypothesis to be tested, which may not lend itself to randomized control samples. Second, in some low probability – high risk events (i.e. terrorism) it is difficult to assign random controls as this would leave some communities unprotected, with ethical implications (Laycock, 2012:105). Pawson and Tilley (1997) believe that the level of extraneous variables occurring in a field setting make it important to be realistic about evaluation, and to recognize the importance of different actors in the process. They argue that evaluation should observe the phenomenon in its entirety.

Implementing national approaches

The advent of evidence-led approaches and the willingness of the police to use more proactive policing styles has encouraged governments to consider changes to crime control policy. Previously, when crime reduction programmes have been established and proven successful, they have acted as a catalyst to replicate the initiative in a much larger area. However, as has already been discussed, it has been difficult to transfer such examples. This has not deterred politicians who have tried to introduce national programmes though. In the UK, two mainstream approaches sponsored by the UK government were The Safer Cities Programme and the Crime Reduction Programme. There have also been national programmes in Sweden, Finland (Savolainen, 2005) and Australia (Walters, 1996; Homel, 2006). Even though the theory upon which they were based was reliable, the method of programme implementation together with the disparity in skills and resources surrounding their implementation often mitigated the impact.

It is interesting to analyze one national programme that did lead to a reduction of crime – the Street Crime Initiative (SCI), executed in England and Wales during 2002. Although street robbery only constitutes about 3% of all crime in the UK, it receives a high profile as it is associated with a lack of order and control of the streets. At the time of the initiative, the UK was experiencing a significant rise in this area, and as such both the government and the media highlighted it as a priority. In line with the pareto principle, the 10 police forces showing the greatest number of robbery offences were provided with funding (approximately 1% of their annual budget), to deploy against street robbery. The resulting SCI was implemented over a 2 year period, at a cost of £48 million and was deemed a resounding success. Machin and Marie (2011), in a careful study of the initiative, discovered that although the trend of robbery was similar across all the forces in England and Wales, the SCI areas saw a significant drop in offences, whilst the non-SCI areas continued to show a rise. Altogether there was a 15–17% drop in robbery, and the annual net social benefits was estimated in the region of £58–127 million compared with an outlay of £24 million.

So why was this multi-agency initiative so successful when others have failed? First, the process involved clear leadership, which designated this issue as the most important priority. In this stance, the Prime Minister took the lead, hosting a number of meetings with government ministers and the police. Secondly, it targeted those areas most significantly affected, rather than diluting the funding across the 43 Police Force Areas. Third, the project had academic support, as Professor Nick Tilley was asked to lead a group of researchers to assist in promoting effective responses. The interventions during the programme were categorized into four key areas:

1. Policing and Criminal Justice mechanisms (to investigate and detect, thereby incapacitating or deterring offenders).
2. Social interventions (to divert criminals and to improve social control mechanisms).
3. Individual treatment (such as reducing illicit drug dependency associated with offending).
4. Situational mechanisms (increasing the risk and effort for offenders through such interventions as target hardening).

However, perhaps the most critical implementation variable was the project management. One of the Chief Officers in command of an SCI area at the time commented,

> We were under no illusion this was a priority. The PM took personal control of this and the Home Office personnel who monitored our performance clearly took it seriously. Every day we looked at the figures and reported them to the Home Office. Every month we chaired a meeting, attended by all the senior personnel including someone from the Home Office. As such all the people who could make a difference were present – and we couldn't blame anyone else. We were held to account for what we were doing, and whether it was working.
> (Chief Officer, UK Police)

Section summary

Crime Scientists and the evidence-based policing movement share similar principles. They believe that using scientifically evaluated police interventions are the most appropriate method to increase the effectiveness of policing. Over recent years, more is becoming known about crime prevention and crime reduction approaches. Of course many gaps remain in this knowledge, specifically, 'how we can move beyond lists of effective and ineffective strategies evaluated in isolation, in order to draw generalizations about effective policing approaches, and apply those generalizations across different jurisdictions, settings, policing units and crime types?' (Lum et al., 2011). Nonetheless, what this section has shown very clearly is the importance of implementation. It is not just *what* should be done, but *how* it is done that promotes success. Across the world there are significant budgets invested into policing crime reduction initiatives. More study and focus on implementation issues appears to be a cost effective way to increase performance.

Brown and Wildavsky (1984:254) acknowledge this very point and contend, 'What an organization devoted to learning can do about implementation failure is to utilize it as a route to implementation success – successful exploration [...]. The learning society views the implementer as a source of new information. On this basis, a case may be made for the reconceptualizing of implementation as an exploratory rather than an unquestioning, instrumental and even subservient type of behaviour'.

Conclusion

This chapter has concentrated on the role of the police in reducing crime. At the outset, it highlighted that the use of crime statistics in evaluating performance is not without its risk, and that police forces can only realistically be evaluated when all agencies record crime in the same manner. The other point to consider is that the police can be viewed as having some impact in relation to crime, but there are also much larger forces in play, that range from vehicle security to the role of the family.

What research has shown is that police staff working on specific crime problems can have a significant impact if they follow a systematic approach. These early studies proved that putting visible police officers in hot spot areas, has a noticeable impact on crime by disrupting offenders from committing crime in the area. However, this style of proactive policing often relies on enforcement, therefore it does not provide a sustainable solution to the problem. A sustainable solution is more likely to use an evidence-based approach that blocks the opportunity for the crime to be committed and reduces the reward.

Models that facilitate this process generally revolve around four critical stages (although some models expand these stages). Whilst in theory these stages are relatively simple, in practice they become much more complex. There are now many studies that highlight the propensity of implementation failure, which revolves around theory, effective project management skills and evaluation.

When reflecting upon these findings, it is useful to consider how we deal with our own personal challenges or problems. When we consider what car to buy, where to go on holiday, or which school to place our children in, we rigorously analyze our needs and survey the options available. Indeed, we spend time researching the Internet and speaking to the right advisors. When prioritizing our options, we establish whether they are value for money and whether we can afford them. Once the research is concluded and our decision is made, we make sure it is implemented as efficiently as possible, and later review whether we made the right choice. To think that we can get away with less effort when dealing with complex reoccurring crime problems is simply unrealistic.

4
Investigating Crime and Bringing Offenders to Justice

Introduction

This chapter is divided into three sections and deals with the ability of the police to investigate crime and bring offenders to justice. The first section explores the role and capability of the wider Criminal Justice System (CJS). The second looks at the general rules and procedures surrounding investigation, and the third concentrates specifically on major crime investigations, such as homicide. The final section examines two publicly criticized murder investigations to examine what went wrong. This leads into an explanation of how the UK has changed its approach to improve the professionalization of investigation. As with other chapters, the reader is asked to consider the importance of implementation in relation to the investigation of crime and in bringing offenders to justice.

Section 1: The criminal justice system

The process of bringing offenders to justice

The UK CJS website explains its purpose is, 'to deliver justice for all, by convicting and punishing the guilty and helping them to stop offending, while protecting the innocent' (cjsonline.gov.uk, 2012). Within this short definition, there are a number of concepts: investigation, detection, conviction, punishment, rehabilitation, deterrence, fairness and protection. Farrell and Clark (2004) estimate that, across the world, approximately $424 billion (£281b) is spent on the CJS, with the majority spent on the police (62%), followed by Courts (18%), prisons (17%) and prosecutions (3%). Although each of these individual agencies work towards a central objective, there are many studies that illustrate the process breaks down at a number of stages, notably:

- Many victims do not report the crime – this could be due to the inconvenient process or lack of confidence in what it achieves.
- The police choose not to record the crime – this may be for legitimate reasons (i.e. it does not fit the technical or legal definition of crime) or illegitimate reasons (the victim is not believed).
- Although the crime may be recorded it may not be investigated. Many crimes are screened out for no further action due to the lack of resources or deficiency of clues.
- The investigation may be unsuccessful due to police ineffectiveness (i.e. poor use of forensic evidence or the inability to find a witness).
- Even if a suspect is identified he or she may not be prosecuted because the victim either: withdraws the complaint; there is insufficient evidence to proceed; or the prosecutor decides it is not in the public interest to prosecute.
- If the offender is charged or summonsed to appear before the Court, he or she may abscond and the subsequent arrest warrant is not enforced.
- The case breaks down when it reaches Court. This may be for witness-related issues, late or inadequate disclosure of evidence to the defence, prisoner or escort problems.
- The judge may discharge the case due to the omission of an essential legal element.

Owing to these reasons the conviction rate can be low. In England and Wales, only 20% of all crime recorded during 2000–01 resulted in the potential offenders being brought to justice (CPS, 2012). Similarly, in Los Angeles County, a study of 25 police agencies showed less than 50% of felony arrests resulted in convictions (Petersilia et al., 1987). This attrition rate varies across police jurisdiction and offence category; for example, violence (where the offender is more likely to be known) has a higher detection rate than criminal damage, which often takes place anonymously and in isolated areas (CPS, 2012), Sexual offences are notoriously difficult to prosecute for a variety of reasons, often surrounding the vulnerability of the victim. Daly and Bouhours (2010), studied five countries between 1970 and 2005 (Australia, Canada, England and Wales, Scotland and the US), and established only 11.5% of sexual assaults reported to the police resulted in a conviction. Burman et al. (2009), found a similar conviction rate when looking at rape convictions across Europe. Ratcliffe (2008) graphically illustrates this attrition process using general crime data from the British Crime Survey (BCS) and UK police crime records. Using a hypothetical sample of 1,000 crimes, he argues only 410 (41%) would be reported to the police; 287 (28.7%) would subsequently be recorded; 75 (7.5%) offenders would be detected; 37 (3.7%) of these would receive criminal charges; whilst 21 (2.1%) proceed to the court; and of the 15 (1.5%) found guilty only 4 (0.4%) would receive a custodial sentence.

The reason why a system operated by educated professionals leads to such poor outcomes has been vigorously examined in the UK. Lord Chief Justice Auld (2001:315) stated, 'The word "system" in the expression "criminal justice system" is misleading. There is no "system" worthy of the name, only a criminal justice process to which a number of different government departments and agencies and others make separate and sometimes conflicting contributions'. Berry (2010:13), stated the words spoken by Auld remain true and argues that the CJS in the UK requires a common purpose, a shared business case, and compatible IT if it is to improve. However, flaws continue to emerge and recent inspections reveal gross inefficiencies in the system. A randomly chosen case of minor assault was seen to take 242 days to pass through the system, requiring 44 hours of processing, with five copies of case papers generated across three IT systems (HMIC 2010a:20). It appears the CJS, similar to other multi-agency partnership initiatives, suffer problems of implementation. Understanding the theory of what to do is not the problem – it is the process of putting it into practice that often breaks down.

The CJS encompasses a group of professional organizations that have the joint responsibility of bringing offenders to justice. Research shows that the UK system (as well as others worldwide) achieves notable results although more effective implementation would bring a further change in performance. However, it is unfair to blame the ineffectiveness of the Criminal Justice process entirely on the police (who consistently get the highest public confidence rating of all Criminal Justice partners). As such the section now looks at an area they are responsible for – the investigation of crime.

Section 2: The investigation of crime

Introduction

One of the central roles of the police is to investigate crime – a process that focuses upon the search for truth, rather than just identifying the offender. This section illustrates that the investigative process can be viewed as a trade-off between the potential of what can be achieved, against the moral and financial cost of achieving it. It is also shown that investigative performance can be plotted on a continuum; ranging from *highly effective* when investigating low volume, high profile crime – to *administrative detection techniques* when investigating high volume, low profile crime. It is acknowledged that most crimes will not be investigated, either because they are not reported or recorded by the police or because the police feel there is little point in an investigation (Carson, 2005). For those that are investigated the level and outcome of the process will be determined by the rules of investigation, the seriousness of the crime, the competence of the investigator, and the tools and resources available. It is useful to take each of these in turn.

The rules of investigation

All criminal investigations occurring in the developed world should take place within a legal and ethical framework that protects human rights. This means investigators are not permitted to abuse the human rights of the suspect or intentionally introduce flawed evidence that may later result in a miscarriage of justice. A further point to note is that the English Justice system is based on an adversarial system rather than an inquisitorial system (observed elsewhere in Western Europe). The purpose of the adversarial system is to ascertain whether the prosecution evidence is sufficient to prove the offender has committed the offence *beyond all reasonable doubt*. In this way, the prosecution are asked to disclose their evidence first, as well as provide any other material they feel may be relevant to the defence. The defence is then allowed to challenge the material before deciding whether they want to bring evidence themselves – a process that may see the victim open to robust cross-examination. There are other legal protocols that also provide guidance on what evidence is required to prove the offence, and these also direct how evidence should be gathered and presented.

Different countries have different approaches when dealing with suspects. This may change over time as specific procedures are deemed no longer acceptable. When a civilized society experiences a crisis involving a miscarriage of justice it often responds by increasing the control on the police and the investigative process. In the UK, there has been a significant amount of legislation, in this area (Table 4.1).

The Police & Criminal Evidence Act 1984, for example, increased protection for the suspect as well as clarifying how evidence should be obtained. Specifically, PACE 1984 established that suspects should be

Table 4.1 Recent legislation affecting the investigation of crime in the UK

Year	Legislation	Purpose
1984	Police & Criminal Evidence Act (PACE)	Clarified police powers; set out investigative procedures and defined rights of suspect
1985	Prosecution of Offences Act	Established the Crown Prosecution Service to take responsibility from police in relation to prosecution
1996	Criminal Procedure and Investigation Act (CPIA)	Defines criminal investigation and role of investigator. Introduced statutory disclosure process
2000	Regulation of Investigatory Powers Act (RIPA)	Defined process of covert investigation and placed it within regulatory regime
2003	Criminal Justice Act	Gave CPS responsibility for selecting charges

cautioned about self-incrimination, have the right to free legal advice, and if they are under 18 years (or otherwise vulnerable), have the right to have an 'appropriate' adult present. Since its introduction, the *codes of practice* outlined in this legislation have been updated to deal with concerns regarding ambiguity or to deal with changing circumstances. As with other legislation, if there is non-compliance with these codes of practice, the courts are entitled to reject the evidence and the offending police officer may be sanctioned.

Although legislation and procedure define the investigative framework, adherence to this process will not routinely deliver an effective and efficient investigation, as a considerable amount of expertise is needed regarding operational implementation. For example, ethical judgment is extremely important and is difficult to codify. Ethics has been defined as 'the set of beliefs, values and standards by which people regulate their conduct' (Wright, 2007:586). Wright argues this is important as investigations can be complex and involve conflicting views as to the correct course of action. He argues that doing the *thing right* (a technical act) is different to *doing the right thing*, and within any investigation there are moral judgments to be made. For example, although informants have been heralded as cost effective (HMIC, 1997), their usage can be counterproductive and deliver unintended consequences, as they may be motivated by the wrong reasons. For example, they may want revenge against the person they are incriminating, they may wish to disrupt a specific investigation by providing false information or they may want to continue with their own offending and obtain information from the police. There are also concerns that potential informants could obtain money from the police in other deceptive ways. Consider the following scenario – a male offender (henceforth referred to as the informant) is in possession of an illegal firearm that he wants to dispose of. The informant approaches a police officer (now referred to as the informant handler) and tells the officer that he can recover an illegal firearm from an offender. The informant also says he cannot reveal the name of the offender for fear of reprisals and will only obtain the gun if he is given sufficient money to pay for it, as well as something to compensate for the risk involved. In this way, although the informant appears to be receiving money to take an illegal firearm off the street, he is, in reality, selling his or her own illegal firearm to the police. Examples such as these illustrate a small sample of the investigative dilemmas that detectives will face in the investigation of crime. Over the years, there have been many checks and balances put into the system – in this example only experienced officers are now allowed to deal with informants and they are assigned an 'informant controller' to supervise this interaction. Even so, many of these investigative dilemmas depend on an investigators' professional judgment and strong ethical code to navigate safely through.

An Ethical Dilemma

There is a vendetta between Mr. Yellow and Mr. Green. Intelligence sources inform you (as the investigator) that Mr. Yellow is going to kill Mr. Green. You cannot use that information as evidence. What do you do? If you tell Mr. Green will he take pre-emptive action and kill Mr. Yellow? If you don't tell Mr. Green how can you defend your position if he is killed?

The seriousness of the crime

Crime can be subdivided into many types and can be committed at many different levels of seriousness. The highest proportion of committed crime involves: theft (shoplifting, vehicle crime), burglary, and assault. These are known as volume crime offences. In a study across eight police areas (Basic Command Units) in England and Wales, burglary and car crime were found to account for nearly 30% of all recorded crime (Tilley et al. 2007). Volume crime is an important category because, as it involves large numbers, a high level of detection in this category will have a positive impact on the overall detection rate. In a system where quantitative measurement is the only way to judge effectiveness, this becomes an extremely important measure of performance (see Chapter 2, on New Public Management (NPM)). Different types of volume crime are associated with different detection opportunities. For example, shoplifting and assault are often only reported when the victim wants the offender prosecuting and as such they enjoy a high detection rate. Conversely, bicycle theft historically has a low detection rate (5% in 2004–05).

During a busy working day, police officers will make decisions to maximize the chance of detecting volume crime. This may mean spending more time on crimes with positive lines of inquiry and not pursuing those they are unlikely to detect. Eck (1983) said there were three types of investigations: self-solvers, cases able to be solved with some investigative effort and those crimes that cannot be solved without a reasonable amount of effort (or cannot be solved at all). Tilley et al. (2007:234) explains this generates a triage process as the police prioritize different responses based on the answers to the following questions:

1. Which cases warrant police attendance at the scene?
2. Which cases warrant an immediate response?
3. Which cases warrant the expenditure of extended investigative effort?
4. Which cases warrant forensic examination?
5. Which cases warrant prosecution?

In this way, attrition naturally occurs throughout the volume crime investigation process. Gill et al. (1996) reported that car crime rarely receives a secondary investigation, whilst most domestic burglary does (Coupe & Griffiths, 1996). Tilley et al. (1997:240) discovered 18% of all volume property crimes were detected, the reasons for which could be classified into 20 categories, the most prevalent being:

- Offender caught at or near scene of crime (34%).
- Physical evidence, including CCTV (27%).
- Information from victim or witness (18%).
- Possession of stolen goods (12%).

There also appeared to be less effective investigatory methods. Informants, for example, only led to detection in 0.5% of all volume crime cases. Similarly, the efficiency of criminal investigations has often been questioned, with secondary investigation often criticized as leading only to the duplication of effort. Although in recent years, efforts have been made to improve investigative processes these continue to receive criticism, with HMIC (2010) citing a burglary case in which 30 different individuals were used to prepare one case for court, and a rape offence where 24 people were involved in the first 24 hours.

As aforesaid, most volume crime investigation suffers from a low resource allocation. This has resulted in practitioners introducing a degree of gamesmanship into the system, whereby volume crime detections are achieved through minimal effort, thus utilizing administrative practices. There have been numerous scandals surrounding this practice. Arguably the most common relates to already incarcerated offenders accepting offences *taken into consideration* (also known as *write offs*), for which they receive no further sanction, only to later discover the individual was incapable of committing them. Resultantly, further rules have been introduced in the UK in an effort to prevent any additional exploitation of the system, and there are now different categories for counting detections in an effort to ameliorate the incentive to engage in unethical practices. Detections are now divided into sanctioned and non-sanctioned detections. The former is where:

- A person is charged, cautioned, issued with a summons or given a formal reprimand or final warning.
- The offence is admitted and taken into consideration by the courts.
- A fixed penalty notice is issued in relation to a notifiable offence.

Conversely, a non-sanction or administrative detection is where the police have gathered sufficient evidence to charge someone but charges are not brought. This can be because:

- The offender or a key witness is dead or too ill to proceed.
- The victim refuses, or is unable to give evidence.
- The offender is below the age of criminal responsibility.
- To proceed with the case would not be in the best interests of the public (i.e. the offender is already serving a term of imprisonment and is unlikely to get an extended period if brought back before the Court).

NB: At the time of writing these categories were under review.

Even with these rules there remain numerous manipulations of the crime recording system. The latest review by HMIC (2012b) discovered many police forces were classifying some incidents on their system as 'no crime', when in fact there was evidence a crime had occurred.

Section summary

This section has shown that volume crime suffers resource and time restrictions that impact greatly on investigative techniques. However, in low volume, major crime categories (such as homicide or serious sexual assault) resources are more likely to be available. It is in these cases that the full investigative skills of the police are revealed. The following section uses major crime investigation (i.e. homicide investigation) as an example.

Section 3: Major crime investigation

The competence of the investigator

In the UK at the start of any major investigation, a Senior Investigating Officer (SIO) will be appointed and made accountable for the investigation. Here, good practice regarding the investigative process has been developed by the ACPO Homicide Group (a national group of senior police investigators), and published by the National Policing Improvement Agency. This procedure is now articulated in numerous documents; the foundation of these are the Core Investigative Doctrine, the Murder Manual and the Major Incident Room Standard Administrative Procedures (MIRSAP). These documents consist of hundreds of pages, of which a few critical elements are outlined here.

The first point relates to the investigative mindset and evaluation of material, set out in the Core Investigative Doctrine (Stelfox, 2009:154). At the start of any investigation, the Senior Investigating Officer outlines specific objectives in relation to the search for material. This varies according to the type of crime and the particular stage of the investigation. Initially, these objectives are likely to be wide: has a crime been committed, are there any witnesses and can a suspect be identified? As the investigation continues these may narrow, i.e. can a particular suspect be placed at the scene or can a suspects' alibi be corroborated? Second, the SIO grades incoming information against the following criteria:

- *Relevancy:* (the Criminal Procedure & Investigations Act 1996 sets out that relevant information also includes material that would be useful to the defence);

- *Reliability:* investigators also look for independent corroboration, and;
- *Admissibility:* (the rules of evidence exclude certain types of information thought unreliable). In essence, the police will not find all available information and not all gathered evidence will be admissible.

Using the '5WH' formula, the investigator can *organize* the information *to* establish what information is present and what is missing (Stelfox, 2009). This can be summarized as follows:

- Who: Can the victim(s), witnesses and suspect(s) be identified? Is there a physical description or other evidence that may assist in identifying the suspect? Are there any characteristics of the victim that suggest a possible offender?
- Where: Is it clear where the offence took place? Is there any evidence of selectivity? Does there appear to be an element of planning or does the choice of location and victim appear random? Are there characteristics of the location that may be significant, e.g. sheltered housing or vulnerable commercial premises?
- What: It is important to establish what has occurred by piecing together all available information and building a hypothesis of how the offence took place.
- When: It is useful to establish a timeline highlighting significant events prior to, during and after the crime.
- Why: For what reason was this offence committed in this location, against this victim, at this time?
- How: Is there sufficient information to explain how the offence was committed? Can the level of skill or knowledge used by this offender inform the investigation as to his/her identity?

The experience, knowledge and leadership skills of the SIO are important. This is made more difficult due to the limited time period the investigator has to achieve results, a factor that can constrain thinking and decision making. In a number of illuminating studies, Tverskey and Kahneman (1974) and Kahneman and Tverskey (1973) have illustrated how decision making can be affected by heuristics and bias. The former can be classified as cognitive short cuts, which are more likely to be used in areas of uncertainty when information is ambiguous or unavailable. Although generally used when little time is available they can lead to severe and systematic errors. The most commonly observed heuristics within an investigation are the base rates fallacy, representativeness heuristic and the availability heuristic. For instance, studies have shown that people often use stereotypes rather than baseline information to inform quick time decisions. This is similar to the representativeness heuristic; it is extremely helpful to say something is similar to X as it permits a quick judgment, allowing the issue to be dealt with using past experience. For example, despite limited information, the media illustrated this by quickly linking the Yorkshire Ripper offences to the murders of five women in Ipswich during December 2006. Finally, there is the *availability heuristic*; this involves assessing events according to the ease they can be retrieved from memory. People often assume if something is easily recalled, then the event occurs regularly and is more probable (and vice-versa). However, studies show availability is open to cognitive bias and individuals are most likely to remember things that are familiar or distinctive. The danger is if a detective has experienced a recent murder that he/she feels is similar to the current investigation, then he/she can quickly make similar assumptions based on limited evidence (Alison & Crego, 2008:159).

The SIO is also open to bias, a phenomenon traditionally regarded as the biproduct of heuristics (Keren & Tiegen, 2004), which inclines the investigator to one judgment rather than another. These may not always be errors in judgment but the result of cognitive limitations, processing strategies, specific motivations and cognitive styles. The biases most pertinent to an investigation include *belief persistence*, where once a belief or opinion is formed it can be difficult to override. This is obviously important when investigators (and jury members) try to make sense of who-did-what, and why. Additionally, there is *confirmation bias*, where decision makers actively seek out and assign more weight to evidence that confirms their hypothesis and ignore, or place less emphasis on, evidence that refutes it. *Confirmation bias* can be said to operate through two mechanisms – selective information search and biased interpretation of available information. Confirmation bias significantly affected the investigation of the Yorkshire Ripper when *Wearside Jack* sent in a recording confessing to the murder. Confirmation bias led the investigators to only look for those with Wearside accents, which was later found to be false. Finally, there is *Hindsight bias*. This is where events are thought to be predictable only after they have already occurred. These hindsight experiences often happen when the event has a well-defined alternative outcome (i.e. win/lose), and can play a significant part when apportioning blame after the event. A hypothetical example may be when the police are called to an incident where it is alleged a man is brandishing a firearm. A police firearms officer sees the subject pointing something at him and shoots the suspect, who is later found to be carrying a chair leg. If the person assessing the incident has no understanding of the stress associated with the situation then they may be biased towards thinking the officer acted unlawfully.

In complex investigations, the SIO will delegate various parts of the process to other specialists, who determine the strategy for such areas as Search, Forensic, Intelligence and House to House inquiries. Having highlighted some of the complexity affecting SIO decision making, it is useful to establish some of the implementation difficulties surrounding the tools used in the investigation.

Tools and resources for the investigator

The investigator has many methods of obtaining information. However, unlike the media depiction of investigation, the circumstances in which this evidence is gathered is besieged with practical dilemmas that requires careful judgement. This subsection deals with some of the most common areas.

Witnesses

Witnesses are crucial to most court cases. However, they create a number of difficulties for investigators. Research into false convictions (often shown when DNA evidence exonerates a convicted person) shows the most common reason is inaccurate witness evidence (Connors et al., 1996; Huff et al., 1996). Witness testimony relies on memory, which can be fallible at the stage of: *acquisition* (witnessing the event), *retention* (storing the memory in its original form) and *retrieval* stage (recalling the original memory). Using the mnemonic ADVOKATE, Kebbel and Wagstaff (1999) describe the case of R. V. Turnbull 1977 that list the variables most associated with the quality of acquired memory:

- Amount of time under observation
- Distance between the witness and incident
- Visibility at the time of the observation
- Obstruction between the witness and incident
- Known or seen before (witnesses are more able to recognize the features of those they already know)
- Any reason to remember (if the incident happened on a birthday the witness may place specific relevance on it)
- Time lapse between the incident and being asked to recall it
- Errors or material discrepancies.

Studies show that memory recall can be distorted due to various situations; for example, recall is more accurate for non-violent events than violent ones, or those where weapons are used (Clifford & Hollin, 1981). Similarly, in terms of retention, with the exception of facial recognition most memories deteriorate over time. Finally, pertaining to retrieval, witnesses are generally better at describing what happened than describing the physical characteristics of the offender. Unfortunately, studies have also shown that asking leading questions and presenting false information to the witness can make them change their answers or even recall events that have never occurred (Porter et al., 1999). These complications make the investigators approach and judgment critically important. The investigator may be under severe time and media pressure to find the offender and may be interviewing a victim who desperately wants to assist the investigation. In these situations, care needs to be taken to prevent the witness making assumptions or being inappropriately led.

The nature of these pitfalls has led academic research to assist with helping witnesses recall events, as well as perform more accurately in identification tasks. The Cognitive Interview, devised by Geiselman et al. (1984), uses four techniques to improve witness recall. These are: reinstating context (this involves asking the witness to think about the physical surroundings and personal emotional reactions that existed at the time); reporting everything that comes to mind about the event, no matter how inconsequential; recounting events in a variety of chronological sequences (beginning to end; reverse order; forward or backward from highly memorable points) and adopting different perspectives (recalling events from the view of another person at the scene). These approaches, using social and cognitive cues, assist the witness in gathering information from all aspects of their memory and can significantly increase recall. The system was later improved through emphasizing interviewer skills, such as rapport, empathy, listening and awareness of emotions. Further, Wells and Olson (2003) and others have assisted in the understanding of false identification, which has resulted in significant changes in the process of identifying suspects and the use of identification parades. Although these points show that investigative skills are critical when obtaining accurate information from the witness, none of this assists in the practical matter of securing the witnesses' attendance at Court. Some witnesses may be reticent to attend court due to intimidation or their drug/alcohol dependency. Often officers are engaged in cajoling, shadowing and otherwise supporting individuals so they can attend and provide their evidence. This again is problematic, as the prosecution team should not inappropriately induce the witness to give evidence.

Scientific support

In recent years, the media have promoted the use of scientific support in investigations, especially in relation to individualization – the process of showing whether *trace material* is attributable to a single unique source. This principle comes from Emile Locard, who famously said,

> No one can act with the intensity that the criminal act presupposes without leaving numerous marks in his wake; either the criminal will have left traces of his identity at the scene, or by an inverse action, he will have carried indications of his stay or his actions on his body or on his clothing.
>
> (Locard, 1923 cited in Broeders, 2007:320)

History shows the use of scientific evidence had a ponderous start. Whilst Professor Marcello Malphigi noticed ridges, spirals and loops in fingerprints in 1686, it wasn't until 1935 when the Metropolitan Police established their first forensic laboratory, and a further 30 years later when it was recommended a specialist officer should attend the scene of a crime (Broeders, 2007). However, since Sir Alec Jeffreys discovered DNA profiling in 1984, progress has been swift. Although scientific evidence is not infallible, irrefutable or inarguable, it is often the best evidence presented before the Court. The central question for the Scenes of Crime Investigator (CSI) or the Forensic scientist is whether that particular fibre, footprint, glass particle blood or saliva came from one particular source. Similarly, further advancements, such as the analysis of bullets or gunshot residue, when coupled with blood distribution, also allow crime reconstructions to be created.

Even with these advancements much depends on the practitioner; more effective examiners have a greater understanding of where burglars have been and will harvest more *trace material*. However, practitioners are fallible and also subject to bias, leading to significant performance differences between individual CSIs or forensic scientists. A considerable amount of money has been invested in forensic examination and debate continues to surround its economic efficiency and the ethical context of the approach. Recently, in the UK, the productivity of scientific support appears to be falling. Between 2003/04 and 2008/09 the number of detections made by both fingerprints and DNA has fallen, whilst the total cost of delivering the service has risen by 21% to just under £350 million. Indeed, the peak period for scientific support–related detections was in 2005/06 (93,996 detections), whereas in 2008/09 this had dropped by 20% (HMIC, 2010a:11). Similarly, controversy currently surrounds the effectiveness of the approach, as in a relatively small number of cases scientists have missed evidence, most prominently in the Damilola Taylor case (Rawley & Caddy, 2007). This has been interpreted as human fallibility, rather than technical error, as it was pointed out, '... whereas missing one area of blood might be explicable, missing at least four areas of blood was not consistent with a careful and diligent inspection' (Rawley & Caddy, 2007:1).

These concerns notwithstanding, it is clear the use of scientific evidence has provided some of the most significant breakthroughs in crime investigation. However, the retrieval and analysis of scientific evidence (like other examples in this chapter) relies on good implementation and must be acted upon; fingerprint identification is of little use if a police officer fails to arrest the suspect. However, whilst Locard devised the principle of *every contact leaves a trace*, he could not have predicted the evolution of this concept through technological developments.

Passive intelligence sources

Individuals moving through different locations often leave electronic traces, which police investigators in the UK refer to as passive intelligence sources, for example:

- Public CCTV (street, garage forecourts, department stores)
- Automatic Number Plate Recognition (ANPR) for motor vehicles
- Credit and debit card transactions
- Telephone calls
- Satellite navigation systems
- Movement through ports
- Timed transactions at stores.

Each category of passive intelligence source can provide a wealth of information that can reveal different elements of the suspects' lifestyle; where and when he/she travels; hobbies, interests and habits; affluence and disposable income.

> The use of passive intelligence sources has been particularly effective in 'no body' murders. In 2005, David Guilfoyle went missing in Lancashire and murder was suspected. Passive intelligence sources showed he was not in a hospital; neither had he: attended appointments; travelled abroad; spent or collected money; paid for food; or

> phoned business colleagues or friends. This convinced a jury he had been killed and a suspect was convicted of his murder. After his conviction the offender admitted his guilt and led officers to the body.
>
> (Senior Detective, UK Police)

Kirby and Turner (2007) have also shown the particular benefits of ANPR. To clarify, ANPR can either involve static or mobile cameras that photograph a vehicle's number plate and check it against police (and other agency) databases. Its use was highlighted following the investigation into the fatal shooting of Constable Beshenivsky in November 2005, when ANPR was used to assist in the identification of a suspect vehicle and those associated with it. However, in their compilation of good practice, Kirby and Turner (2007) showed the technique can be associated with many innovative examples. One involved an investigation into three linked armed robberies taking place on separate days at Maidstone, Ashford and Margate. The subsequent ANPR analysis showed 40,000 vehicles were recorded in these areas at the relevant time although only two vehicles were in the vicinity of all three robberies. This allowed a much more focused investigation and it was soon discovered one of these vehicles was directly involved in the crimes. A further example used *post incident analysis*, following a road rage incident at Heathrow Airport that culminated in serious injury. Witness accounts at the scene pointed to a multi-purpose type vehicle (MPV) being used and subsequent analysis of the ANPR data found such a vehicle following the victim's car. Within an hour, detectives had the name and address of a suspect and a quick arrest enabled the speedy retrieval of vital forensic evidence. Further inspection of the ANPR data at the time of the incident enabled the identification of 128 other vehicles in the vicinity of the crime, from which more witnesses were found.

Offender profiling

No chapter on the investigation of crime would be complete without some mention of offender profiling. 'Offender profiling' attempts to draw inferences about an offender's characteristics from examining the behaviour at the crime scene.

Although the FBI popularized the term the concept predates their usage. During the 1400s 'Malleus Maleficarum' was written to identify and eradicate witches. Woodworth and Potter (1999:243) say it was one of the first '... systematic approaches for identifying and making inferences about supposedly guilty individuals'. The technique rose to prominence in 1956 when the New York police consulted with psychiatrist Dr James A. Brussel to compile a profile of a serial bomber who was believed to be responsible for over 30 bombings. Following a successful profile, the concept gained popularity, and in the 1970s Howard Teten (who had previously consulted with Brussel) started teaching psychology to the FBI. In 1972, the FBI Behavioural Science Unit (BSU) was established, and its task was to assist murder investigations by either reducing the overwhelming list of suspects or by opening new lines of inquiry. The BSU based their profile research on the indepth interviewing of 36 convicted murderers, which categorized offenders into organized and disorganized killers. They argued, for example, organized offenders would: plan the offence, control the conversation and general scene, use restraints and hide the body. Conversely, the disorganized would display spontaneous offending, use minimal conversation, leave a disordered scene, use sudden violence against the victim, may engage in sex after death and leave the body at the scene. The profilers stated each of these categories correlated with personal characteristics. Consequently, the BSU could determine that the organized offender would be highly intelligent, socially adequate, sexually competent, live with his father; and have a masculine image. Equally, the disorganized offender would be below average intelligence, socially inadequate, have an unskilled occupation, low birth-order status; have received harsh/inconsistent discipline, lives alone, lives/works near the crime scene, and have poor personal hygiene.

Recently, there has been an attempt to elevate the scientific integrity of this research and widen its scope. Pioneered by Professor David Canter and colleagues, this work has used large databases of offenders and tested their behaviour against psychological principles. One study tested the organized/disorganized dichotomy used by the FBI and extrapolated that this theory could not be verified in an operational setting (Canter et al., 2004). However, problems surrounding the offender profiling approach being used inappropriately were seen most clearly following the murder of Rachel Nickell on Wimbledon Common. Paul Britton, a clinical psychologist, was asked to profile the potential offender. When a suspect emerged Britton was employed to assist in the deployment of a female undercover operative who allegedly tried to persuade the suspect to confess to the killing. Although the suspect was eventually charged with the murder, this was later dismissed by a judge who criticized police action. Ormerod and Sturman (2005) argue police failings related to three points:

- The Criminal Procedures and Investigations Act 1996 (CPIA) specifies that the police must investigate the crime and not the suspect. This includes an obligation to pursue lines of enquiry that point away from the suspect.

- The case illustrates the problem of *confirmation bias* as the investigators only sought information that would implicate the suspect as the murderer.
- A criminal law case must be proved beyond reasonable doubt. The profile shows the type of person who could do it, *not* the person who has done it.

Ormerod and Sturman (2005) also highlight the US experience. In the cases US versus Sokolow, 1989 and US versus Quigley, 1989, it was held that whilst such measures are acceptable in assisting the direction of an investigation, such predictions are not admissible as evidence in any subsequent trial. It was stated that for something to be admitted as scientific evidence it must have *general acceptance* in the scientific community. As a result of this the judge affirmed that 'profiles identifying the defendant will be excluded as insufficiently relevant, unreliable, prejudicial and unscientific'. Although the academic effort invested in offender behaviour has revealed considerable insight, this investigation serves as another example of where useful knowledge is implemented poorly.

Section summary

The changes to investigation have been significant. The tools and information available to the investigator are much more advanced in contemporary society. When used effectively they can achieve some excellent results, especially when sufficient resources are available. The many successes in high profile murder investigations illustrate the level of expertise held by the UK police. However, the investigative process is inherently complex and when this process breaks down it is often due to human fallibility in implementation, rather than a lack of knowledge or equipment. This point will be continued in the next section.

Section 4: Implementation failure and the professionalization of investigation

This final section examines two high profile investigations that have been publicly criticized in the media. It evidences how incidents such as these, coupled with other drivers for change, prompted the British police to make changes in their approach to investigation, and establish a more professional footing.

Implementation failure

The first case study relates to Operation Ruby, which investigated the disappearance and murder of Milly Dowler (13 years). The second relates to Operation Fincham, which dealt with the murder of Hollie Wells and Jessica Chapman (10 years). These cases had a number of similarities both occurring in 2002 and involving young females. Furthermore, although the investigations resulted in the arrest and conviction of the offenders, the police were criticized over their handling of the investigation and subsequently apologized for their actions.

Milly Dowler went missing on the 21 March 2002. She had followed her usual midweek routine, finishing school, travelling home by train and spending time with her friends in a café, before starting her walk home. She never arrived and her father reported her missing at 7 pm. The investigation surrounding her disappearance was not brought to a swift conclusion. During the mandated 28 day review, the author (DCS Payne) was critical of the ongoing investigation. He argued the incident was being treated as a 'missing from home' enquiry when everything pointed to it being an abduction and murder; he also said the command structure was poor and that there was a general lack of CID experience available in the force to assist on the investigation. It was 6 months after her disappearance that Milly's body was found in woodland some distance away, and a further 9 years before the offender, Levi Bellfield, was convicted of her murder. Following this conviction, the investigation was thoroughly re-examined and a number of failings were highlighted. Most notably, the day before Milly's disappearance a man was reported trying to lure a 12-year old schoolgirl into a red car. The communications operator logged this as a suspicious incident and passed it to the local intelligence officer; neither member of staff brought it to the attention of the Operation Ruby investigation team. This incident was particularly significant as Bellfield was living with his girlfriend in this area and had access to her red car. Twenty-four hours after Milly vanished this exact car was reported stolen. The second major failing in the investigation was that officers, whilst engaged on house to house enquiries in the area, knocked on Bellfield's door 10 times but received no reply. When they did get a response there were new tenants in the flat, and no attempt was made to identify or speak to the previous occupants. The final criticism was that the investigators placed a considerable amount of effort investigating Milly's father, which diverted them from other enquiries (Wright, 2008).

The second investigation related to the disappearance and murder of Holly Wells and Jessica Chapman in Soham. At approximately 6.15 pm on the 4 August 2002, the two friends left a family barbeque to walk to the local sweet shop. During their walk back they encountered Ian Huntley, the local school caretaker, who persuaded them to enter his home, where he then killed them. Concerns about this particular investigation followed two routes. The first was that the offender found himself in a position of trust as the school caretaker on unwarranted grounds. The resulting inquiry, chaired by Sir Michael Bichard, established that although Humberside Police had received numerous allegations linking Huntley to sexual offences against women and children, they had not kept any records. Indeed, although a constable had voiced concerns that Huntley was a 'serial attacker' those views had been erased from the intelligence system a few months prior to him applying for the job at Soham (BBC News, 2004). There were further human errors, as Huntley's real name was not linked to his alias. This meant a further check failed to find a second allegation relating to burglary. Additionally, the North East Lincolnshire Social Services Department also failed to associate three allegations of underage sex from 1996 with Huntley, whilst Soham Village College failed to check his references. A second area of criticism focused on the police investigation and was led by HMIC (Flanagan). It criticized the police for a 'lack of grip', especially in the 2 days following the disappearance of the children. This period is referred to colloquially as 'the golden hour' and highlights the critical period immediately following the offence, where the best intelligence and evidence can often be found. Equally, the longer the investigation goes on the more potential there is for the offender to distance him/herself from the crime. The police admitted a number of mistakes during their investigation. One related to the early public disclosure of specific lines of enquiry, an action that resulted in them being deluged with irrelevant leads. Such was the impact of this that the media presence threatened to overwhelm the investigation as 500 journalists arrived at Soham, requesting information from a relatively small police force with limited resources. As Matt Tapp, the force media liaison officer said, 'The media may also have forced police chiefs to direct the enquiry in directions they really did not want to go' (BBC News, 2004). Thirteen days later, the bodies of the two girls were found 6 miles away and Ian Huntley was arrested and later convicted for the crimes.

The investigations illustrated similar problems. The first was in relation to the management of information, a frequent issue in contemporary society. It is often discovered that although the information may be in the system it can frequently be poorly recorded or not shared. Second, the prioritization of leads is an issue that requires critical judgment. One of the phrases that was consistently repeated following both reviews was, 'clear the ground beneath your feet'. In major investigations, there are many reasons for investigative focus to be diverted so it is imperative the SIO focuses the early stages of the investigation on the area where the answer is most likely to be found; the immediate vicinity of the crime. In Milly Dowler's case it was the red car that was initially missed, whilst in the Soham case it was the school caretaker, whose house was on the sweet shop route. The third issue is that the investigators may be following the correct process but they are doing so with insufficient rigour (what Flanagan referred to as 'lack of grip'). This was shown in the inability to get a swift response from Bellfield's address or the perceived lack of haste in the 2 days following the children's disappearance in Soham.

These two cases came at the end of a period when drivers for change were converging (Stelfox, 2009:33). Two Royal Commissions followed a number of high profile miscarriages of justice in the 1970s and 1980s. These had precipitated numerous legislative changes relating to the way criminal investigation was to be conducted. Furthermore, there were technical and procedural changes (already discussed) that had changed the format of the investigation due to the increase in the number of specialists involved. Finally, there were a number of internal reviews that questioned the effectiveness of the police, particularly in major crime investigation. Indeed, historically, there have been a range of blunders and allegations of corruption (Maguire, 2003:375).

All these factors assisted policy makers in realizing that improvements in investigation would not be generated merely through new and enhanced legislative and procedural measures, but through enhancing the skills of investigators. As HMIC (2004:173) argued, 'Policing is now highly complex and spans a massive spectrum of activities requiring a similarly extensive range of skills and competencies in those taking up the challenge'. When investigations go wrong (either they remain undetected or result in a miscarriage of justice), the most common factor in that failure is flawed decision making (Irvine & Dunningham, 1993; Smith, 2003; Nicol et al., 2004).

In the UK, it was established investigators required skills in the following areas:

- Crime scene management
- Forensic investigation

- Searching
- Victim and witness management (including locating, interviewing and care)
- Intelligence management
- Passive data management (i.e. data gathered by automated systems)
- Elimination enquiries
- Communication
- Covert policing
- Suspect management (Core Investigative doctrine, cited by Stelfox, 2007:638)

The Professionalising Investigation Programme (PIP) was therefore introduced in September 2005 by ACPO, who sought 'to enhance the crime investigation skills and ability of police officers and staff involved in the investigative process and to drive through new standards of investigation at all levels' (NCPE, 2005:1). PIP looked to provide a 'cradle to grave' curriculum for investigators. This started at level 1 for general patrol officers who are required to investigate volume crime and antisocial behavior. Level 2 was aimed at dedicated investigation roles (i.e. detectives and specialist investigation roles such as child abuse). Level 3 was focused on the SIO, who would head murder or other complex crimes. The achievement of each of these levels was as a result of formal training, and independent assessment based against National Occupational Standards (NOS). As Stelfox (2009:39) notes, 'The NOS describe competent performance in relation to the outcomes of investigations and the knowledge skills and understanding investigators need to perform effectively'. Alongside these tiers of investigation grew a range of training courses together with advice regarding investigative practice, which was developed and written with the support of the National Police Improvement Agency. This developed the knowledge, techniques and understanding that investigators required to carry out their role.

The critical question is whether these developments have made UK investigators more effective. At the time of writing there was no published evaluation of PIP and as Tong et al. (2009:219) state 'there is a lack of understanding and research on the effectiveness of new training regimes for uniformed officers and detectives'. However, these commentators have also considered how far criminal investigation has progressed as a profession and they have come to the conclusion that, '... the role of the detective is an expansive one requiring multidisciplinary knowledge in order to conduct comprehensive and appropriate investigations. It is from this perspective that we would argue that the task of the detective displays the characteristics of a profession, but that the infrastructure and knowledge generation in place for established professions are not yet in place for the modern day detective' (ibid.:220).

This appears a fair assessment and one that is generally supported by senior practitioners who were spoken to when researching for this book. Although in the UK the detection rate for murder has always been high (92% for 2008/09), they were of the opinion that the role and professionalism of the detective has improved significantly over the past 20 years, albeit there is considerable scope for further improvement.

> As a process PIP is conceptually strong, and is based upon Continuous Professional Development. However with regards its application there is a disparity in how it's applied; so you can still go into different CID offices across the country and find officers with different levels of knowledge and expertise. However we've come a long way from where we were twenty years ago. We no longer learn by just telling war stories; we do formal debriefs, extract the learning, and make sure it's applied. Where we need to improve, in my opinion, is more scientific rigour to our findings, we still rely to much on experiential learning.
>
> (Senior Detective, UK Police)

Asked why there was such a high detection rate in murder investigation the interviewee said,

> Arguably every crime could be detected if it was dealt with in the same way. Homicide is commanded at the highest level; it has the highest degree of accountability; the detectives involved are the most competent, tenacious and enthusiastic of all investigators, and the event is resourced to the highest level too. Coupled with that are the advances in investigative techniques, such as DNA.
>
> (Senior Detective, UK Police)

Conclusion

This chapter discussed the investigation of crime and the ability of the CJS to bring offenders to justice. Although many efforts have been made to standardize investigative practice the permutations are significant and are dependent on: crime type and severity, SIO and practitioner competence, as well as the technology and level of resources available.

The chapter has also shown how the external and internal influences highlighted in Chapter 1 have affected the investigation of crime. In the external environment we have seen:

- Late modernity has changed public and stakeholder expectations. This has influenced the standards of investigation, specifically in relation to Human Rights. It has also facilitated improvements to investigation through technology and research.
- Bringing offenders to justice is the responsibility of many agencies and not just the police. This complex partnership suffers implementation issues, resulting in a significant attrition between the crime being committed and the conviction of the offender.
- The media have become more enquiring and demanding with the ability to influence the direction of an investigation.
- The public is critically important in providing investigators with information and evidence to solve crime.
- Conscious opponents attempt to destroy evidence to evade their capture.

The evidence from internal influences included:

- The investigation is influenced by organizational culture. Whereas enthusiastic and tenacious staff are more likely to detect crime, unethical approaches lead to miscarriages of justice and the inappropriate recording of crime detections.
- SIOs can make a significant difference to the outcome, with poor leadership ('a lack of grip') associated with poor outcomes.
- Practitioners are trained and developed much more effectively than before.

This chapter also illustrated that when failure occurs this is more likely to be due to poor implementation caused by poor decision making or other human fallibility, rather than a deficiency in knowledge or technique. Often this wasn't a single failing but a chain of events that enabled these failures to occur. The chapter has also shown that the investigation of major crime has generally been very effective. As HMIC (2000:115) has previously said, 'the investigation of murder should set clear standards of excellence that all other criminal investigation can follow'. It is unsurprising the UK has such a high detection rate for homicide, as the police appear to deal with *critical incidents* more effectively than routine incidents. These events are often associated with successful practice and this is especially true of major crime investigation. New standards and improvements have been introduced and embedded in a variety of ways, specifically:

1. The ACPO Homicide working group is a highly regarded team of senior investigators, representative of UK law enforcement agencies and led by a senior Chief Constable. It acts on behalf of the service setting out the areas for development.
2. Homicide incidents are probably one of the best resourced of all police events.
3. There is a systematic 'cradle to grave' program in place to train and develop investigators.
4. Investigating homicide has a significant amount of practice advice. It has its own periodic journal that highlights trends, changes and good practice. There is also an annual SIO conference where good (and bad) practice is shared.
5. The investigation of homicide within the UK has a clear accountability structure. Once a homicide is committed a review by an ACPO officer takes place after 24 hours, and then a further review will take place after 28 days if it remains undetected. Additionally, legislation requires the formal review of all child and domestic homicides. Peer review is also recommended in this process.
6. The major incident room procedures facilitate checks and balances to reduce human fallibility (i.e. all information is reviewed by three people: SIO, Statement Reader and Receiver).

5 Policing Critical Incidents and the Use of Force

Introduction

Consider this scenario. Early one midweek morning, a man visits his ex-partner at her home address. The doorstep discussion escalates into an argument, culminating with him brandishing a handgun. His ex-partner dashes back inside the house to telephone the police, whilst our subject runs back to his car and drives away. A short time later, he is seen and pursued by a specialist firearms team, driving a liveried police vehicle. The subject drives into a residential area and stops on a grassed area in close proximity to a number of houses. As the police ask him to get out of the vehicle, he puts the gun to his head and threatens to shoot himself. A crowd gathers, and the police officers hold their position and inform the communications room of the circumstances.

One way of conceptualizing policing is by separating the management of serious incidents from more routine day-to-day events. It is these serious incidents, often referred to in the UK as *critical incidents* that this chapter focuses upon. The first section will explore the management of firearms incidents, and explain why the recent phenomenon of *active shooter* incidents has made the policing of these events even more challenging. The second section will provide an overview of how the police deal with serious disorder, specifically showing how the implementation of police action can promote or reduce disorder within a crowd. Furthermore, it will provide a police perspective on how public order policing has changed in recent years, using London as an example. Before these sections are presented, two issues need to be explained in more detail – the *police use of force* and the *critical incident*.

The police use of force

One of the noteworthy elements that distinguish the police from other organizations is their ability to use legitimate force against citizens. Judging when and how to use reasonable force is difficult, as Kuhns and Knutsson (2010:3) point out,

> When used legitimately, respectfully, consistently and lawfully, police use of force is a functional and necessary aspect of living in a safe and healthy society, regardless of the form of government, culture or society. But when police use of force is considered illegitimate, disrespectful or unlawful, real or perceived, it can quickly erode the confidence of citizens in their own government, increase crime and violence, and generate wider dissent and dissatisfaction across communities and countries.

Lanagan et al. (2003:3) highlight the fact that although most US citizens are generally satisfied with the police service, this level of satisfaction drops on the specific issue of force. Terrill and Paoline (2010:11) argue that police use of reasonable force can be analysed from different perspectives, specifically: public, legal, police organizational and street cop perspectives. In the first case, the public appears to employ a mix of legal (i.e. resisting arrest) and extra-legal factors (potential of offender to escape), when deciding whether the use of force was legitimate, albeit they always expect the officer to act professionally. A legal perspective uses a framework of protocols and legal precedent to establish whether the police use of force was reasonable and proportionate. A police organizational viewpoint explains how police leaders formulate policy and advice on what is proportionate and reasonable in various scenarios, as well as explaining how excessive force is identified and dealt with (albeit interpretation can differ across different agencies). Finally, a street cop views the incident through a variety of lenses; for example, he/she will consider public expectations, legal authority and be aware of how their organization would expect them to act. Of course, a further complication is the media, who are able to inflame public concern by highlighting police use of force in particular circumstances (i.e. against a female or child).

In the UK, a risk management approach, coupled with specific legislation such as the Human Rights Act, made it inevitable that the level of individual police discretion would be reduced (Buttle, 2010). The subsequent development of a conflict resolution model (CRM) proposes a doctrine of reasonable force (rather than a doctrine of minimum force), which is determined by subject (offender), officer and impact factors. Although the *National Decision Model* ACPO (2012), now acts as the overarching model, the CRM still provides the rationale to be considered prior to any decision in this area. The subject behaviour category is simple to understand, and relates to whether the individual is compliant, verbally resistant, passively resistant, actively resistant, aggressively resistant, or shows serious or aggravated resistance. The next stage is for the officer to decide upon a proportionate response to counteract this, considering: Is the officer's presence sufficient to diffuse the situation; is a restraining hold needed; or does he/she need to consider deadly force? However a third issue, referred to as impact factors, relate to the unique factors of the interaction, and can include the age, gender, size and skills of the officer or offender. For example, a police officer who is a black belt in karate may feel that a drunk and aggressive man of a similar size will cause him few problems, and may be controlled using a restraining hold. Conversely, if the aggressor was the black belt, the officer may decide to reach for the CS incapacitant spray. As with most areas of policing, attempts to define ambiguous situations still allow a considerable amount of discretion to be used.

The critical incident

In the UK, 'any event where the effectiveness of the policing response is likely to have a significant impact on the confidence of the victim, his or her family and/or the community' will be designated a *critical incident* (Grieve, 2008:70). A critical incident can revolve around numerous events, such as a terrorist incident, a child who goes missing in suspicious circumstances, a train or aeroplane crash, leakage from a nuclear facility or even the aftermath of flooding. Conversely, they can relate to internal issues, such as a police officer accused of corruption. What personifies these incidents is their potential to highlight poor police professionalism (if handled incorrectly), thereby creating significant public mistrust and dissatisfaction. These events are also epitomized by being complex and high in profile, occurring in a rapidly changing environment and requiring fast decision making. It is also true that these incidents generally require a clear command structure, supported by a wide range of resources and specialist staff.

In the UK, once a senior police officer formally defines the event as a 'critical incident', a predictable and well-rehearsed procedure is generally followed, which involves a Gold, Silver, Bronze command structure.

In this command hierarchy, the Gold Commander initially sets out the overarching strategy for the policing operation, which will include unambiguous objectives. It is then the role of the Silver Commander to operationalize this strategy by considering what tactics could be used to achieve these objectives. Once this is decided, the Silver Commander will appoint a series of Bronze Commanders to supervise the delivery of each operational element within this tactical framework. Although there would only be one Gold Commander and (in most cases) only one Silver Commander, there can be a plethora of Bronze Commanders. Gold and Silver are unlikely to attend the scene as they need to maintain an overview of the situation, and be in a position to collate and disseminate information in a relatively calm environment. As such, they are likely to be placed in an appropriate *Operations Room*, assisted by suitable communication facilities and those who can provide specialist expert advice. Conversely, Bronze Commanders are likely to be at the scene, supervising and supporting the much smaller teams who implement tactics. The benefits of the Gold, Silver and Bronze approach are that even in very complex situations (including operations that utilize many agencies, such as terrorist incidents), clear responsibility, accountability and communication can be maintained for each element of the operation.

Critical incidents vary according to the type and scale of the event, and also require different levels of resource. The response to many critical incidents can be planned in advance, and police forces in the UK are constantly scanning for vulnerable locations and situations where these problems can occur. For example, a nuclear power station will have a contingency plan to deal with leakage, whilst football grounds will have plans to deal with crowd safety issues. As most types of serious incidents can be anticipated, the police will often devise general or specific contingency plans in response. These contingency plans are regularly reviewed and tested, often in 'table top' events, where practitioners are brought together to consider hypothetical problems and rehearse their response.

Since December 2011, the British police have adopted a single National Decision Model to 'provide a simple, logical and evidence based approach to making policing decisions' (ACPO, 2012:1). It is viewed as suitable for all decisions, be they planned or spontaneous, by individuals or teams, and to both operational and non-operational situations. The five stages, all influenced by the ACPO statement of mission and values include:

1. Gather information and intelligence.
2. Assess the threat and risk, and develop a working strategy.

3. Consider powers and policy.
4. Identify options and contingencies.
5. Take action and review what happened (return to stage 1 if appropriate).

It can also be used for specialist areas of policing (such as firearms or public order incidents), with practitioners deciding what questions and considerations are relevant at each stage. For pre-planned operational events, this clarity will be further improved by the use of an operational order, established under the IIMAC format (Information, Intention, Method, Administration, Communication), that is supplied before the event to all those taking part. Once the emergency is under control, there can also be post-incident phases, such as a criminal investigation. Having now set out the background to critical incidents, the first section will outline one particular type – those involving the criminal use of firearms.

Section 1: The police management of firearm incidents

Incidents involving the illegal use of firearms are commonplace around the world, and each country develops their own approach to counteract them. Whilst on one level international comparisons are useful, care needs to be taken due to different operating environments. For example, firearms are much more pervasive in the US than in the UK, leading to many more offenders and police officers being shot. Similarly, a number of commentators highlight serious concerns regarding the police response to firearms incidents throughout various parts of the world. For instance Belur (2010:55) explains that in Mumbai, the term 'Police encounters' is used to explain an exchange of fire between the police and alleged criminals where the police shoot to kill in self defence'. However, Belur continues, '... during the course of this research, it became evident that the word encounter signified a legitimized cover-up for what were essentially police killings of alleged hard core criminals'. Unlike the inquiries that follow police shootings in the UK, Belur argues that these incidents receive apathy, acceptance and even approval from both public and police leaders. Further, Glebbeek (2010) highlights the worrying use of firearms by police forces in Central America, as they attempt to deal with the exceptionally high levels of violence, crime and insecurity. Generally speaking, whilst the murder rate is extremely high in this area, trust in the police is very low; which has led to both an increase in private security patrols and more repressive security policies, known as mano dura (zero tolerance). These approaches are 'associated with illegal detentions, severe punishments for minor offences, military style occupations, and collective punishment of entire neighbourhoods' (ibid.:70). Finally Higgins (2010:73) reports on systematic police violence in Brazil, disclosing that 'a combination of official and unofficial statistics indicate that on-duty Brazilian police are responsible for up to 70% of all civilian murders in Brazil', pointing out that inappropriate police violence is normalized and institutionalized.

Police procedure in the UK is explained by the *Home Office Code of Practice on Police use of Firearms and less lethal weapons*. This document sets requirements on Chief Officers to adhere to standards of equipment, training, tactics and post-incident procedure (Perks, 2008). To explain how these procedures work in practice, it is useful to return to the scenario outlined at the start of the chapter, which involves an armed man in a residential area. The event that actually occurred was deemed a *critical incident* at the time, as it was felt that the potential outcomes could involve: (a) the subject shooting himself in full view of local residents (including children); (b) a police officer being shot or shooting the subject; (c) the subject threatening or shooting into the crowd; (d) someone in the crowd trying to disarm him; or (e) the subject escaping and shooting someone else.

At this early stage, the role of the officers at the scene is to contain the situation until further assistance can be found. All UK police forces have a Chief Officer (ACPO rank), and other senior officers (Superintendent/Chief Inspector) either on duty or *on call* who are authorized to act as firearms commanders. In this particular example, the *on call* Gold and Silver Commanders are contacted and informed of the situation. The Gold Commander then sets the strategic objectives, focusing on the peaceful resolution to the incident, with particular emphasis surrounding the safety of the public, police officers and subject. Once the Silver Commander is aware of these objectives, he or she will decide on the tactical interventions, and list the resources required to achieve them. For each of these tactical elements he/she will often select a Bronze Commander, who has the specialist skills to supervise their implementation. In our example, the Silver Commander chose Bronze Commanders for the following areas of responsibility:

- *Intelligence*: Information is required about the subject and the firearm (including an explanation for his current behaviour, his propensity for violence, etc.).

- *Police negotiators*: These officers are deployed to try and persuade the subject to peacefully hand over the weapon. In this example, a psychologist was also in attendance to assist the negotiators in interpreting the subjects behaviour.
- *Firearms officers*: These officers contain the situation by preventing the subject from moving around with a loaded firearm, thereby reducing the danger to others.
- *Cordons*: Police officers create an inner cordon within the immediate proximity of the subject, signifying a sterile area where only firearms officers and negotiators are allowed. There will also be an outer cordon, behind which members of the public and journalists will be safely situated. The area between the two cordons is where police officers actively involved in the operation will be stationed.
- *Media liaison*: An individual will coordinate the information provided to journalists at the scene, or remotely via electronic means. The speed of this information flow becomes even more important, as the media are now using a host of other information sources (e.g. aerial surveillance, social networking sites). This means they are continually probing the police for a response, which requires regular and systematic briefings.
- *Logistics and catering*: As critical incidents can continue for a significant period of time, plans need to be made to find both relief staff and refreshment.

The example provided would be seen as a relatively common *critical incident* and will probably be replicated across the UK every day. This particular incident continued for 20 hours and required over 70 staff. Later on in this scenario, a further bronze commander was needed to liaise with the housing department, in order to evacuate nearby residents; other emergency services were also utilized. Unfortunately, this particular scenario had a tragic outcome, as after many hours of negotiation, the subject took his own life.

Although in this case, the incident was spontaneous, unpredictable and fast moving, all of the specialist staff used were practised in their particular role. For example: the firearm officers had been previously trained to contain volatile firearm situations, negotiators were trained to engage with suicidal/dangerous people, catering staff had procedures in place to quickly mobilize hot food deliveries, administrative support had protocols to obtain relief staff from a wider area and other support staff had procedures to count the financial cost of the operation. One further point that distinguishes critical incidents from routine incidents is that they are debriefed on their conclusion. Of course in practice, this evaluation may range in intensity; so, for example, a routine firearms incident, where no one was arrested or harmed, may result in a simple debrief chaired by the senior officer who authorized the police to use firearms. A more complex firearms incident, such as the example given here, is more likely to involve a structured debrief, covering specific areas highlighted during the operation. This particular case (as with all police-related deaths in the UK) was referred to the Independent Police Complaints Commission and the Coroner, who also reviewed the police actions.

The potential for firearms incidents to result in a fatal outcome is obviously high, so it is reassuring to note that those in the UK generally culminate with a peaceful resolution. It is accepted that there are obvious exceptions to this (i.e. the De Menezes case, which will be discussed in a later chapter), however, compared to other countries very few citizens are shot by the police, and vice-versa. When considering why the UK police would be effective in this type of incident, three points emerge. First, a firearms incident is a relatively unambiguous event (again it is accepted there are exceptions), and has a clear start and end point. Secondly, the UK police have a very clear method to deal with these incidents, abiding by a robust command structure and deploying well-trained specialist officers who use the best equipment. Thirdly, effective implementation is at the forefront of delivery. Built into this process is a continuing improvement mentality, where performance is scrutinized and any lessons learnt are fed back into the operational environment. Indeed, this level of detail often separates success from failure. The ability of Commanders to remain calm when problems surround them, the constraint shown by firearms officers when facing armed subjects, and the ability of negotiators to identify the reason for extreme behaviour, is only achieved with significant levels of training and experience. However, these scenarios are constantly changing, and the next example highlights a new phenomenon known as *active shooter* incidents, that present new challenges for the police.

A new phenomena – active shooter incidents

Spree killings in the form of 'active shooter' incidents are a relatively new phenomenon that have emerged within late modernity. Spree killings involve offenders who tend to kill three or more victims in different locations, during one single event, over a very short period of time (Keeney & Heide, 1995). After the incident, the offender is unlikely to kill again and often commits suicide, or dies at the hands of the police.

Indeed, some explain spree killing as 'suicide with hostile intentions' (Preti, 2008), and studies on school shootings have found the offender to often express their suicidal intention through a note or message left on the Internet. Studies show that spree killings often start with an identifiable victim, and then become random as the killings continue (DeLisi & Scherer, 2006).

The UK first experienced the phenomenon of an active shooter during 1987, when a 27-year-old man called Michael Ryan shot and killed 16 people, injuring 15 others, in just a few hours whilst walking through Hungerford. Similarly, Thomas Hamilton shot 16 children and their teacher whilst injuring 17 others in a single episode at a school in Dunblane; both cases ended in suicide. *Active shooter* incidents have become more prevalent across the world in the 21st century. In July 2011, Norway saw a lone male (Anders Breivik) set off a car bomb killing 8 people, before opening fire 2 hours later on a youth camp killing over 85 people (Meo et al., 2011). Moreover, just a few months later in December 2011, Nordine Amrani, 33, opened gunfire and set off grenades in a busy Belgian city centre, killing 4 people and injuring over 120 more, before then committing suicide (Traynor, 2011). In 2008, such was the prevalence of these incidents that Preti warned about the danger of increased media coverage sparking copycat events. Indeed, the study showed that after the Columbine massacre, 350 American students were arrested for posting similar threats against schools. Media guidelines, aiming to reduce the sensationalism of these events, have now been proposed (Preti, 2008).

Research has identified that the classic spree killer is a white male, aged between 30 and 40 years (Meloy et al., 2004), with no previous criminal behaviour (Gresswell & Hollin, 1994). DeLisi and Scherer (2006) further explain that typical spree killers are usually sane males, who experience feelings of isolation, violation and hatred towards others; although Hempel et al. (1999) found that some suffer from depression or paranoia (DeLisi & Scherer, 2006). They are also described as failed, lonely, angry, resentful individuals who are ready to explode (Gresswell & Hollin, 1994). Spree killers have occasionally been referred to as resentment killers, taking revenge on individuals or an element of the community who have caused them upset (Preti, 2008). It is also important to acknowledge that emotional stressors in the form of situational and environmental factors can act as triggers for these incidents to occur. These can include prior arguments; significant money loss; unemployment or marital conflict – all factors that can lead to paranoia, depression or panic, causing an individual to lose control (Salfati et al.,

2006). Other studies note that offenders frequently have a fascination and preoccupation with weapons, particularly guns (Mullen 2004 as cited in DeLisi & Scherer, 2006).

Active shooter incidents are less predictable than other violent events, as such they are rarely anticipated and therefore difficult to prepare for. One scenario that illustrates the difficulty of responding to such events took place on the 2 June 2010 in the English Lake District. Derrick Bird, a taxi driver and lawful firearms holder with no history of violence, had mistakenly come to the conclusion that he was going to be sent to prison for tax evasion. On the day in question, he rose early, shooting and killing his brother at his home before driving to his solicitor's house where he took the same action. As information started to come to the police, he drove to a nearby town centre taxi rank where he shot three acquaintances. He then continued driving calmly around Cumbria, randomly shooting at further victims. Between 10.13 am and 12.15 pm he drove 52 miles across an area of rural beauty, murdering 12 people and injuring 11 others. As the police started to tighten the net around him, he stopped his car and killed himself (Chesterman, 2011).

Political leaders were quick to highlight the bravery and good work of both the local community and emergency services on the day. As with all critical incidents, the event was thoroughly debriefed and included an independent police review to establish lessons for the future. As with other similar incidents, it was quickly established that the events could not have been predicted or prevented. It was also acknowledged that even though the incident occurred in an isolated location, within an hour of receiving the initial information there were over 30 armed police officers deployed to the area. This incident provides a tragic but insightful example of the ongoing challenges regarding the implementation of operational tactics. First, Bird was the ultimate conscious opponent. A keen gunman, he was operating in an area he had intimate knowledge of, and used numerous isolated roads that were often obscured from aerial surveillance by thick woodland. Secondly, the complex nature of the incident meant that the effectiveness of the operation depended on other agencies. One unexpected problem involved the ambulance service, which was expected to go to the aid of casualties. However as Bird's exact location could not be identified the service felt unable to deploy staff in specific areas as their safety could not be guaranteed. This created further dilemmas for the police, forcing them to consider between stopping to assist casualties, or carrying on in pursuit of Derrick Bird. In essence, the operational challenges of this situation were all amplified because of the mobility surrounding it. Compare the difficulty of policing this event with the one described earlier, when the subject was controlled within the police cordon. This level of difficulty was captured by the incident's Gold Commander, who reported:

> I was in command, but unlike other incidents there wasn't the same level of control. It was impossible to predict Bird's movements or actions, especially in those early stages. Police officers were coming across an unprecedented level of violence and were required to make immediate decisions. We needed an approach that could match the speed and variation this situation provided. The tried and tested Gold, Silver, Bronze command and control approach was slow in reacting to the demands.
>
> (Chief Officer, UK Police)

The Gold Commander also made reference to the proactive nature of the media. By coincidence, another event had been taking place that day in Cumbria, meaning there was a strong media presence in the general area; however, their ability to quickly reorganize and cover the event was highlighted by the Gold Commander who said:

> As I am commanding the incident from the HQ operations room I look over at the TV and see a live news bulletin is being broadcast regarding the events unfolding in Cumbria. On the screen I see the Prime Minister briefing the House of Commons and hear him say there have been five fatalities. At this early stage even I didn't know the number of fatalities and I believe this information came from the media.
>
> (Chief Officer, UK Police)

As this incident shows, unexpected events will continue to emerge, which the police will be asked to respond to. Mobility – a byproduct of late modernity – has presented significant challenges to contemporary policing, including firearm related crimes. A further example was the Mumbai terror attack on 26 November 2008, where 10 Pakistani terrorists stormed 2 luxury hotels, a Jewish religious centre and a Cafe in south Mumbai. Their indiscriminate firing resulted in 166 people (including 18 foreign nationals) being killed and many others injured. Similarly, the De Menezes case (described later) is another that demonstrates the difficulty of dealing with mobile subjects. There is no doubt new problems will emerge in the future, which cannot be envisaged at the moment, meaning that the police will need to be more flexible in their approach; for even though they may not be anticipated or trained for, public expectations will require they are dealt with to the same exacting standards.

Section summary

It is clear that police officers in different countries face different challenges surrounding the criminal use of firearms, generated through the variation in laws, levels of criminality and standards of policing. Examples from the UK generally show the police to be proficient in dealing with such incidents, for in the case of a clear threat, the police use a clear command structure, as well as trained personnel and evaluated tactics. However, the comparison between the two firearms incidents brings into sharp relief just how important implementation is. The *what* to do was similar, it was to bring the incident to a peaceful conclusion as quickly as possible. The *how* to do it was much more difficult, especially in the *active shooter* incident, which was a new challenge for the police officers involved. Nevertheless, no matter what the level of performance, due to the dynamic nature of confrontational situations, there always appears room for improvement, a factor illustrated in the next section.

Section 2: Policing disorder

Introduction

The role of the police as guardians of the state and their importance in maintaining public order has a long history. As Adlam (2000) points out, historians agree that the British police were formed in 1829, to protect the seat of capitalism at a time of increased urbanization and industrialization. This is a sentiment explored by Robinson et al. (1994:6), who said that 'A society dominated by a ruling class needs a coercive instrument to maintain its control over basic resources and over a labour force necessary to produce the surplus product to support and sustain the ruling class'. Before the public police existed, governments relied on the army to quell protests. In the UK, these confrontations were often brutal; the Gordon Riots of (1780) resulted in over 400 people being shot and killed (Palmer, 1988; Zedner, 2006), with the protests at Peterloo, Manchester (1819) culminating in 15 deaths and hundreds of injuries (Thompson, 1964). The irony was that this brutality was often counterproductive, as it caused opposing political protesters to forge new affiliations.

The tragic consequences of policing protest continue to occur across the world. The death toll from citizens in the *Arab spring* uprisings, or the 34 miners shot dead by South African police during unrest at a platinum mine in 2011, are a constant reminder of the impact such confrontations can have. Although across the world, disorder is more likely to occur in economically deprived areas, fuelled by multi-faceted issues, history shows that they are often ignited by police actions. The acquittal of the officers who assaulted Rodney King prompted the Los Angeles riots of 1992; the death of two youths allegedly chased by the police precipitated the extensive rioting in the Paris suburbs during 2005; and more recently the shooting of Mark Duggan triggered the London riots of 2011. It was the same in 1981 when a new Conservative government led by Margaret Thatcher stirred social unrest through their approach to economic reform. At the same time, the London police implemented 'SWAMP 81' – a street crime operation that attempted to curtail robbery in Lambeth. It was an individual search during this operation that prompted the conflict, from which 299 officers were injured. Similarly in July 1981, an allegedly heavy-handed arrest provoked 9 days of serious disorder in Toxteth (Liverpool), and it is this particular event that we explore further.

The strategic and tactical response by police to the disorder at Toxteth was severely criticized in the reviews that followed. Taylor (2007), a Police Sergeant at the riots who later became a successful PhD student, provides a vivid account of the scene, saying, 'It has only been a matter of minutes we have been there but my world has changed irrevocably. I am weary, physically and mentally. ... There is no plan, there is no discipline – it is on the hoof decision making at its worse'. Taylor later goes on to explain that lines of officers holding riot shields remained static, waiting to be assaulted by flying missiles, a burning milk float and individuals with machetes. It was later accepted by the Chief Constable that the response to the riots had been 'totally and utterly inadequate' (ibid.:138), a view endorsed by official figures that recorded 468 injured officers and damage to 70 buildings; although it was felt this figure was seriously underestimated.

Taylor's description is illuminating for many reasons, and epitomizes the ineffective policing of serious disorder at this time. First, from an organizational perspective the police were too reactive. They showed no organizational learning from other similar events, and failed to predict and prepare for serious disorder. Second, the solution to stop the violence (the use of CS gas) was already known to be both legal and effective in those situations. However, as it had only been previously used in Northern Ireland, police leaders and politicians debated its use as the disorder continued around them. Third, Taylor provides a fascinating insight as to what undisciplined officers are capable of. He explains that soon after the CS has been used and dawn begins to break, the groups of rioters start to dissipate. As police officers observe the retreat, they spontaneously run in pursuit of their attackers, bent on revenge and willing to use *unreasonable force*. Finally, Taylor speaks of the legacy left by the disorder, including the impact on people and careers, some of who did not fully recover. Often, accounts of policing are snapshots, revealing little of these long-term consequences or their impact on organizational culture.

In essence, these riots were a striking example of a chain of events that resulted in police ineffectiveness. The political environment created the unrest, police behaviour generated the spark, police leadership was lacking in terms of preparation and critical incident command, and practitioner skills and equipment were also lacking. This systematic ineffectiveness was mirrored in numerous other events around this time, such as the Hillsborough football stadium tragedy that resulted in the death of 96 Liverpool football supporters. Such momentous events are often opened to formal public scrutiny, and just as the Hillsborough tragedy caused significant improvements to the safety of football stadiums, so too have advances been made in relation to the policing of disorder. The next section will explore this theme in more detail.

The policing of crowds

Increased mobility, generated by late modernity, has allowed individuals to gather at large events more easily. Madensen and Knutsson (2011) divide crowds into three generic sections: political demonstrations (i.e. G20 summit), sporting events (i.e. American Superbowl) and festivities (i.e. midsummer eve in Sweden, Oktoberfest in Germany). Madensen and Eck (2011) acknowledge that crowds make some illegal behaviours easier to commit; they can encourage bad behaviour, reduce the risk of detection, provide opportunity and excuses, and even make offending more rewarding.

Reicher (2011:11) argues that crowd events are emblematic of defining the wider relationship of the police with the public, suggesting that day-to-day relationships are played out in crowd relationships. However, crowds are diverse, bringing together a variety of people with different values and attitudes. For example, the G20 protests have the potential to attract people from all over the world – from sophisticated and potentially violent *conscious opponents*, to peaceful law abiding citizens who merely want to highlight their concern.

The 1999 World Trade Organisation meeting at Seattle was a symbolic turning point in policing protest, as approximately 50,000 individuals converged from all over the world to successfully disrupt the negotiations. The police blamed the catastrophe on their lack of preparation, insufficient resources, well-coordinated protestors, and the lack of police powers (Gillham & Marx, 2000). Since then, the police have responded robustly. Australia's largest security event – the APEC summit in Sydney generated a significant response from the government, including 3,500 officers on duty, 500 vacant cells ready for mass arrests, a 2.8 m steel and concrete fence erected to protect a 5 km area of the business district, the implementation of extensive exclusionary zones and police snipers on rooftops. Only 5,000 protestors arrived, and the policing was criticized as disproportionate by civil rights lawyers and some politicians (Baker 2012:68).

Baker (2012:62) states that the Australian approach personifies the evolution of policing protest, saying, 'Research in many countries indicates the proliferation and the increasing use of police paramilitary units and special weapons and tactical teams. When economic and trade interests are at stake, policing has tended to be openly coercive'. della Porta and Reiter (2006) support this analysis, arguing that the last decade has seen the police revert to a tougher style of policing, relying on increased technology, improved powers, covert surveillance and the use of more force. Indeed, commentators are concerned that police tactics can exacerbate violence by changing the disposition of peaceful crowd members. Stott (2011:28) explains the importance of understanding crowd dynamics using the Elaborated Social Identity Model of crowd behaviour (ESIM). He looks at how individuals distinguish between personal and social identities, and argues that crowd members usually adhere to their own norms, values and ideology. However, if the police take disproportionate or illegitimate action against the group, the individual can change their mindset to accommodate an 'us against them' mentality, facilitating collective action from the crowd. Stott, therefore, asserts that a graded tactical approach, which avoids disproportionate and indiscriminate use of force, is critical to maintain the peaceful disposition of protesters (ibid.:43); in this way it is more effective to proactively manage the maintenance of public order, rather than react to the resulting disorder. There appears considerable evidence for this assertion. Recent protests across the USA surrounding the *occupy* and *tea party* movements have seen a variety of police responses, with the more aggressive tactics associated with more violent crowd behaviour. Reicher (2011) summarizes the four principles required to police crowds, which have been accepted in principle by British Chief Officers (ACPO, 2003) although not always followed in practice. These include the following:

1. Facilitating the legitimate aims of crowd members. This is a critical issue, as researchers argue that by knowing the intentions of the group, it is feasible to empower and give responsibility to group members, so they can achieve their objectives lawfully. This is more effective than trying to control them.
2. Understanding social identities within the crowd. There needs to be an insider's knowledge of the group culture, which can be used to pre-empt conflict. This focuses around cultural intelligence, i.e. how the group sees the world – a process that can be gleaned from open sources, rather than concentrating solely on criminal intelligence (often obtained through covert means).
3. Differentiating between the various psychological groups in a crowd event. This means police should not deal with the crowd as one (i.e. all criminal or all hostile). Although difficult to implement in practice, failure to achieve this can cause the group to become hostile (for the reasons provided earlier).
4. Communication. Negotiation and communication are critical, to ensure that people in the crowd know what is being done and why it is being done.

In this way, different types of strategy and tactics can be considered against these principles. So for example, *kettling*, a controversial tactic that contains the crowd for a significant period with the aim of allowing aggression to dissipate, is against many of these principles. Reicher argues that if *kettling* is used indiscriminately, it can negatively affect crowd dynamics. This is not to say that police should not use the tactic, but they should consider the unintended consequences if implemented badly.

Madensen and Eck (2011) use an environmental criminological perspective to highlight those police interventions that can facilitate peaceful crowd behaviour. Basing their proposal on Cornish and Clarke's (1986) Rational Choice Theory, they consider police interventions to: increase the effort required by protestors to behave badly; increase the risk of sanctions if they are caught behaving badly; reduce the rewards of behaving badly; as well as reducing the provocation and removing the excuses for behaving badly. Using these principles as a framework to devise appropriate interventions, Madensen and Eck highlight the good work of Las Vegas Police Department, who safely managed the New Year's eve celebrations of 400,000 people, on the Strip.

Holgersson and Knutsson (2011:192) also examine the lessons established from the policing of approximately 25,000 protestors at the Gothenburg European summit in June 2001. In the violence and damage that followed, 459 people were arrested, with 150 needing treatment (50 of which were police officers). Ironically, whilst the National police commissioner was criticized for inaction, the Operational Commander was tried (and later acquitted) for too much action (mass arrests). On reflection, it was felt that the police were poorly trained (or not trained at all), had no experience and poor equipment. Police allegedly caused conflict by creating chaos, negatively stereotyping, or provoking the crowd. As a result, during 2004, the National Police Board introduced a new approach, based upon the good practice observed in Denmark that looked to facilitate the legal aims of the demonstrators. The process involves the following: facilitation (assist the demonstrators to reach their legitimate goals), dialogue (communicate and mediate with protestors), counterpart perspective (recognize the impact of police action, always attempting to promote de-escalation), differentiation (differentiate the actions of individuals and subgroups within the crowds), signal value (show there is a capability to use force if necessary) and identifying 'state' (in this model, crowd behaviour is identified as three states: green – relaxed with no confrontation, yellow – a tense situation that could develop into a confrontation and red – confrontation with physical attacks and use of force (ibid.:196)). Perhaps the most significant change is that of the importance of dialogue with protestors. In fact, such is the emphasis on this element that specific operational officers are clearly identified to the crowd as being responsible for this task.

So far, this section has provided academic and media accounts of disorder. The final element will place more emphasis on the police perspective.

Policing crowds and protest in London

Maintaining order during 2011 and 2012 was particularly challenging for the Metropolitan Police Service (MPS), and this was a period in which they received plaudits and criticism. In a city such as London, the police are constantly planning for and dealing with crowds. The period saw inner city riots and looting, student protest marches and associated disorder, a myriad of high profile processions (including the English Defence League and Anti-facist party), the Notting Hill Carnival, the Olympics and Para Olympics, and New Year festivities.

In researching for this book, an interview was conducted with the Commander responsible for public order policing within the MPS, and this was supplemented by many discussions with other police leaders and practitioners. This section will concentrate on the London riots, the Notting Hill Carnival and the G20 summit. Although the G20 summit had occurred prior to this period, its legacy was continuing and being actively discussed during this time.

The period between the 6 and 10 August 2011 saw rioting break out in several districts of London, at an estimated cost of £0.5 billion. Over 5 days, approximately 15,000 people were involved in the rioting that led to five deaths and numerous other injuries (including 186 police officers). The disturbances were sparked following the police shooting of Mark Duggan, a local man suspected of involvement in firearms (Riots, Communities and Victims Panel, 2012). The protests that followed his death saw arson, looting and significant confrontations with the police; and from that evening, the disorder spilled out to other areas of London, and then onto other UK cities (Birmingham, Liverpool, Manchester and Bristol). However, the characteristics of these riots were dissimilar to other incidents of serious disorder. The most obvious difference was that disorder took place in city centres, rather than inner city areas, where retailers could be looted and damaged. The events were also called the 'Blackberry riots', as individuals used social media to organize their activity. This enabled potential rioters to mobilize in large numbers, as instant communication allowed them the flexibility to change shape, constantly scattering and re-forming in smaller groups to probe vulnerability in police tactics. This approach initially appeared to overwhelm the police although in the days that followed, increased officer numbers allowed the police to regain control. Police also started to monitor social media, enabling them to become more proactive in their public disorder tactics as well as allowing them to communicate and reassure members of the public. Another effective tactic was the focused use of CCTV to quickly identify and arrest offenders, an approach often supported by the Courts, who gave swift custodial sentences. In the investigation that followed, 4,000 rioters were arrested, 90% of whom had previously come to the attention of the police. By February 2012, 827 of these had been sentenced – 85% of whom received an immediate custodial sentence (Riots, Communities and Victims Panel, 2012).

The second example relates to the Notting Hill Carnival, the largest street festival in Europe, which originated in 1964 as a way for Afro-Caribbean communities to celebrate their culture and tradition. The carnival takes place in a small area of London over the August bank holiday weekend and has in the past resulted in serious disorder and death. The carnival is now subjected to intense advanced planning and approximately 4,000 officers are used to police the event. The planning starts with a thorough debrief of the previous carnival (utilizing both police and community representatives). The operation then adheres to a Gold, Silver, Bronze model (described earlier) and uses the rationale of the conflict management model to establish proportionate responses. Once details of the event are provided by the organizers, the threats are assessed together with the likelihood of them taking place. The Gold Commander then sets the event strategy, the Silver Commander outlines the tactics and the Bronze Commanders (of which there are several) are chosen and made accountable for the implementation of those tactics. The operational plans are also discussed with legal teams, to guarantee their compliance with the Human Rights Act.

During his interview, the Commander explained how the operation had developed significantly over the past 5 years, due to the use of community consultation, operational debriefs, various external inquiries, litigation and a general increase in transparency. One of the processes to aid transparency has been the meticulous use of decision logs to explain why a particular decision was made at a particular time. In this way, police leaders, whilst engaged in the policing of the carnival, explain and dictate their operational decision to a loggist, who records it contemporaneously. Decisions as such may include the supply of water to the crowd or portable toilets being requested for a particular location. Even apparently innocuous decisions are recorded, as their significance is often unknown until the event finishes. This process may require the operational commander to have a support team, that includes a driver, a loggist, and someone available for general support. Although the Commander acknowledged the need to constrain bureaucracy, he felt transparency had made it easier to defend incoming complaints, as legal challenges were now synonymous with contemporary policing.

The potential problems that can occur on carnival days are diverse, and may include the coming together of rival gangs, who can involve themselves in 'steaming' (running and converging as a group to steal from a victim), shooting rivals, or various other gang confrontations. Here, policing of the event has become more proactive, with a significant level of effort invested into obtaining criminal intelligence through a variety of means, including speaking with community members. This information generally culminates in an operation taking place a month before the carnival, to seize weapons and disrupt some of the planned gang activity. Similar searches continue up to the carnival date, to find bottles that can quickly be adapted into Molotov cocktails or missiles. The *London Evening Standard* (2012) reported this proactivity, explaining that the police intercepted 36 gang members at King's Cross Station, who were intent on confronting rival groups at the carnival. Fifteen of the group, some of whom were wearing body armour, were arrested and released only after the carnival had finished. The newspaper also reported a safe carnival environment, interviewing one waitress who said 'We did not see one fight break out. In the 1990s it had a reputation for being very dangerous, but it was happy and everyone was up for having a good time'.

Although the MPS deal with approximately 1,000 protests every year, the most significant protest had occurred some years earlier, with the G20 protest in 2009. This event was still relevant, as proceedings were on-going in relation to the death of Ian Tomlinson who had been confronted by a Metropolitan Police officer. The Commander used this event to explain some of the wider issues involved in policing protest. He initially explained that protests occur in a much wider environment, where others make decisions that subsequently affect the policing of the event. For example, the location is always important when dealing with protest, and in some countries the initial G20 conference location has been moved to less vulnerable locations (Redekop & Pave, 2010). In this case, the London location created significant problems due to its city and river location. Each delegate travelled with copious staff and equipment, all requiring numerous safe routes to and from the venue; in fact the difficulty of preparing viable routes was seen the following year, when protestors attacked the Prince of Wales' official vehicle. Even the day chosen for the G20 summit, the 2nd April was symbolic, as the day after April fool's day is internationally recognized as a protest day and would automatically generate more demonstrators.

During the interview, the Commander stated that all of these decisions were accepted by the police, and he explained the months of preparation that took place to prepare for the event – the vast majority of which would never be seen by the public. He acknowledged that although the summit and the city were never disrupted to the extent seen in other countries, the tragic death of Ian Tomlinson dominated public perception of policing during that period. In fact, the ICM poll highlighted that 59% believed the police to have used unacceptable violence (*London Evening Standard*, 2009). The Public Order Commander also mentioned that since G20, the public order landscape had been consistently changing, through means of legislation, legal precedent, public views and police policy. Clearly aware of all the good practice that surrounds the policing of protest, he explained that the policy of the MPS is to try and facilitate as many of the 1,000 annual applications as they can. Their approach is to work with the organizers to establish what they want, and negotiate how this can be achieved with the least disruption to others. As HMIC (2009c:5) said, 'Balancing the rights of protesters and other citizens with the duty to protect people and property from the threat of harm or injury defines the policing dilemma in relation to public protest'.

Section summary

The public order environment is one that shifts constantly. Since the Public Order Act 1986 came into Force, there have been 29 pieces of legislation in relation to policing disorder, and 90 amendments to the Act itself (HMIC, 2009c). The policing of disorder shares many of the characteristics found when policing firearm incidents. First, there is a significant difference across countries concerning the police management of crowds, and unfortunately many deaths can be associated with this when viewed at an international level. Secondly, it has been shown that the implementation of tactics is vitally important, as indiscriminate actions can exacerbate aggression, whereas thoughtful and proportionate policing can reduce disorder. Thirdly, the policing of disorder in the UK demonstrates the evolution of good practice. Here, the ineffectiveness of the 1980s has subsided through adherence to a continuous improvement approach that has implemented good practice within a clear and robust command structure. Again, like other aspects of policing there appears no finishing line in terms of effective public order policing. For example, a thematic inspection by HMIC (2009c:7) pointed out that variation exists across British Police Forces in relation to the understanding of public order powers, as well as their use of tactics; and also that training and guidance was not keeping pace with changes in society.

Conclusion

Critical incidents and the use of force often define police legitimacy. As with the delivery of other elements of operational delivery, 'The use of force varies widely across officers, situations, organizations, and political systems at multiple levels' (Maguire, 2010:200). Although this chapter has focused on the UK, there have been sufficient examples to show the different approaches by other countries. As Bayley (2010:xiii) worryingly argues, 'out of 192 countries within the United Nations there are only 15–16 I don't fear from illegal and unprincipled use of force'.

Studying the use of force and how the police deal with critical incidents is illuminating, as it conveys a significant amount of information regarding the police as an organization. Of course, in the challenging environment of a critical incident, it would be unrealistic to expect that the police were always effective. Sharf and Binder (1983) argue that when officers are frightened, they are prone to making mistakes that result in the use of excessive force. Eyre et al. (2008) established that poor outcomes in critical incidents result from inaction or failing to establish that actions had been implemented, distributing blame and hiding from accountability and a lack of compatible thinking and cooperation. However, critical incidents, especially when involving confrontation, can often illustrate the strengths of the police institution. This is because such events are accepted as *real policing* within the culture of the organization. Secondly, it generally involves clear objectives that rely on enforcement as the solution. Thirdly, the focus is on implementation, with operational interventions constantly practised and improved; each utilizing a clear command structure with specialist officers to deliver evidence-led approaches. Perhaps the most significant finding with critical incidents though is the process of learning that accompanies them. These operational events are debriefed at various levels, with subsequent findings being re-invested into future tactics.

6
Investigating Serious Organized Crime and Terrorism

Introduction

This chapter focuses on ways in which the police deal with more serious problems, specifically terrorism and organized crime. On first examination, there appear obvious differences between the genres. Whilst terrorism is politically motivated and aims to bring social change using extreme violence against people, locations and events (Hoffman, 2006), the fundamental aim of organized crime is to achieve personal profit. However, on closer inspection some overlap is apparent. Organized crime offenders may engage with terrorists if it adds to the profitability of their actions, whilst terrorists will reciprocate if the liaison either assists their activity or provides them with the necessary illegal goods or services to facilitate their actions. Further, as terrorists and organized crime offenders are sophisticated *conscious opponents*, and often transnational in nature, they also share operational characteristics; meaning that the law enforcement approach to tackling these crimes also share similarities.

Section 1: Terrorism

Defining terrorism and terrorists

For academics, the subject of terrorism is difficult to study due to its clandestine nature (Silke, 2004). It is defined by UK law as the 'Actual or threatened acts of violence against people and/or property designed to influence the government, to intimidate the public or a section of the public, or to advance a political, religious or ideological cause' (Section 1, Terrorism Act, 2000). However, it is worth highlighting that the label 'terrorist' has been described as pejorative, applied by powerful groups onto opposing political groups weaker than themselves (Innes & Thiel, 2008:556). An example of this would be the Taliban in Afghanistan, who were previously supported by the USA, yet are now labelled by some as *terrorists*. A further complication emerges when trying to quantify the scale and type of terrorism, as again this is diverse, ranging from state-sponsored terrorism (e.g. The Pan Am flight, Lockerbie), to domestic extremism (e.g. extremist Animal rights groups). One similarity that all terrorist groups share though is their requirement for public support, which provides them with the legitimacy they need in order to survive. This means that terrorists can often achieve more by targeting democratic countries, from which supporters, recruits and lobbyists are easier to recruit (Richardson, 2006; Sluka, 1989). Indeed, public support is critical to both terrorists and those they target, leading to careful selection of their actions, words and symbols (Smelser, 2007); because of this, terrorists frequently target symbols of state power or economic greed. Furthermore, terrorists often rely on the state response being unreasonable or disproportionate, in order to endorse their role as the persecuted victim.

Terrorism is not a new phenomenon: the term dates back to 1798 and has long had an association with many countries (Laqueur, 1987). In the UK for example, the 'Special Irish Branch' (later becoming Special Branch) was formed within the London Metropolitan Police in 1883, to deal with fenian terrorism. However, the terrorist approach has changed since then. Prior to the 1970s, terrorism was very much localized, as terrorist groups focused grievances on their own governments; yet the advent of late modernity, globalization and enhanced mobility facilitated the introduction of nonterritorial terrorism (Sloan, 1978). One early example of this was in November 1979, when 53 American hostages were seized at their embassy in Tehran. This trend has accelerated in recent years, and is referred to as *international terrorism*, the most prominent threat emerging from groups who associate themselves under the name of al-Qaeda (AQ). These groups include the following:

- Core al-Qaeda – leaders and main members (Burke, 2004);
- Loosely coupled affiliates – personal acquaintance and family networks (Wright, 2006);
- AQ inspired terrorism – which begins as self-radicalization operating for ideological reasons (Kirby, 2007).

The most infamous of AQ's attacks occurred with the coordinated suicide of 19 terrorists, who, on the 11 September 2001, hijacked and crashed four aircrafts in the USA, culminating in the death of nearly 3,000 victims from across 70 countries. This incident was followed by other atrocities across the world, including attacks on the London Transport system on the 7 July 2007, where 56 people died and 700 were injured. A further significant factor is that this latter attack involved three bombers from Pakistani families in the UK, signalling the first *homegrown* UK terrorists. In essence, AQ-related terrorism has changed the nature of the terrorist threat across three criteria: the increase in the scale of the attack, the involvement of mass casualties and the willingness of the terrorists to die in the process (often through suicide attacks). These changes required new policing strategies, tactics and skills, coupled with an enhanced level of consciousness and cooperation from the public. As mentioned throughout this book, late modern society has embraced a risk-based approach whereby potential harms are quantified, prioritized and responded to, through rational and measurable interventions. It is, therefore, useful to quantify the risk that *international terrorism* poses, before examining the policing responses to it.

The threat from international terrorism

There was no lack of academic or political leaders to voice concern about the new terrorist threat. Following the Tokyo subway sarin gas attack by the terrorist group Aum Shinrikyo, Laquer (1996) predicted that there would be a more concerted use of weapons of mass destruction. Following the attacks of 2001, this rhetoric increased with Giuliani, the mayor of New York saying, 'We're looking at dozens and dozens and multi years of attacks like this'. As Sheehan (2008:7) writes, 'No terrorism expert or government leader wants to appear soft on terrorism. It's always safer to predict the worst; if nothing happens, the exaggerators are rarely held accountable for their nightmare scenarios'. Unfortunately, for those addressing the threat, there appears no typical terrorist profile, as individuals exhibit a range of age, nationality, residence and socioeconomic status. Furthermore, the journey to radicalization also appears ambiguous, as different people have negotiated different pathways before emerging as a terrorist. Wiktorowicz (2005) appears to encompass the most commonly held view that young men become radicalized through radical friends and family members, often following some personal crisis or feelings of alienation brought on by perceptions of discrimination.

Concerns about international terrorism generated a change of philosophy for police and government agencies, turning from a *need to know* to a *right to know* approach when providing information. This was precipitated by the view that the wider community would be more likely to identify suspicious activity linked to terrorism if they knew what to look for. In November 2006, the British Security Services (MI5) stated that they were monitoring 200 terrorist networks, containing 1,600 individuals, who were involved in over 30 potential terrorist plots (BBC, 2006). This was followed up in July 2007, when the UK Prime Minister revealed this number to have increased to 2,000 individuals (Brown, 2008); in fact, during that particular year 203 people were arrested on suspicion of terror offences in the UK compared with 201 across the rest of Europe. In the same year, 42 people were convicted of terrorist offences in UK courts (half pleaded guilty), following 16 separate police operations. It was later published that between July 2005 and April 2008, a total of 15 terror plots been intercepted within the UK (Europol, 2011).

Terrorism obviously poses a significant threat to society; however, there are a growing number of commentators who argue that the response is disproportionate. Carle (2008), a previous Deputy National Intelligence officer with the Central Intelligence Agency (CIA), stated that AQ consisted of 'only a handful of individuals capable of planning, organizing and leading a terrorist organisation', adding, 'its capabilities are far inferior to its desires'. Sageman (2008) also suggests that the centre of AQ consists of less than 150 people although these individuals are supplemented by thousands of sympathizers and potential jihadists that engage in rhetoric with each other. It is also reported that the USA and UK authorities generally feel there are no active sleeper cells, and voice more concern surrounding homegrown terrorists.

By analysing terrorist incidents, certain cycles and trends also become clear. At an international level, between 1968 and 2006, there have been an average of 420 terrorist-related deaths and 1,249 injuries each year, with these statistics peaking during the 1980s – a time associated with the trend in state-sponsored terrorism (Sandler et al., 2008). A more recent examination has established that only a proportion (between 200 and 300) of these deaths are specific to Islamic extremism, emanating from atrocities such as the bombings in Bali or London in 2005 (Cordesman, 2005, cited in Mueller & Stewart, 2011). From this follows the probability that being killed or injured by a terrorist today is essentially zero (Treverton, 2009), with terrorist incidents on American Airlines flights estimated, over the previous decade, as one in every 16.5 million flights (Mueller & Stewart, 2011). Furthermore, there is evidence to show that fatalities emanating from domestic and international terrorism have been declining since 1998 (Mack, 2008). Compare these findings with road-related injuries. Even Britain, who boast one of the best road safety records in the world, reported 1,901 people killed and a further 23,122 seriously injured in 2011 (RoSPA, 2012). This makes responding appropriately to terrorism (a relatively small problem in quantitative terms, but extremely high in generating psychological fear) a difficult task to get right. One would assume it to follow a logical risk-based model that generates cost effective solutions.

Unfortunately, there is considerable evidence to suggest that the response to terrorism is not risk based. In the USA, the RAND Corporation (a think tank that analyses terrorism and counterterrorism interventions) has been critical over the lack of systems to objectively manage the threat. The president of the corporation, James Thomson, pointed out that although the Department of Homeland Security (DHS), was based on a crisis management model, their programmes were implemented '... with little or no evaluation as to their performance or effectiveness' (Thomson, 2007 as cited in Mueller & Stewart, 2011:3). In essence, although significant sums had been invested, no quantifiable risk reduction could be established. Indeed, Mueller and Stewart (2011) discovered in 2010 that the DHS refused to do a cost benefit analysis surrounding the use of full body scanners at US airports, costing $1.2 billion per year, because it was 'too much of a burden on agency resources'. Further to this, the scientific validity of counterterrorist initiatives, such as data mining and behaviour detection have also been questioned by the National Research Council. Although it is accepted that judgements are notoriously difficult to make in this area, other organizations have successfully achieved a risk-based approach. Risk and cost-benefit analysis is used widely in low probability high-risk events, such as those found in the nuclear, aviation and environmental protection industries. Indeed, insurance companies are now gaining expertise in being able to judge the probability of these events occurring and to then set appropriate premiums. Unfortunately, a critical review by the National Research Council showed the DHS to have no risk analysis approach in place to adequately support their decision making.

It is widely acknowledged that terrorism is a difficult area to navigate, and that deficiencies in intelligence are problematic if counterterrorist interventions are to be proportionate and cost effective. One of the ways decision making can be distorted, however, is through the use of the *precautionary principle*. Many definitions of this principle exist, but the central point is that a 'lack of decisive evidence of harm should not be a ground for refusing to regulate' (Sunstein, 2005:18). In this way, the *precautionary principle* is legitimately used by nations to intervene when insufficient information is available. So, for example, laws and agreements may be made on environmental concerns, such as pollution, before the complete impact of the potential pollutant is known. Although widely used, this approach varies in implementation across nation and subject; as Sunstein (2005:20) points out, 'Europe has been more precautionary about hormones in beef, whilst the US has been more precautionary about mad cow disease (BSE)'. Although the approach is a perfectly rational position to take, the critical element relates to the level of precaution deemed appropriate for the circumstances. In this, Sunstein (ibid.:20) argues that at certain times the principle can be paralyzing, as decisions are not made on the grounds of probability but on the basis of possibility. Sunstein highlights five underpinning issues that influence the decisions surrounding the precautionary principle:

1. The *availability heuristic,* whereby exposure to recent information makes some risks feel especially likely, even when they aren't;
2. *Probability neglect,* which makes individuals focus on the worst case scenario, even when this is highly improbable;
3. *Loss aversion,* which makes people dislike losses from the status quo;
4. A belief in the benevolence of nature, which makes human decisions and processes seem especially suspect;
5. *System neglect,* an inability to see that risk is part of the system. Indeed, changing elements of a system can create risks of their own.

Studies consistently indicate the term terrorism to be so emotive that it can block out objective probability assessment. The 9/11 Commission report shows that between 2001 and 2004, the US Federal spending on defence, homeland security and international affairs was approaching US $200 billion, a 50% increase compared with a similar period before. To give another example, the London Metropolitan Police Service, which leads on counterterrorism policing in the UK, also doubled resources during that time (Australian National Audit Office 2010); whilst costs have also increased dramatically in Australia and Canada (Mueller & Stewart, 2011).

Has the increased funding to counteract terrorism been spent wisely? There has undoubtedly been an improved level of security; however, there are doubts whether this outlay has always been cost effective. A particular example can be observed within the Australian

Federal Police (AFP), who are in essence Australia's specialist protective security supplier. From 1979 to 1999, their resources remained relatively stable. However, the rapidly changing environment saw a significant increase in investment to deliver New Policy Initiatives (NPI), which are government-based initiatives, introduced to deliver specific operational outcomes. The increase in funding was huge. The Australian National Audit Office (2010) estimated that over the previous decade, the overall budget had seen an overall increase of 250%, and a staffing increase of nearly 140%, with an overall budget approaching AUS$1.4 billion. Since 2001, the government has asked for over 140 NPIs to be introduced, with an associated budget which at times equated to around 75% of the AFP total budget. By accepting this money, the role of the AFP was to clearly articulate the programs they were implementing, to translate the theory into practice and to disclose the results of the investment. Not surprisingly, the National Audit Office was asked to inspect the AFP to establish whether these measures had been implemented. Specifically, they were asked to ascertain whether the NPIs 'were being delivered in accordance with time, quality and cost expectations articulated by government' (NAO, 2011:43).

As NAO (2011:60) state,

> A policy initiative is most likely to achieve the best possible outcome when the question of how the policy is to be implemented has been an integral part of policy design and when arrangements for NPI development provide that:
>
> - The means of, and barriers to, the effective and efficient implementation of the policy are considered when new policy initiatives are being developed;
> - The priority of a particular policy initiative relative to others is considered and properly understood;
> - The proposed initiative is aligned with the strategic direction of government and is well integrated with, and supportive of, other related policy initiatives; and
> - The business case for the proposal is sound, the risks understood and the desired outcomes clear.

As the Australian National Audit Office was quick to acknowledge, the implementation of these projects was not a simple task; however, their initial review during 2007 found a distinct lack of oversight systems. Following these comments, the AFP agreed to improve their project management and performance reporting, yet when later inspected, the NAO (2011:16–20) found little change had been made, saying:

> However while the broad strategy developed in 2008 to improve project management and oversight in the AFP was sound, its implementation has not been effective ... In particular, implementation planning has been generally poor, with no consistent approach to, or clear policy on, project management across the organization; and coordinated executive reporting on NPI implementation has been neither comprehensive nor rigorous. In essence less than a third of surveyed project managers were managing their initiatives as set out by the AFP which meant only a minority had implementation plans setting out milestones, success indicators, costs and risk management strategies.

In this way, the AFP was unable to provide the government with any significant oversight information as to how they had used the increased resources to deliver outcomes that were sought. As the Audit Office said, 'A policy which is embraced by a Minister, approved by Cabinet, announced publicly, but inadequately delivered is worse than no policy at all' (NAO, 2011:20).

Of course every decision has implications and not all are benign. Spending money unwisely means there is less money being channeled to other needy areas, and this is especially concerning in times of recession. As highlighted earlier, there can also be iatrogenic effects (unintended consequences) and one such example was discovered in the area of counterterrorism. Blalock et al. (2007) estimated that increased security measures at airports had resulted in increased cost and inconvenience, causing many more people to drive. The study estimated that this change could be associated with 500 or more fatalities a year, far more than those associated with AQ.

The International policing response to terrorism

Counterterrorist policing is perhaps one of the most complex and challenging areas for policing. It involves a multi-agency approach, whereby numerous government services provide different pieces of the intelligence jigsaw. This next section tracks the policing response to international terrorism, from a multinational to a local perspective.

Since international terrorism has proliferated, there have been numerous attempts to establish an international response. Romaniuk (2010) highlights that as far back as the anarchy movements of the 1800s, governments have found it difficult to sit down together and reach consensus on counterterrorist measures. He observes that in the period between 1970 and 2000, approximately 100,000 terrorist attacks have taken place, some of which were high profile (i.e. Black September at the Olympic Games), with terrorists using increasingly innovative approaches (e.g. highjacking). Although governments were aware that significant counterterrorist measures could be achieved by concentrating on migration controls, financial regulation, movement of goods, and communication technology, they remained concerned about the interference this may have on their domestic policies. Even when multi-lateral agreements were made, the governance systems surrounding them generated so much bureaucracy that they often obstructed effective implementation.

Despite this, the atrocity of 9/11 created greater unity, especially in the immediate aftermath. Although negotiations continued to stutter, due to concerns about intrusiveness regarding domestic affairs and breaches of international human rights law, there was sufficient motivation to implement change. The ambition for change resulted in a multifaceted response, covering financial regulation, migration and custom controls, restrictions on movement of weaponry, and the use of communications technologies. Furthermore, multi-lateral counterterrorism has extended beyond the United Nations, resulting in a proliferation of regional, sub regional or theme-based affiliations. The impact of this multi-lateral approach is difficult to establish, as problems surround the measurement of terrorism and the impact of the response. However, history now provides greater detail as to what cooperative arrangements can achieve. It also shows that terrorist attacks inevitably bring nation states back to the negotiating table.

A national response to terrorism – implementing the UK Contest strategy

National strategies in relation to terrorism propose interventions that lie somewhere on a continuum between military and criminal justice models, varying in emphasis between clandestine to overt approaches. In recent times, a transparent approach has become increasingly more popular, as attempts have been made to engage wider society in helping to make the environment more hostile to the terrorist, as well as managing the perception of a social audience. Innes and Thiele (2008:559) argue how this response can also be understood on a range between *high* and *low* policing. In this way, *high* approaches commence with military interventions (i.e. the declaration of war, civil emergencies); and then start to gravitate to less violent arrangements. This may incorporate the use of various security services (mi5, mi6, CIA, etc.); progressing to include Special Branch or other police counterterrorist specialists. Conversely, at the other end of the continuum, *low* policing embraces the wider concept of policing, and incorporates the involvement of civilian communities together with Community safety partners (such as local government); it then incorporates uniformed officers and general police detectives. In the UK, the terrorist strategy is known as the CONTEST approach, which implicitly incorporates all of the elements mentioned above, and has four specific legs:

1. *Prepare* – To mitigate the impact of terrorist attack by developing political, economic, social and technical resilience.
2. *Prevent* – To stop people becoming terrorists or supporting terrorism (e.g. deradicalization).
3. *Protect* – Strengthen protection against a terrorist attack (e.g. target harden the national infrastructure.
4. *Pursue* – To stop terrorist attacks by bringing offenders to justice.

In this way, the Contest strategy encapsulates both a proactive preventative approach, together with a reactive response of arrest and prosecution. However, the significant question relates to how this approach is put into practice.

Implementing the Contest strategy – some unintended consequences

Although counterterrorist approaches can be constructed rationally, it is often the way the strategy is implemented that becomes the critical issue. In fact, terrorist responses have created significant concern across the world, including the following: detention without trial, questionable interrogation techniques, trials without a jury, the use of *supergrasses* to obtain convictions, control orders to curtail the movement of unconvicted terror suspects, *shoot to kill* policy and the increase of policing powers: specifically stop and search, arrest and surveillance powers.

In broader terms, the investigation of terrorism-related offences are probably the most challenging of all investigations because the stakes are so high and the collation of intelligence so difficult to attain. The intelligence community are historically protective of human sources, as they are in danger of being killed or seriously injured should they become exposed as an informant. Similarly, an intelligence operative would not want to divulge a particular tactic, as this knowledge could assist other suspects in devising counter surveillance measures.

As a consequence, investigation often becomes a contest between surveillance and counter surveillance measures, where knowledge is key to achievement. However, once sufficient intelligence is gathered, the next stage of the process is the response, and again the stakes are clear. If a terrorist attack takes place then it will probably result in mass casualties. The main objective, therefore, is to prevent the attack from taking place, and this takes priority over bringing the offender to justice (although ideally both can be achieved). As such, prevention and disruption are key strategies in the counterterrorist field, and many successful operations in the past have no doubt involved the seizure of cash, commodities or the arrest of peripheral actors, without being publicized as a counterterrorist operation. The increased funding to support the counterterrorism approach has been associated with a growth of legislation and powers, and this in turn has led to an associated increase in gathered intelligence and counterterrorist interventions. However, this increase in productivity has also created a number of concerns.

One example of this was provided by an East Lancashire focus group that included five people engaged in de-radicalization work (East Lancashire is an area with a higher proportion of Muslims and has been subjected to increased interest by the authorities). Initially, the group provided some context by pointing out that religion is central to the daily life of practicing Muslims, and that their culture is fundamentally charitable. They also highlighted that Asians living in East Lancashire had a diverse heritage, originating from different areas of India, Kashmir and Pakistan. This is coupled with widespread concern about what is perceived as persecution of Muslims across the world, in areas such as Palestine, Afghanistan, Kashmir, Chechnya and Iraq. They explained that one of the difficulties for British police (who are generally non-Muslim) is their lack of understanding regarding Islam and these issues. Having explained this context, they went on to explain that during 2009 a peace convoy of nine well-respected Muslims set off from East Lancashire, heading towards Gaza with humanitarian aid. They then said that the authorities assumed this money was in support of terrorism, which resulted in their arrest by the police. Although later released without charge, the Muslim community was outraged by the way these law-abiding community members were treated. As one of the focus group said, 'It set us back 10 years in terms of trust and relationships with police and communities', going on to explain that an edict was released instructing local Muslims to avoid talking to the police.

This incident does not appear isolated, as there have been widespread concerns about the number of arrests that do not lead to prosecution.

The Institute of Race Relations highlighted that between 11 September 2001 and 30 June 2004, 609 people were arrested under new powers of the UK Terrorism Act, with only 15 convicted (three Muslims). In the UK since 9/11, there have been 19,623 terrorist-related arrests overall although these have been decreasing in recent years. Of the 121 terrorist suspects arrested in 2010/11, 45 were charged, 63 were released without charge and 13 had some other disposal (i.e. deported). Of the 13 convicted, four were given life sentences, with two jailed for between 10 and 30 years, and seven jailed for less than 10 years. Of the 87,000 individuals currently incarcerated in British jails, 97 are held for terrorist offences (Povey et al., 2011; *Daily Telegraph*, 2011). To the uninformed observer, these figures illustrate disproportionality when comparing the numbers who are arrested with those who are convicted. This perception is of critical importance, as it can cause law abiding Muslims to feel unfairly treated by the police. This point relates to the concept of procedural justice discussed in Chapter 2, which can reduce the legitimacy of the police and therefore the withdrawal of public consent, which is critical to their work.

A further issue has been voiced concerning the use of stop and search powers. As has been previously argued in this book, areas that allow the police to use high levels of discretion can sometimes be abused. In the UK, Section 44 of the Terrorism Act allows police officers to stop and search anyone in a designated area without reasonable suspicion of being involved in an offence. In 2010, there were 210,013 cases that resulted in only 9 arrests (0.004%). Concern over this led to sections of the Terrorism Act 2000 being repealed and replaced by more limited powers in March 2011. This led to a reduction of 90% in stop and search powers under the Terrorism laws in 2010/11 although the resulting arrest rate remains under 1% (Povey et al., 2011; Parmar, 2011; *The Daily Telegraph*, 2010).

Parmar (2011) continues in this theme by showing the unintended consequences of poorly implemented counterterrorism stop and search powers. Working alongside London police officers, who stated their support for these new powers, he also interviewed those youths who were at the receiving end. He found those affected to believe that the only reason they were searched was because they were Asian, Black or perceived to be Muslim, asserting that 'ethnic minorities firmly believed that they were unfairly targeted' (ibid.:375). Parmar pointed out that it was ironic for the police to be requesting better engagement with Muslim men, when they were subjecting them to this level of intrusion, adding that Sikh men were also caught up in this process when mistaken for Muslim. From the interviews he conducted, Parmar

(2011:377) concluded that 'the enforcement of S44 was found to at best, stifle and at worst, reverse the development of mutual trust between British Asians and the Police'.

Further controversy has been associated with the *PROTECT* leg of the UK Contest strategy, involving increased security around the UK's critical infrastructure. There have been numerous examples of innocent bystanders being challenged for taking photographs of iconic tourist attractions (*The Daily Mail*, 2010). On a similar theme, whilst researching for this book, a police initiative was observed where over 4000 bus drivers in an English County were briefed in relation to transport related terrorist bombings. Although a significant level of effort went in to the initiative, carried out by committed and enthusiastic practitioners, the benefits can be questioned. For example, this was a local initiative and few transport-related attacks had occurred in the UK and none in that specific region. Similarly, although a considerable number of transport staff was briefed, it could not be taken for granted that these operators would be on duty if such an attack occurred, nor was there any plan to educate new recruits. This was a further example of well-meaning practitioners, in difficult situations, using blunt responses to deliver questionable outcomes in relation to effectiveness and value for money.

Perhaps the most controversial element of the UK strategy has revolved around the PREVENT leg of the CONTEST strategy, which in essence has attempted to identify and divert those individuals who are vulnerable to radicalization. Although conceptually simple, this activity has been particularly difficult to implement, as limited understanding exists concerning the radicalization process, or about those who are particularly vulnerable. At an overall cost of £70m in 2011/12, shared across three government departments (Department for Communities and Local Government (DCLG), Foreign Commonwealth Office (FCO) and Home Office (HO)), this approach has been shrouded in controversy. Some argued that the process has presented Muslims as a *suspect community*, as well-meaning individuals have sought to identify those who are at risk (Panzatis & Pemberton, 2009, 2011). An evaluation of the initiative has not been complimentary, saying it has served to 'legitimise ... the views of the Far Right and other Islamophobes', making it difficult to engage with a critical element of the community (Communities and Local Government Committee, 2010:8). Although some limited success was highlighted within the government evaluation, there was fierce criticism that this funding did not get to the areas for which it was intended and subsequently resulted in a waste of resources (May, 2011). In essence, the de-radicalization strategy has been costly, at best delivering some limited return, whilst at its worst, considered as counterproductive in making mainstream sections of the public more suspicious and less likely to engage with the police – a further iatrogenic effect of the strategy.

Finally, we turn to the *PURSUE* leg of the strategy. History shows 18 individuals to have been killed by police officers in the UK since 1920 (not including the Royal Ulster Constabulary). A number of these have been terrorist related, with the most recent involving the death of an innocent Brazilian man, Jean Charles de Menezes, living in London. Following the failed bombings on the 21 July 2005, officers were conducting surveillance on flats linked to a suspect. A soldier assisting the police announced that Mr de Menezes fitted the description of the suspect and was evidently leaving the premises. Due to the operative allegedly using a makeshift toilet to relieve himself at the time, he was unable to relay pictures back to the operations room, which would have shown that Mr de Menezes was not the suspect. A surveillance team followed the subject into Stockwell underground station, where authority was given to the firearms team to confront him. Using *Operation Kratos* tactics he was pulled to the ground, and police officers discharged seven shots at point blank range, into his head. Although there have been many concerns surrounding this tactic (which became known as a 'shoot to kill' policy), the police defended their actions by arguing that a suicide bomber could not be prevented from detonating a bomb unless he was killed immediately (nevertheless accepting they had killed an innocent man). An inquest delivered an open verdict, and although individual charges were not pressed, the MPS were found in contravention of the Health & Safety at Work Act 1974 (failure to provide for the health, safety and welfare of Mr de Menezes). This finding culminated from criticisms surrounding the implementation of the command structure, communication and surveillance procedure throughout the operation, which was no doubt exacerbated by the time pressures. As could be seen from the inquiry, this outcome did not emanate from a single individual event, but from a chain of events where (in hindsight) the correct interventions were not made.

Section summary

The threat of international terrorism has been associated with atrocities that have generated widespread fear across the world, also creating a complex problem for security agencies. From an objective standpoint, however, evidence suggests that the rhetoric and response may have been disproportionate to the threat. Although policing interventions have no doubt reduced terrorist activity, some of these approaches have been less effective and even counterproductive. It is important to understand that the UK-based Muslim population is approximately 1.6 million, and comprises 56 nationalities that speak 100 languages; approximately 74% of these are from an Asian Heritage, predominantly Pakistani and Bangladeshi. They also have the youngest age profile of any religious group and incorporate 50% of the under 25 years in this country. If, as has been argued, this section of the community unfairly and disproportionately suffers from powers generated by the Counter Terrorist response, this could have significant consequences. In Parmar's view (2011:379), 'A spectre of terror was used to legitimate unfair policing practice and this is difficult to reconcile in the context of efforts which were said to be being made to engage with ethnic minorities and in particular Muslim Communities'. As has been seen, policing in democratic countries relies on consent and legitimacy, and this can only be achieved if the public perceive the police to be fair.

Section 2: Organized crime

Defining organized crime and Organized Crime Groups

Commentators are of the opinion that an increasingly mobile and interconnected world (both physical and virtual) has created the criminogenic potential from which illegal entrepreneurialism can prosper. Castells (1996, 1998) believes that Organized Crime Groups (OCGs) have seized the wider commercial, political and social opportunities available in society, to generate increased profits. In recent years, research into this area has increased in prominence, as governments become more aware of the scope, costs and dangers surrounding organized crime. Similarly, as Ayling and Broadhurst (2012) point out, the global financial crisis now makes legitimate business more vulnerable to approaches from OCGs. Despite this interest though, a unified definition for organized crime remains elusive (Finckenauer, 2005). Indeed, von Lampe, who at the time of this research had collected 185 separate definitions from academics and institutions across the world, argues that authors face a task akin to 'nailing a conceptual pudding to a wall' (von Lampe, 2002:191). Not withstanding these concerns, Albanese (2008) sets out the prospect that organized crime can be understood either by listing criminal activity or by describing the characteristics of the group involved. In relation to criminal activities, these have been categorized into the following groups: (a) the provision of illicit services (e.g. human trafficking or subcontracted services such as illegal dumping); (b) the provision of illicit goods (e.g. controlled drugs, counterfeiting); or (c) the infiltration of business (e.g. extortion, money laundering, fraud). However, most policing agencies focus on the criminal actors rather than the illicit markets and products.

Conceptualizations of OCGs have often fallen into either hierarchical or enterprise models; the former epitomized by the Italian, American and Russian Mafia, Chinese Triads and Japenese Yakuza (Paoli, 2002). However, the advent of globalization generated significant changes to organized crime, making it a more fluid and dynamic affair. As such, the 'enterprise model' developed by Smith (1980) places emphasis on profit, where actors seek to find opportunities to exploit, through interaction with those who can assist in their aim. An enterprise crime is therefore a process, a series of linked criminal acts relying on an ability to forge fresh contacts that bring new opportunities for profit (Europol, 2011).

Efforts have also been made to define OCGs, and after lengthy negotiations, the United Nations came to the conclusion they were a '... structured group of three or more persons existing for a period of time and acting in concert with the aim of committing one or more serious crimes or offences in order to obtain, directly or indirectly, a financial or other material benefit' United Nations Convention Against Transnational Organized Crime (2000). Albanese (2007) analysed existing definitions and highlighted the four most prevalent characteristics as: a continuing organizational hierarchy, the use of force or threat, the corruption of public officials to maintain immunity, and obtaining rational profit through crime. Similarly, van der Heijden (1996) suggested that OCGs can be identified by recognizing six characteristics from the list below (the top three of which must be included):

- Collaboration of more than two people.
- Suspected of the commission of serious criminal offences.
- Determined by the pursuit of profit and/or power.
- Each having their own appointed tasks.
- For a prolonged and indefinite period of time.
- Using some form of discipline and control.
- Operating across borders.
- Using violence or other means suitable for intimidation.
- Using commercial or business-like structures.
- Engaged in money laundering.
- Exerting influence on politics, the media, public administration, judicial authorities, or economy.

There remain gaps within all these definitions, however. For example, how can an OCG definition accommodate paedophile rings that swop rather than sell images, or differentiate between the severity of the crime committed? Due to these issues, most governments establish a very simple definition such as that coined by the British Government (2011:5) who define an OCG as '... individuals, normally working with others, with the capacity and capability to commit serious crime on a continuing basis, which includes elements of planning, control and coordination, and benefits those involved'.

As research has increased, further attempts have been made to try and identify the career criminal, as well as those who engage in more harmful behaviour. As such, the notion of *serious crime* has now been included in many of these discussions and has been defined by the United Nations (2004:5) as 'an offence punishable by at least four years in prison or a more serious penalty'. Similarly, The UK National Criminal Intelligence Service (2005) also included a period of imprisonment in their description of organized crime, saying it encompassed 'Those involved on a continuing basis, normally working with others, in committing crimes for substantial profit or gain, for which a person aged 21 or over on first conviction could expect to be imprisoned for three or more years'. The procedure of defining seriousness using a term of incarceration is now a common approach, and is currently used as a discriminatory factor in the UK Regulation of Investigatory Powers Act, to establish whether the use of covert surveillance techniques are proportionate.

Research has also established that organized criminals are qualitatively different to their general crime counterparts. As Ayling and Broadhurst (2012:41) point out, 'Very risky activities such as drug trafficking, require a high degree of trust between offenders, so the structure of such groups tends to be denser and involve a larger proportion of affective relationships than groups involved in less risky enterprises'. More recently, studies have started to explore the criminal careers of organized crime offenders. Much of this work has emerged from the Netherlands and the research has established the following characteristics:

- In terms of offending history, there are clear differences between organized criminals and general offenders.
- Organized crime offenders exhibit a more persistent offending pattern than general offenders.
- Those who commit organized crime are unlikely to do it as a first offence.

- The average age of organized crime offenders, on first conviction, is in the mid-20s, and a significant proportion is even older, indicating a 'late starter phenomenon'. It, therefore, appears that criminal opportunities can act as a precipitator for organized crime involvement at a variety of ages (Kleemans & de Poot, 2008).
- On first conviction, organized crime offenders (if imprisoned) generally receive a sentence three times longer than general offenders.
- Organized crime offenders spend twice as long in prison as general offenders (van Koppen et al., 2010).

The level of organized crime

Although the sums involved are ambiguous, the problem of OC is significant enough to threaten the stability of many international governments, with the United Nations estimating that US$125 billion a year is generated through illicit transnational crime flows (UNODC). Similarly, the British Home Secretary reported organized crime to have cost the UK between £20 and 40 billion a year (Home Office, 2011). Duborg and Pritchard (2007) have attempted to quantify the financial cost of organized crime categories, in both market size and in the economic and social costs for the UK. In this way illegal drugs was by far the most significant category in relation to organized crime, with a market cost of £5.3 billion and a social/economic cost of £15.4 billion. This was followed by excise fraud (£3.7 billion market cost; £3.7 billion social/economic cost); fraud (£1.9 billion market cost, £2.7 billion social/economic cost); people smuggling (£250 million market cost, £1.4 billion social/economic cost); people trafficking (£275 million market cost, £1 billion social/economic cost); and non-excise intellectual property theft (£840 million market cost, £300 million social/economic cost). The authors were keen to point out the difficulty of quantifying these areas, resulting in approximate estimations that are often based on HM Revenue and Customs data. Therefore, they do not take into account qualitative measures such as exploitation and misery.

The challenges of organized crime to policing

The next area of focus will highlight the challenges that organized crime is causing the police. Prior to doing so, it is useful to consider the profit to be made from organized crime, in order to understand the motivation of those who pursue it. For example, when a kilo of cocaine is produced it will cost approximately £325, and a kilo of heroin approximately £450. The commodity will then go through various traffickers, so that when it eventually emerges in the UK, the street price of cocaine will have increased to around £51,659 a kilo (15,800% profit) and heroin about £75,750 a kilo (16,800% profit) (Wilson & Stevens, 2008). As can be seen, the monetary costs of trafficking and selling drugs are relatively small, with the nonmonetary costs, such as imprisonment and violence from other dealers being a more significant deterrent. Furthermore, the profit surrounding this criminal enterprise is high, making it a viable opportunity for many offenders. The Home Office goes as far as to suggest that there are 300 major importers in the UK, with 3,000 wholesalers and 70,000 street level dealers (Matrix Knowledge Group, 2007).

Back in 2001, Roger Gaspar, Head of the UK National Criminal Intelligence Service said: 'Organized crime bosses have embraced globalization every bit as enthusiastically as the heads of legitimate international conglomerates. Which means Colombian, Italian, Chinese, Russian and Jamaican gangsters are doing business in London, Manchester, Glasgow and Belfast'. Many commentators have highlighted the numerous economic, political and social opportunities that globalization has presented to OCGs, with the rapid transit of humans, goods and information across the world. In fact, Europol (2011:38) highlight five strategically placed European hubs that collate and disseminate illicit drugs, trafficked people or counterfeit goods. These include the North West (Netherlands and Belgium), North East (Lithuania, Estonia, Latvia and Russian Federation), South East (Bulgaria, Romania and Greece), South West (Spain and Portugal) and Southern hub (Southern Italy). Such hubs change in terms of capacity and capability due to fluctuations within the markets, as well as a variety of other factors such as corruption and quality of policing. Of course, improved connections can also be made in the virtual environment, assisted by communication technology. Internet banking has allowed 'fast and anonymous transfer of huge amounts of money' (UNODC, 2007:46), allowing money laundering on an unprecedented scale. Similarly, the cyber network has allowed for an increase of fraud (phishing) and trafficking of illegal pornography, allowing opportunities to be exploited in both the material and virtual world. There is no doubt that individuals within society are travelling further, and this also includes offenders; for example, a third of the 72,505 individuals arrested in London during 2011 were foreign nationals (Evening Standard, 2012), whilst HM Prison (2008) shows foreign nationals to account for 14% of the prison population. The challenge, therefore, emerges as to how law enforcement agencies can face the increasing threat of organized crime, when confronted by budget reductions as a result of the worldwide recession (Gilmour, 2008). The current strategy of instigating a lengthy investigation and prosecution to incarcerate OCG members has a number of deficiencies. These deficiencies have been set out in a number of documents (Kirby & Penna 2010; Penna & Kirby, 2012); however, there are three main concerns:

(a) *There are too many organized criminals for law enforcement agencies to pursue and arrest.*
Put simply, organized crime is now evolving at a quicker pace than ever before. During 2007, a Constabulary in the North of England identified five large scale hydroponic cannabis factories within its jurisdiction. A year later, the same Constabulary had identified 42 separate factories. They had proliferated because a Vietnamese organized crime group had exploited a niche, only requiring rented accommodation, a power supply, and some knowledge of hydroponic cultivation to deliver their product to an expanding market. In fact, the impact of organized crime is not just found at an international level, but is increasingly observed throughout each tier of criminality, from transnational to national to regional to local. Whilst many countries have limited intelligence to accurately assess the level and diversity of OCGs operating in their country, the UK has recently engaged in a national mapping exercise (Gilmour, 2008). They estimate approximately 38,000 offenders were operating within 6,000 organized crime groups (Home Office 2011), and in 2005, it was estimated that 'less than 6 per cent were being targeted' (HMIC 2006: 5).

(b) *Increasing diversity, complexity and problems of jurisdictional accountability.*
Conceptually and operationally, organized crime has become more complex. The enterprise model has allowed organized crime to diversify, and also to integrate with some elements of legal activity. Offences can include vehicle theft, drugs, firearms, people trafficking, fraud, money laundering, pornography and child exploitation. Due to the secretive nature of this crime, it is difficult to establish the level of harm associated with it, and therefore how crimes or offenders should be prioritized. Whilst late modernity has provided increased opportunities to commit organized crime, Beck (1992) argues that offenders (similar to terrorist groups) have exploited modernization more effectively than the police, who are still constrained within the institutional organization of the late 19th

and early 20th centuries. It is a useful exercise to unpack this observation to ascertain the level of the challenge that faces the police.

At one level of analysis, it is clear the police are able to exploit the same transportation and communication systems as their *conscious opponents*. As was shown in an earlier chapter, offenders will often leave electronic traces as they move, therefore legitimate travel by sea or air allows personal details to be recorded; whilst road movements can be captured by CCTV, ANPR (Automatic Number Plate Recognition) and satellite navigation systems. Phone usage can also be traced, revealing where and when the phone was used. Coupled with this, internet browsing and bank account details often reveal personal and professional interests. In the 21st century, the investigator has access to computer hardware and software that allows him/her to interpret patterns across this data much more effectively; similarly, secure systems of communication allow that investigator to speak with anyone across the world. However, whilst the physical technology has improved in this way, the process of transnational investigation has barely altered. Different jurisdictions continue to use different legislation, whilst rules, procedures and bureaucracies are often slow and costly to negotiate. Formal permission is required to investigate, question, arrest and seize evidence in foreign countries. Finally, many will have no extradition process agreement, and even Europe, which uses the European *arrest* and *evidence warrant* to speed up the process, still has 27 different legal systems to negotiate.

Along a similar thread, more professional police officers now exist across the world, who are increasingly able to communicate more effectively with each other, and yet cooperation remains limited in practice. This is due to the many human factors that surround the investigation. For example, different agencies are affected by different objectives and methods of working, as illustrated by a senior detective on disclosing that, '... we were interested in speaking with a man detained by immigration services as he was involved in an organized crime network over here. However the immigration services just shipped him back, and we were unable to complete that piece of the jigsaw'. Another case had to be withdrawn when one of the suspected offenders was found to be registered as an informant to another law enforcement agency; disclosing this fact in court would have endangered his safety. There are many practical reasons like these that prevent police officers from fully cooperating, even when appropriate policies are present. These include: insufficient time or resources, trust surrounding the sharing of information, concern that other investigations will be compromised or otherwise affected and the safety of witnesses or informants. As the 9/11 commission said, 'There are no punishments for not sharing information. Agencies uphold a 'need to know' culture of information protection rather than promoting a 'need to share' culture of integration' (National Commission on Terrorist Attacks in the United States, 2004:417). In essence, compared with their *conscious opponents,* the investigator is at a disadvantage as he/she does not benefit from a market environment and is unable to go anywhere else for information or assistance.

Unfortunately, due to these implementation issues, the law enforcement infrastructure has generated more tiers and adjuncts to facilitate cooperation and intelligence transfer. United Nations Office on Drugs and Crime assists states in their bid to tackle drug, arms and people trafficking; Interpol (1923) emerged as the first transnational unit, and continues to act as an intelligence clearing house for its 188 member countries; whilst the Europol Drugs Unit (1993) looks specifically at drug trafficking. There also exists, as an intergovernment body, the Financial Task Force, formed under the OECD to look at policies to prevent money laundering across its 34 member states. However, many of these agencies have little or no enforcement powers, and international agreements for action do not guarantee implementation. This was shown clearly in the UN Convention against corruption agreement in 2005, which has made limited progress, despite 151 countries having signed up to it (Ayling & Broadhurst, 2012). Likewise in the UK, national structures in the form of the National Criminal Intelligence Service emerged (later morphing into the Serious Organised Crime Agency [SOCA], and latterly into the National Crime Agency [NCA]). However, national structures – even with supporting provincial offices – have proved insufficient, so that new Regional Agencies have now emerged. In the UK, these include the Regional Asset Recovery Agency, the Regional Organised Crime Unit and the Counter Terrorist Regional Units. Such changes are seen worldwide, and are illustrated by the United States, who have a proliferation of national and state agencies, such as the FBI and DEA. Following 9/11 however, even these were considered insufficient and as such, Fusion Centres were added as a further tier to collate and disseminate intelligence from various agencies. These have since been criticized on the grounds of ineffectiveness, mission creep and the infringement of civil liberties (Monahan & Palmer, 2009).

Perhaps the most significant difference between investigators and organized criminals is the individuals themselves. Entrepreneurialism is a major factor with organized crime, as offenders are willing to accept much higher levels of risk due to the rewards on offer. As one detective said,

> We had an offender who always kept one step ahead. He started off trafficking drugs and when he got enough money he cut out his dealer and bought them wholesale. To mask his tracks he crossed over to the continent using a jet ski. That ended one day in him crashing, writing off his jetski, ending up in hospital and losing his drugs in the process. Not deterred he bought a microlight and did the journey by air. When he raised even more money he bought a fast boat and made the journey with less risk and more comfort.
> (*Senior Detective, UK Police*)

This is another critical difference between the conscious opponent and the investigator; whilst the offender is rewarded for taking risks, the investigator receives no such rewards, only sanction if he or she fails.

(c) *The investigation of organized crime has increased dramatically in terms of cost.*

As was mentioned earlier, mobile data and telecommunications play a significant part in evidence gathering although this can be time consuming and costly. During research for this book, a British detective revealed that a recent proactive investigation into drug trafficking involved the analysis of over 180,000 individual telephone calls. In transnational investigations providing evidential continuity, to the standard required by British courts, is challenging, especially when complying with legislation regarding the disclosure of foreign-based unused material. A further challenge is the physical act of travelling to these countries to conduct enquiries, which is time consuming, bureaucratic and expensive. For example, imagine collecting evidence for a human trafficking case. The crime process involves suitable women being identified and recruited (often through fraud), who require fraudulent identification documents, transportation (air, sea land) and bribes to facilitate passage. This requires a diversity of offenders with different skills – often negotiating in different languages and currencies – who are able to source their contacts from anywhere in the world.

The police response to organized crime: Prosecution, disruption and prevention

As was shown in the previous paragraph, the traditional response to organized crime has been the pursuit and prosecution of offenders. This has a significant benefit in that it brings offenders to justice; however, in terms of reducing the overall impact of organized crime, it has limited impact for a number of reasons. First, any prosecution is protracted and expensive. The police therefore have to decide which groups to target – and this can only relate to a small percentage of the overall number of OCGs due to finite resources, making the risk of arrest to organized crime offenders very low. The second reason is that the organized crime event rarely stops; indeed, when an offender is arrested, it can be viewed merely as providing a vacancy for other offenders to compete over. In fact, in some cases the organized crime offender is able to continue their illegal business whilst in prison (Ayling & Broadhurst, 2012).

The policing of terrorism provides a useful analogy as to how organized crime can be dealt with in a different way and with more effectiveness. The counterterrorism paradigm has at its heart the prevention of the offence. The impact of a bombing or other atrocity has such devastating consequences that the paramount objective is to prevent the harm, rather than arrest the offenders. As such, the investigative process revolves around the ability to understand who the terrorists are and how they operate. Interventions to prevent the incident can be activated at a number of levels and in a number of ways. These can include: the arrest or deportation of the offender, increasing the difficulty of the terrorist act through target hardening or the removal of the facilitating mechanisms (explosives, funding, chemical precursor, personal contacts). The point is that the policing of terrorism relies first on understanding the constituent parts of the terrorist process, and secondly by using this knowledge to prevent it from occurring through disruption of the offender's networks or operational plans. Three questions are particularly important when deconstructing the organized crime process:

- Where are the profits made? Profit (mainly financial) is the key motivator for criminal involvement in organized crime.
- Who are the actors in the process? These may be offenders, victims and/or facilitators. As has been seen, a legitimate business man (solicitor or haulier) may become involved in organized crime, due to the financial inducement involved.

- Who are the stakeholders or guardians of the environment that the crime takes place in? For example, a corrupt official or officials may facilitate organized crime.

(Kirby & Penna, 2010)

Knowledge of this process allows organized crime to be tackled by other means, specifically by using disruption or prevention. Disruption, 'is a more flexible, transitory and dynamic tactic, which can be used more generally to make the environment hostile for the organized crime group ... this approach focuses on disrupting the offender's networks, lifestyle and routines'. Conversely, Situational Crime Prevention (SCP) 'is taken to refer to those interventions that successfully stop or dismantle a single organized crime event, specifically those that change a process of environment in a sustainable manner' (Kirby & Penna, 2010:205). In essence, whilst disruption concentrates upon the *offender*, SCP concentrates on the *crime*. However, they both work on the principle of reducing the opportunity for the offender to commit organized crime.

The success of SCP and crime disruption, as viable strategies, has increased over recent years. However, Levi and Maguire (2004) mirror most views when they say that there is still insufficient research surrounding the implementation of SCP, in relation to organized crime. Others are concerned that removing the opportunity will merely cause displacement. Kleemans et al. (2010) showed this by explaining that when the main ingredient for ecstacy (PMK) was restricted in the Netherlands, it prompted Dutch OCGs to work with Chinese OCGs, in order to obtain an alternate supply. This not only rendered the restrictions useless, but generated an extra crime of smuggling. Notwithstanding these concerns, during July 2011 the UK Government published their latest organized crime strategy, 'From the local to the global' (Home Office, 2011:6), which embraced these alternative methods. Specifically, its approach was based upon three principles: stem the opportunities for organized crime to take root; strengthen the use of enforcement against organized crime (using the full range of lawful interventions); and safeguarding communities, business, and the state, by examining and reducing vulnerability. The alternative approaches of disruption and SCP will now be looked at in more detail.

Kirby and Nailer (2013) followed a Police Force in Northern England over a period of 3 years in relation to their disruption approach to an OCG. The OCG was comprised 13 core members, who were supplemented by a wider network of 17 others. There was a clear hierarchy in the group, and interestingly this appeared to correlate with the level of previous convictions. Whilst one offender had no criminal convictions, three others accounted for approximately two third of the total convictions, with one offender alone accounting for 39% of convictions. Analysis showed that the high conviction offenders were predominantly used as enforcers within the OCG.

The disruption approach completely inverts the normal approach of prosecution (normally facilitated by a covert proactive specialist team). Rather than keeping the operation secret, it was publicized to the community, partner agencies and even the OCG themselves. This is because the objective had changed from the prosecution to the reduction of organized crime. The approach mobilized both commercial and public sector agencies to share information, pool resources and deliver the most effective response. The most common partner was local government, which included the building planning department, environmental services, rights of way department and antisocial behaviour officers. Other partners included the Land Registry, The Environment Agency, Her Majesty's Revenue and Customs, Driver and Vehicle Licensing Agency, The Fire and Rescue service, Department of Works and Pensions, Vehicle and Operator Services Agency, the Crown Prosecution Service and voluntary agencies.

The disruption approach aims to generate a hostile environment for the OCG to operate within. Kirby and Nailer (2013) listed all of the interventions implemented by the agencies, and categorized them using the 'rational choice theory' framework, as postulated by Cornish and Clarke (1986) (Table 6.1). This model, as explained in the previous chapter, was devised to deal with the reduction of volume crime, yet has been observed to work effectively in this area as well. It argues that the costs of committing the crime could outweigh the benefits, if interventions:

- Increased the effort needed to commit the crime,
- Increased the risk of being caught,
- Reduced the rewards from the crime,
- Removed the excuses to justify the crime.

One of the most interesting anecdotes to explain this process was provided by a Chief Officer from the Police Force concerned. He explained that at one of the partnership meetings, a representative from the Environment Agency conveyed suspicion that members of the OCG were dumping illegal waste, though they had insufficient resources to catch them in the act. The police allowed the Environment Agency to direct their surveillance unit for a day, which immediately

Table 6.1 The disruption interventions used against OCG members, categorized in accordance with Cornish and Clarke's (1986) Rational Choice Theory

Increase effort	Increase risk	Reduce rewards	Remove excuses
1. Increased police visibility in area of OCG residences to challenge low level criminal behaviour	1. Use of ANPR on all OCG vehicles. Providing information as to movement of OCG-related vehicles	1. Use of the Proceeds of Crime Act 2002 to seize and confiscate money obtained from crime by OCG members	1. Traffic calming measures and notices
2. Inform legitimate business that their products and services are being used to facilitate crime (i.e. transport)	2. Extensive monitoring of OCG's movements and dealings to identify any wider offending	2. Preventing the development of houses and removal of unlawful buildings through the enforcement of planning regulations (no response results in demolition). Take legal action against unlawfully constructed buildings	2. Notices issued by County Council to all residents of the village relating to antisocial behaviour (noise nuisance). These establish what is and what is not appropriate
	3. Zero tolerance of minor infringements by OCG members		
	4. Decrease anonymity of OCG members by supplying photos and information regarding OCG members to partner agencies		

Source: Adapted from Kirby and Nailer (2013).

provided the evidence to convict and incarcerate members of the group. The approach, when taken overall, had a significant effect. More information was revealed about the OCG and their offending level was reduced. The approach also appeared a very popular method with police, and with partner and public representatives, who through this confident and robust approach saw a fresh confidence in the community. This example is not isolated, and similar approaches have been seen across other police agencies across England, and no doubt further afield. In another area of the UK, police working with Inland Revenue and local government services targeted premises that were used by the OCG to launder money. The premises were closed down once their tax and operating procedures were inspected. The most effective response will obviously vary according to the organized crime process, and will always be highly context specific.

The remainder of this section will look at a SCP approach to organized crime. Again, there is growing evidence that these approaches can work in practice (Bullock et al., 2010) although this is seen in isolated good practice, rather than common practice. A useful example is provided by Kirby and Penna (2010), who describe an incident that occurred in February 2004, in which 23 illegally smuggled Chinese nationals, from the Fujian province, drowned whilst digging for cockles in Morecambe Bay, Lancashire. Following the tragedy, the initial response was to bring the offenders to justice. The investigation that followed generated a considerable level of work, as enquiries were made with business and government representatives from China, European cockle processing plants and haulage companies. Government departments included Fisheries, Department for Environment, Food and Rural Affairs (DEFRA), the Department for Work and Pensions and Immigration. Overall, the investigation created 1½ million pages of documentation (including Mandarin, Spanish and French languages), approximately 2,900 statements, and 2,500 exhibits, with approximately 20,000 phone calls analysed for evidential purposes. The three suspects (each supported by their own Queens' Counsel, barrister, solicitor and interpreter) were convicted of offences involving manslaughter, conspiracy to pervert the course of justice and immigration following a 6-month trial, culminating in a total sentence of 20 years in prison (Lancashire Constabulary, 2006). Unfortunately, even though millions of pounds had been spent on this prosecution, the organized crime environment remained unchanged. The money laundering contacts remained in place, as did the potential profits. Cockle prices soared from around £200 a ton 4 years earlier to £1,300 a ton, and with 35 miles of coastline to harvest there were significant profits available. Secondly, cheap labour was still available as more were willing to be smuggled from China. Thirdly, the vast shoreline provided anonymity to illegal workers and their controllers, with official guardians of the cockle harvesting process apparently apathetic to enforcing the licensing procedures (at the time of the tragedy only 160 permits were issued when it was estimated that 800 individuals worked on the sands). On an average day, 100 vehicles (of which 79% were found to be un-roadworthy or overloaded) were transporting up to 400 cocklers. Also, the Department for Work & Pensions were of the view that nearly a third of the cocklers were fraudulently claiming benefits, costing the state £1,216,800 a year (Lancashire Constabulary, 2006). Finally, immigration authorities had insufficient resources to detain or deport illegal immigrants.

As with the last example, all partner agencies met to discuss the way forward. The Departments of Environment, Fisheries, and Rural Affairs; the local Crime and Disorder Reduction Partnership; the Department for Works and Pensions; the Maritime and Coastguard Agency; the North West Chinese Council; the Health and Safety Executive; the Sea Fisheries Committee; the City Council; the Immigration Service; and English Nature were all brought together. All those involved improved their audit systems to prevent inappropriate or illegal practices, especially with regards to the permit scheme. However, the innovative change was to relax a local by-law, thereby allowing a catering caravan to park at a strategic location on the sands. As this was used by most of the workers, it became a natural point where people could gather, allowing information to be circulated and workers identified. There were considerable benefits. Within a short period, 1200 regulated workers were recorded on the licensing scheme, and benefit claims were reduced, saving HM Treasury £828,000 in the first year. Un-roadworthy vehicle usage was reduced by 84%, and all workers started to carry personal life-saving equipment, resulting in lifeboat deployments reducing from 34 in 2004 to 1 in 2005. The cocklers went on to form their own shellfish association that convened weekly and started to self-police standards on the sands (Lancashire Constabulary, 2006).

Section summary

Organized crime is a problem increasing in scope and threat. More sophisticated *conscious opponents* are exploiting the opportunities provided by late modernity to increase illegal profits. In a period of tightening public sector budgets, the traditional response of prosecution appears an expensive strategy to follow in relation to the potential outcome. By analysing organized crime in more detail, especially from an offenders' perspective, it is clear that opportunities exist to disrupt or prevent such criminality at much less cost and greater speed. By joining up other agencies in this endeavor, *policing* can be seen as a wider concept, and not just the responsibility of the police institution. However, such an approach appears to be observed as good practice rather than common practice. Why aren't these approaches used more often? The main difficulty appears to emanate from an organizational culture that values arrest and enforcement approaches more than prevention (Murray, 2005; Read & Tilley 2000). This approach relies on good leadership, and tenacious and energetic activity by practitioners. It is also clear, as many commentators have observed, that research in this area is limited (von Lampe, 2011), and that more is required to ultimately test the efficacy of this approach in different locations and on different OCGs.

Conclusion

Although there is evidence of significant achievements by the police in the field of terrorism and organized crime, there remain opportunities for greater levels of effectiveness. Late modernity has been associated with an increasingly sophisticated conscious opponent, who uses the opportunities presented by globalization. As this chapter has shown, these opponents are able to seize these opportunities much more effectively than law enforcement practitioners. In responding to this new threat, the implementation of policing approaches is seen as a constant challenge. It has been shown, especially in the terrorism section, that legislation may fail to predict unintended consequences. Using blunt instruments without sufficient consideration as to their outcome can lead to a sense of injustice, thereby affecting the legitimacy of the police – a critical factor when policing a democratic country. Furthermore, those larger strategic projects would benefit from a greater adherence to project management – in this way obtaining clarity on what the investment is trying to achieve, how it will be achieved, and the benefits that accrue. This chapter also shows some excellent multi-agency work that reduces harm by preventing and disrupting organized crime. Although it is a logical approach, offering great potential to increase effectiveness, the existing police culture makes it more difficult to implement than more traditional enforcement approaches.

7
Conclusion

Introduction

On arriving at this stage of the book, it won't surprise the reader that the simple question, 'Are the Police effective' doesn't generate a straightforward response. As such, this conclusion spreads over three sections, traversing between the general and the more specific. The first section will explore the parameters on which 'effectiveness' could be judged, and discuss how the Police Service compares across these measures. Section two will explore the general factors that could improve effectiveness and efficiency within policing; while section three emphasizes the importance of implementation, a critical element within Praxis (the process by which theory is enacted or realized). Finally, the conclusion of this chapter will verify that improvement to implementation would lead to a step change in police performance.

Section 1: Are the police effective?

The term 'police' is often used to explain 'state organizations employed specifically to maintain order and control crime' (Newburn 2007:218). When considering the question of police effectiveness, it is important to acknowledge that although all police agencies have similar identifying features they cannot be viewed as a single entity when considering performance, as they vary between and within agencies. Diverse government priorities and legislation, together with different procedures and operating environments, mould police forces in different ways. For example, victims in Latin America, Asia and Eastern and Central Europe are far less likely to report crime than elsewhere in the world (Van Dijk, 2012). In these countries, the way police agencies obtain their legitimacy to operate, the services they provide and the way they are structured, will vary from agencies in Western Europe or North America. In fact, as Chapter 1 has shown, the standard of policing even varies between and within agencies from the same country, due to the way individuals and organizations respond to external and internal influences. It is also important to understand that there is no finish line in terms of effectiveness, due to the dynamic and rapidly changing environment that the police institution operates within. Even if an agency were to be viewed 'effective', this does not mean it will remain so.

Having concluded that all police agencies differ and should be evaluated in their own right, and at specific intervals, this chapter will focus on British police forces. The next challenge is to identify the measures on which effectiveness should be judged. This book has highlighted the difficulty of measuring the police, due to their diverse role. Punch and Taylor (1973) referred to the police as the 'secret social service', Banton (1964) emphasized the peace keeper role and Bittner (1974) summed up the diversity by asserting that, '... their competence to intervene extends to every kind of emergency, without any expectations whatever. This and this alone is what the existence of the police uniquely provides, and it is on this basis that they may be required to do the work of thief catchers and of nurses, depending on the equation'. Whilst the effort and money invested in New Public Management provided insight into organizational performance, no matrix was developed to present an objective score that determines success or failure.

One obvious performance indicator would be the government priority '... to cut crime, no more no less' (May, 2010a). Using the Crime Survey of England and Wales as a gauge, the police would undoubtedly be judged effective (as would most law enforcement agencies across the developed world, when considered against their crime statistics). Although diluted by evidence that the police aren't the exclusive reason for this reduction, it is nevertheless clear they can play a significant role by reducing reoccurring community problems surrounding particular people, places, events and products. Unfortunately, police performance on this particular objective (the reduction of reoccurring crime problems) was never monitored in the list of government indicators.

Few, however, would support the judgement of effectiveness on one exclusive indicator, and most commentators would look across a wider suite of services. This view is apparently endorsed by the British government, who, when faced with impressive crime reduction figures, continue to drive through significant police reform. Unfortunately, identifying a consistent suite of suitable comparators has also proved too difficult to establish. An alternative approach would be to compare the effectiveness of the police against other public sector entities. At the time of writing, this approach regrettably did not extend the debate much further, as the British media were voicing criticism about politicians (i.e. brawling, expense fraud, perverting the course of justice); the National Health Service (i.e. deficiencies of care and unethical practice); and the clergy (i.e. sex scandals affecting the Catholic church). This leaves education, which again is not exempt from criticism. Bayley (2011:313), a University Professor and respected police academic, compares the two professions; he starts in rigorous fashion by saying,

> It is the fashion in writing about police organizations to describe them as being rigid, unreflective, ineffective, wasteful, unaccountable, bureaucratized, self-serving and hide bound. This characterization is deserved, as my own writing has tended to show.

Bayley continues, however, by arguing that the police are not unique in this regard, and no worse than other institutions. He points out that higher education has a rigid strategy, counted in time (credit hours) and numbers of students, rather than what it achieves. In his opinion, Professors have considerable discretion and are rarely trained or evaluated, whilst senior administrators receive little or no management training. He continues by saying that 'Efforts to improve the effectiveness of higher education are superficial as those of police ... In both police forces and universities few reforms affect what happens between practitioners and clients' (ibid.:314). In conclusion of this, Bayley states that the police probably come out on top, or are at least no worse than Universities in terms of practice and management, resolving that the defects in both are institutional.

Perhaps another approach would be to examine the financial cost of the police, and to deliberate whether they provide value for money. Unfortunately, an earlier chapter revealed various statistics, showing either that the British police enjoy extravagant funding, or suffer insufficient investment. In my local area, I pay £220 a year for access to police services and £91 to the fire authority (although national taxation is added to this). Whilst I haven't had the need to call on their help, I know that they offer a 24 hour, 7 day a week service that will respond to just about any crisis or incident. When comparing this against other insurance I haven't claimed against, such as my car insurance, it appears reasonable value. Again this isn't an objective assessment. Perhaps we could quantify the level of things the police get right and compare this against the things they get wrong? Unfortunately though, this doesn't take us very far either. In England and Wales, the police deal with 4.2 million crimes, 3.2 million incidents of antisocial behaviour, and just under 10 million emergency calls a year (ACPO, 2013), of which the majority are dealt with satisfactorily. Overall, national surveys show many more people to have trust and confidence in the police, than those who don't.

This discussion channels us towards a conclusion that police agencies differ as to their level of effectiveness, and that generally speaking the police in the UK are viewed as being reasonably efficient; though previous chapters show they are more effective in critical incidents than day to day management. As such, the question as to whether or not the police are effective cannot be objectively answered on any distinct criteria, and will probably differ relating to who is asked and when. However, when the question is 'Can the police be more effective' and 'can they be more efficient', the resounding answer is yes. It is to this question that the following section now turns.

Section 2: The critical issues surrounding a more effective police service

As commentators have pointed out, demands from society have increased exponentially in recent years. Police Chiefs are expected to manage multi-million pound budgets (for which they have significant autonomy) in an effective manner. As Grabosky (1988:6) says, 'No public sector agency should be able to command an increase in resources unless it can demonstrate that its current allocation is being used efficiently, and that its resources are being targeted at specific, measurable, objectives in a logical manner'. In essence (similarly to other organizations) there is a need to deliver effective police services quicker, with better quality and at less cost.

The senior police officers interviewed for this book all felt that the British Service had improved significantly over the past 20 years, especially in terms of professionalism, accountability, intelligence approaches and critical incidents. They also agreed that improvements could be made in day-to-day management and the use of more evidence-based approaches. Johnson et al. (2008) focus on the management of organizations. They argue that the strategic options and capability of an organization are based on three elements. The first surrounds the threats and opportunities presented by the current and future operational environment. The second relies on the level of resources and competencies the organization holds, whilst the final element relies on the influence exerted by its internal organizational culture and stakeholders. In this way, any preferred strategy can only be feasible if it is within the capacity and capability of available resources and competency, and is acceptable to stakeholders. Frigenti & Comninos 2006 insist that organizations should be clear on their vision, and that once in place this should lead to a mission statement, which in turn would evolve into the objectives and outcomes necessary for success. Generally speaking, in operationalizing any strategy, four areas are particularly important to manage – people, information, technology and money.

In 2005, Sir Ian Blair presented the Dimbleby lecture, and attempted to stimulate a debate by asking the British people's opinions as to the type of police service they wanted. McLaughlin (2007:220) highlights that concerns at the time revolved around the increasing gap between police and public, including anxiety as to how a police and security philosophy could work alongside a service that protected human rights, democratic values and cosmopolitan citizenship. Unfortunately, there was general antipathy to Blair's question, with the general response epitomized by the following quote,

> What the police can do is remove the obstacles to community, such as violence and disorder and public nuisances. What they can do – could do much more – is stay close so close to the community they police that they can anticipate crime and deter it by their close knowledge of who's who and what's going on. Failing that, they are there to catch criminals. You do not need a public debate to discover that, that's what most people think.
>
> (*Sunday Times, 20* November 2005)

In fact this appears the view of the current government. The lack of an overarching vision results in two outcomes. The first possibility is that without any new world to move towards, practitioners can suffer from paradigm freeze, as they are locked into viewing the problem using similar perspectives and methods. The second is that any change can be fragmented, as leaders use their discretion to drive through diverse initiatives that are affected by the myriad of influences in the external and internal environment. However, whilst an overarching vision may be lacking, there still is great appetite for reform, driven by pragmatic economics. As Legrand and Bronitt (2012:1) say, 'Policing is a series of ongoing trade offs between tackling priorities and resource management', and perhaps the great reforming agent in many parts of the world has been austerity measures. On the 20 October 2010, the British government announced that police funding would be cut by 20% in real terms, over the following 4 years (HMIC, 2010b), with almost two thirds of this to take place in the first 2 years.

In the austerity measures that have followed, there has already been significant evidence for 'necessity being the mother of invention'. Police Chiefs interviewed during the research for this book highlighted some innovative practice, as triggered by budget reductions. Thames Valley Police, for example, had conceptualized a new model of dealing with demand that ranges from self-service to shared services. Similarly, representatives of Staffordshire police spoke about the benefits of dedicated teams involved in multi-agency working. Indeed, although none of the senior officers welcomed the austerity measures, all agreed it had prompted new ways of thinking and working. Unfortunately, not all highlighted benefits however. A number of discussions with representatives of partner agencies highlighted that the police had, at times, centralized resources to save infrastructure costs, and had started to focus more on Force wide initiatives to heighten their profile. These changes had the unintended consequences of moving away from multi-agency initiatives and tailored approaches. The lesson was always to focus on the outcome rather than the process.

Of course, prevention is the best way to reduce all forms of demand, be it crime, disorder or wider social concerns. A review of the evidence suggests that prevention remains peripheral to what is regarded as real police work. In 1986, the director of the Police Foundation (UK) stated that 'Whatever the expressed commitment of senior police officers and successive government to the view that prevention is the primary object of policing, the crime prevention job remains an activity performed on the sidelines while the main action takes place elsewhere' (Weatheritt, 1986:49). It is perhaps telling that the former Chief HMIC, in his valedictory lecture, again promotes the importance of prevention in the police mission, no less than 183 years after the birth of the British police (O'Connor, 2012). As such, there remains ambiguity on the most effective way to implement crime prevention; for example, whether it is more beneficial to emphasize primary, secondary or tertiary approaches. The earlier chapters of this book also highlighted other areas of policing that could be improved. These include:

External elements

Late modernity. It is clear that by focusing on the wider concept of policing, society can play a more aggressive role in predicting and anticipating problems. There is very clear evidence for an association between opportunity and crime. For example, although Vancouver and Seattle are similar sized cities – comparable in race, income and age distribution, homicide is 50% higher in Seattle due to the preponderance of firearms (Sloan et al., 1988). Similarly, in developing countries across the world there is a link between crime and the abuse of alcohol by young males (Hartfield, 2009). The challenge is being able to implement the change needed to reduce crime, and to do this in a timely fashion. In 1960, Germany's legislation mandated that there should be high quality steering locks for all cars. This led to a 50% reduction in car theft just 1 year later. In the wider EU, electronic immobilizers only became mandatory in 1998, which 10 years later led to an 80% reduction in car theft (van Ours & Vollaard, 2012). Evidently, with increased knowledge, society can play a much more significant role in reducing crime opportunities through design and technology. In too many examples the 'public police' pick up the expense for the private sector as they attempt to maximize profits, or reduce cost. Major advances could be made if the cause of the crime (the polluter) had the responsibility of implementing or funding the solution.

The Police – Citizen relationship. A further issue that has remained constant in policing has been the importance of the relationship with the public. Research around procedural justice has shown that not only is it important to deliver policing by consent, it can also lead to cost effective crime reduction, as individuals are less likely to commit crime and more likely to stand up against those that do. Implementing a policing approach that emphasizes this issue leads to more effective policing.

Plural policing. Continuing the wider theme of policing, there are now more private security staff than police officers across the world. Greater synergy between the private and public policing sectors can only increase safety and well-being to the public, whilst providing more accountability and value for money to both sectors.

Stakeholders. It is clear that at a strategic level politicians need to understand the ramifications of their actions. Although generated through good intentions, there is considerable evidence to suggest that stakeholder demand has, at times, added limited value or even generated unintended negative consequences. Two elements are critical in this. Evidence shows that when recommendations are produced to the degree at which they have been in the UK, they cannot be implemented. This causes similar problems being encountered again and again (e.g. bureaucracy), resulting in increased costs, but with little to show from it. More consideration needs to be given to what needs changing and what outcomes can be achieved when analyzed against cost. Secondly, New Public management has been an industry in itself, and as Fleming (2009:225) argues the measures 'are not good at capturing the quality and effectiveness of the work involved and the many contributions that Police make to a community's quality of life'. Similarly, Skogan and Frydl (2004:34) asserted that '... governments are more inclined to accept what police do (outputs) as a measure of effectiveness than what they achieve'. There is considerable scope to provide greater clarity on those services and standards that are expected from the police, whilst reducing performance management information.

Internal elements

Leadership. This book, like many others, has shown that leaders are crucial to effective delivery. Unfortunately, there is considerable evidence to show that the police as an institution often becomes embroiled with the process, rather than staying focused on the outcome. As Handy (1994:331) says, 'It is easy to lose yourself in efficiency, to treat that efficiency as an end in itself and not a means to other ends'. The implementation of all police activity highlighted throughout this book depends to some degree on leadership. Often central issues such as effective policing models, quality of service and resource management are not delivered due to poor implementation. Too often this is because the approaches are contrary to the existing organizational culture of the police. Improvements in implementation requires leaders to focus on outcome, have a continuous improvement mentality that prefers to use evidence-based approaches concentrate on successful delivery and evaluate the impact.

Practitioners. Covey (2004) highlights that successful delivery can be associated with three successful approaches: knowledge (knowing what to do, and why to do it), skills (knowing how to deliver) and desire (wanting to deliver). Organizational culture has been seen to affect all of these elements and is sometimes in conflict with organizational goals. Greater clarity in terms of what the organization requires from the practitioner, more accurate appraisal and associated rewards (both implicit and explicit), can only improve implementation, leading to greater effectiveness and efficiency.

The context

Chapter 1 argued that failures can occur even when many opportunities for intervention were possible. For whatever reason, be it organizational culture, poor leadership or poor management, the intervention is not made.

For example, during 2010, a Northumbria police officer was sentenced to life imprisonment for a series of rapes and indecent assaults when he offered to help vulnerable women in return for sexual favours. When convicted, it was revealed he had been subject to previous allegations of serious sexual assault when he was a soldier, though these were never revealed in his police application. He was also disciplined for two separate incidents whilst in the police. Like external problems, internal issues do not occur randomly, but will concentrate around specific people, processes and systems. Often, many individuals know these problems exist, yet accept the status quo. Again this brings us to the importance of implementation, which will be dealt with in the final section.

Section 3: Praxis – implementing theory into practice

Praxis was highlighted as the process by which theory is enacted or realized. The evidence presented throughout this book has demonstrated that implementation failure occurs frequently and at different stages. Consider the following scenarios that illustrate how leadership decisions break down:

1. There are simply insufficient resources to implement the objective required by police or political leadership. Research generally shows that there is no attempt to establish the cost of implementing legislative or policy demands. Furthermore, new demands are rarely associated with extra resources.
2. The political objective (i.e. legislation or policy) is poorly considered and ineffective. The demands on the police are therefore ambiguous, making them difficult to implement or measure. Moss (2009) provides a number of examples for this in the UK. The Dangerous Dogs Act 1991 is one good example, whereby the police experienced difficulty in identifying the type of dog stipulated in the legislation.

3. The policy or objective has insufficient implementation time. This is often due to a change in political or police leadership at national or local level, with the new figure favouring an alternative approach.
4. The legislation/policy may be effective, however, its implementation may have unintended consequences. One example is the UK policy to drastically increase the use of static and mobile speed cameras. The policy reduced casualties, albeit the response from the general law abiding public was overwhelmingly negative. As we have seen, unintended consequences are a constant theme throughout this book.
5. Partners working alongside the police are ineffectual; for example, bringing offenders to justice requires CJS partners to synchronize systems. Similarly, the policing of high profile events (i.e. the Olympics or World Cup tournament) relies heavily on private security and other policing partners.
6. The political objective/policy is legitimate but is not accepted by the Chief Officer. As such, they doom the approach to failure, either by not prioritizing it (an explicit approach) or by devaluing it when speaking to operational staff (implicit approach). This is referred to as the 'say yes, but mean no' approach.
7. The tactical interventions to deliver the objectives are correctly identified; however, the Chief Officer has insufficient ability (leadership/management skills), or resources (people, skills, finance) to implement them.
8. The political priority (outcome) is correct but the senior police officer is unable to put it into practice (identify the operational outputs needed to deliver it).
9. The political priority/objective is accepted by the police leadership but devalued by the organizational culture of front line practitioners. Police leadership (at a variety of levels) is insufficient to ensure compliance and delivery, for example the Problem Oriented Policing model.
10. Leaders inaccurately announce the success of an initiative (evaluation is based on subjective criteria) allowing it to be repeated.

This book has highlighted many malfunctions of execution in both operational and organizational arenas. Consider this further example provided by Cauklin (2012:2) who refers to a central call handling centre in a British police force,

> The first discovery was that 40% of calls on police time were 'preventable'. In the sense that they were caused by someone (sometimes the police, but quite often also another agency) failing to do something or to do something right the first time. In other words if the system worked properly, the reason for those calls would go away. If just a fraction of that 'preventable' demand could be turned off, officers would be freed to carry out more useful activity. They would be doing more with less: capacity would increase.

This book has therefore contrasted examples of outstanding achievement with examples of avoidable malfunction. Whether it is the subject of crime, disorder or managing demand, there is a considerable level of wasted effort and resources, the delivery of less effective services and, at times, unintended consequences. It is disappointing that even when practitioners understand and agree 'what is to be done', and when good practice is established, it may not be achieved due to implementation failure.

Why does the police service find implementation such a challenge? Earlier chapters showed that police appear more effective in tackling critical incidents than in day-to-day management. The analysis behind this finding is straightforward. In critical incidents, the objectives are clear; the approach fits snugly within the organizational culture (as it relies on enforcement). The situations are ostensibly project managed within tight parameters of command and control, and there is a continuous learning loop as incidents are evaluated and fed back into operational tactics. The day-to-day management of incidents is a complete reversal of these factors. As McChesney et al. (2012) has pointed out the daily operating environment can be a whirlwind of noise generated by new initiatives, resource challenges, stakeholder requests and ambiguity.

As the evidence has shown, implementation fails at three levels. There is theory failure: where the wrong choice (mechanism) is made and either it cannot work in practice, or its impact has iatrogenic effects. Secondly, although the mechanism may be theoretically sound, it cannot be implemented in practice. This may be due to inadequate resources in relation to quality or quantity, specifically in relation to time, money and people. Finally, the evaluation either doesn't exist or is inadequate, leading to lessons not being learnt. These principles can be extended over many facets of policing, as this book has shown.

So how can these issues be corrected? How can the focus on implementation be emphasized? Some may argue that when individuals fail, more rules and procedures should be introduced to tighten up the processes involved. There is a contrary argument however, as Latino (2008) highlights that such changes can add more complexity to the working environment and forge a wider gap between procedure and practice. A recent example involved the British police codifying thousands of pages of good practice advice, which was poorly implemented. This has now been recognized, and ACPO together with the College of Policing have vastly reduced the items of guidance, focusing on the areas of high risk. What is required is not new theory, but new ways to concentrate on implementing what is already there. This requires emphasis on two elements: the correct tools and leadership.

Tools to aid implementation

It has been illustrated in earlier chapters that implementation failure occurs in other professions. Here checklists have been used to counteract avoidable errors in construction, aviation and more recently, medical-related complications and fatalities (Degani & Weiner, 1993; de Vries et al., 2010; Gawande, 2010). Sidebottom et al. (2012) highlights the benefits of practitioner checklists in police-related problem-solving initiatives. However, the commentators warn that although conceptually simple, they are difficult to put into practice. Sidebottom and colleagues point out that checklists can be distinguished according to the number of operators they use, and how they confirm the correct action is being taken. They also list the main points of checklist success as that of being concise; unambiguous; sharply defined; specific about what, when, how and who should do what; and being easy to follow and compatible with standard practice (ibid.:201). Checklists have been highlighted throughout this book (National Decision Making Model, IIMAC in critical incidents, Problem-Oriented Policing). Like other disciplines, the most difficult element is choosing the critical elements to populate the list; however, unlike other disciplines, police-related checklists have not been evaluated.

Using the lessons learnt throughout this text, a generic checklist for tackling and implementing both strategic and tactical problems would look as follows:

1. *Outcome*: be clear on what you are trying to achieve, define the desired state and set out the evaluation criteria on which success will be judged.

2. *Examine the current position*: be clear on the capability/resources/capacity/performance already in place. (NB: At this stage the operator should be aware of where they are and where they want to get to. This presents the gap that needs to be bridged.)
3. *Set priorities*: The critical success factors required to bridge the gap can now be identified and set. (NB: Prioritize, what are the most important actions that can be feasibly achieved?)
4. *Implementation plan*: Design the interventions – what is known to work in this context and why? Change mostly revolves around three issues – people (numbers, skills, etc.), processes and structure. Whilst structure is the quickest of the three to change, it often fails to provide a sustainable solution. The implementation plan must set out and provide accountability in relation to activity, milestones and cost.
5. *Implement the plan,* and monitor it is being delivered in the manner required.
6. *Evaluate* whether the intervention has delivered change, and whether this has achieved your outcome.
7. If appropriate, return to step 1.

Wells (1998), in a review of 8,400 projects found that 34% finished in complete failure, 50% had over-run or had been delivered with significant extra cost and only 16% had been delivered according to specifications. The overwhelming majority of these projects fail on basic management practice, rather than technical grounds. This leads us to the importance of project management. As Lock (2001:1) states, 'The purpose of project management is to plan, organize and control all activity so that the project is completed as successfully as possible in spite of all the difficulties and risk'. Project management can therefore clarify the business benefits of the initiative, set out the most efficient way to deliver the project, separate implementation by finding appropriate people to deliver discrete elements and schedule appropriate milestones. At one level the police do this very well, as critical incidents can be viewed as short-term projects, where the organization (represented by the Gold Commander) sets out the requirements. The project manager (Silver Commander) then outlines what is needed, and who will be responsible for implementation. This process of invoking clear objectives, required outcomes, cost management and accountability is seen with firearms, public order and homicide incidents.

On a wider scale, however, this research found that few police forces used project management systematically. Consistent with findings of

Maylor (2010:15), there were examples of 'Ready, fire, aim' (no clear objectives prior to implementation), 'We don't have time to do this stuff'; 'It's all just commonsense'; 'It won't work here'. However, police budgets entail significant resources, and change is both constant and in need of particular management skills. Unfortunately, the management of complex projects are too often given to police officers or staff with limited experience or skills in project management. The ramifications of this have been evident, with too many examples of failed approaches or negative outcomes.

Regrettably, in many ways project management can be interpreted as being contrary to police organizational culture. Its reflective and ponderous style, often exacerbated by the bureaucracy deployed in the approach, does not play to the strengths of the police institution. However, as has been reiterated throughout these chapters, effective implementation is not about preferred styles of working, it is about implementing what works. Project management needs to be a key management competency (Frigenti & Comninos, 2006:91) although it should also be accepted that in the contemporary policing environment, it no longer requires a classic engineering approach. Frigenti and Comninos (2006:2) suggest that 'business redesign and service improvement create management challenges that require a more flexible and organic approach'. Project management within the police context needs to be a more flexible and dynamic affair, whilst still delivering the same benefits. In summary, though checklists and project management offer a positive approach towards more effective implementation, something further is required to motivate practitioners to use these approaches.

The role of leadership in implementation

As a number of commentators have said, 'Management is doing things right; leadership is doing the right things' (Bennis & Townsend, 1995; Drucker, 2002). More effective implementation relies on both leadership and management. For example, Section 44 of the Terrorism Act created greater powers of stop and search. History shows that practitioners will use their powers as flexibly as they can. It is therefore the responsibility of leaders to consider where this flexibility should end, and to decide how these powers should most appropriately be implemented. Similarly, more successful implementation provides the most effective way for managers to reduce waste.

All organizational change relies on leadership commitment. As Weatheritt (1986:120) asserted, '... the Police have been more interested in how they do things than in what those things achieve: in other words they have concentrated on questions of organizational efficiency, at the expense of those of organizational effectiveness'. This indicates that changing the focus onto implementation requires cultural change within leaders and practitioners. This should not be surprising. As McChesney et al. (2012:xxiii) asserts, although business professionals point out that execution is always more difficult than devising strategy, their higher education and training is always focused on the latter; it is execution they require more skills in. However, Scott and Kirby (2012) additionally point out that leadership should also be supported by changes to infrastructure in order to embed cultural change. These changes encompass both people (i.e. selection, training, reward) and systems (i.e. analysis capability, partnerships and tracking systems). On another level, Thaler and Sunstein (2008) proposed a completely different approach with their 'nudge' philosophy. Their method, described as liberal paternalism, tries to steer people into making better choices by understanding what drives individual decision making and behaviour. The UK Government uses a Behavioral Insights Team to promote this approach. Halpern, the director of the unit, provides a useful example, in which police officers attempted to reduce car thefts by getting people to park their cars in garages. When this advice was not followed, they established it was due to people's garages being full of clutter. They, therefore, placed skips in the area, with a notice explaining that they were free – to be used for dumping garage waste. The initiative worked; the cars were moved into the garages and thefts reduced. Halpern explains that through removing the friction that obstructs people's motivation, implementation is encouraged (Bell, 2013). Perhaps such approaches could be extended to counteract the cultural issues that prevent police officers from implementing approaches that work.

Whatever the approach, if implementation is to be improved, it needs to be accepted as an issue by those in leadership positions. It requires an unwavering focus on the outcome to be achieved, the use of evidence-based interventions, flexible project management principles and evaluation of results. This ethos of continuous learning and improvement are key to sustained progress and need to be led from the top. The proposal for direct entry at senior levels within the police may present some opportunities in this particular regard.

Where do academics fit in?

Academics fill an important role in relation to 'implementation'. In their research, they provide the case studies that describe what works and what doesn't work in practice. They have the knowledge, research and evaluation skills that can assist the police. They can also enhance the status of Praxis as a research topic and can emphasize the importance of the subject when speaking to police officers and their stakeholders. If more is understood about implementation failure, more can be done to prevent it.

I remember many years ago, when I was the police representative on a conference panel; I was asked to comment on why the police did not use evidence-based research as much as they should. In defending this position to the academics present, it was pointed out that systematically implementing research across the 43 police forces of England and Wales required the mandate of 43 Chief Constables, supplemented by considerable training and financial cost. To do this for research that was often disputed or challenged by other academics, and was constantly being adapted, was a risky proposition. Furthermore, the research often ignored operational context and implementation blockages. Research has moved on significantly since then, as has the attitude of the police to use it. However, academics constantly need to consider the complexity that surrounds the implementation of their ideas and provide practitioners with a clear understanding of the operational impact that it can achieve. I still read recommendations in academic journals that I doubt could ever be implemented. For example, assessing police performance is a difficult subject, and the principle that policing should be measured in wider terms is to be supported. However, recommending that 'community participation' should be measured highlights numerous implementation problems: it is ambiguous to define, difficult to record, expensive to deliver, and it remains uncertain whether all types of community participation could be associated with police effectiveness.

Conclusion

Pease (2009) once told a story about the Cane toad. He explained that these particular toads are considered a pest in Australia, and that citizens are encouraged to catch and dispatch them. The most humane method is to freeze them gradually until death, a process that apparently causes no discomfort. The point Pease makes is that if things happen slowly and progressively, we are unlikely to notice them at all.

Policing reflects society and adapts to the changes within it. Change is not new; Her Majesty's Inspectorate of Constabulary were suggesting changes to police forces in 1857 (Weatheritt, 1986). However, the current pace and intensity of change is unprecedented and the operating environment is becoming increasingly complex. As Bailey (1986:i) said, 'Unlike manufacturing industries the police service has no identifiable end product, nor do its customers – who range from central and local government to community groups and individuals – all agree on what they want'. As this book has shown, the police, as an institution, often deliver outstanding results and are widely respected by the majority of the population. However in the operational maelstrom, buffeted by ambiguity, and a variety of external and internal influences, execution can break down. This book has illustrated that consensus often exists as to what should be done, and the corresponding information exists to allow its execution. However, delivery breaks down because the correct information wasn't accessed or implemented correctly. Though this book has shown that operator error may be involved, there is often a chain of events that preceded this failure.

This book asserts the level of implementation failure has crept up on police services across the world, and stands as the biggest blockage to increased effectiveness and efficiency. Praxis (the process of translating theory into practice) needs to be elevated in importance by politicians, senior police leaders and academics if this negative impact is to be reduced. As a Chief Constable recently said, 'We should use the best that already exists, because if we used this everywhere it would lead to a step change in good practice' (Marshall, 2013). If implementation were improved it would produce widespread improvements in efficiency and effectiveness, including substantial reductions in crime, increased satisfaction and confidence in the public, as well as produce substantial financial savings. Of course, it is easy to point out issues such as these, without any responsibility to rectify them. As Theodre Roosevelt (1894) pointed out,

> Criticism is necessary and useful; it is often indispensable; but it can never take the place of action, or be even a poor substitute for it. The function of the mere critic is of very subordinate usefulness. It is the doer of deeds who actually counts in the battle for life, and not the man who looks on and says how the fight ought to be fought, without himself sharing the stress and the danger.

It is therefore hoped that a 'doer of deeds' will act upon some of the principles set out in this book.

References

Abrahamsen, R. & Williams, M. (2009) 'Security Beyond the State: Global Security Assemblages in International Politics', *International Political Sociology*, 3, 1–17.

ACPO (2010) *Children and Young People Strategy 2010–2013*, www.acpo.police.uk (date accessed 14.10.12).

ACPO (2012) The National Decision Model, http://www.acpo.police.uk/documents/president/201201PBANDM.pdf (date accessed 14.10.12).

ACPO (2013) Policing in the UK: A brief guide. http://www.acpo.police.uk/documents/reports/2012/201210PolicingintheUKFinal.pdf (date accessed 14.10.12).

Adlam, R. (2000) *Culture Change: An Attempt to Teach Ethics to Police Leaders and Managers within a Traditional Institution and Changing Social Milieu* (Surrey: School of Education).

Albanese, J.S. (2007) *Organized Crime in Our Times*, 5th edn (Newark, NJ: LexisNexis).

Albanese, J.S. (2008) 'Risk assessment in organized crime: Developing a market and product-based model to determine threat levels', *Journal of Contemporary Criminal Justice*, 24(3), 263–273.

Alderson, J. (1977) *Communal Policing* (Exeter: Devon and Cornwall Constabulary).

Alderson, J. (1979) *Policing Freedom* (Plymouth: MacDonald & Evans).

Allen, J., Edmonds, S., Patterson, A. & Smith, D. (2006) 'Policing and the Criminal Justice System – Public Confidence and Perceptions: Findings from the 2004/05 British Crime Survey', London: Home Office Online Report 07/06.

Alison, L. & Crego, J. (eds) (2008) *Policing Critical Incidents: Leadership and Critical Incident Management* (Cullompton: Willan).

Ambady, N., La Plante, D., Nguyen, T., Rosenthal, R., Chaumeton, N., & Levinson, W. (2002) 'Surgeons' tone of voice: A clue to malpractice history', *Surgery*, 132(1), 5–9.

Ascoli, D. (1979) The Queens' Peace: The Origins and Developments of the Metropolitan Police 1829–1979. London: Hamish Hamilton.

Ashton, J., Brown, I., Senior, B. & Pease, K. (1998) 'Repeat victimisation: Offender accounts', *International Journal of Risk, Security and Crime Prevention*, 3(4), 269–279.

Audit Commission (1993) *Helping with Enquiries: Tackling Crime Effectively* (London: HMSO).

Audit Commission (1988) *Administrative Support for Operational Police Officers*, Police Paper No.5 (London: Audit Commission).

Audit Commission (1998) *A Fruitful Partnership: Effective Partnership Working.* (London: Audit Commission).

Auld, Lord Chief Justice (2001) *A Review of the Criminal Courts of England and Wales* (London: Ministry of Justice).

Australian National Audit office (2010) *Management of the Implementation of New Policy Initiatives: Australian Federal Police. Audit Report 29* (Canberra: Australian National Audit Office).

Ayling, J. & Broadhurst, J. (2012) 'The suppression of organized crime', in Prenzler, T. *Policing and Security in Practice: Challenges and Achievements* (Basingstoke: Palgrave Macmillan).
Bailey, S. (1986) Foreword in Weatheritt, M. *Innovations in Policing* (Beckenham: Crook Helm Ltd).
Baker, D. (2012) 'Policing contemporary protests', in Prenzler, T. (ed.) *Policing and Security in Practice* (New York: Palgrave Macmillan).
Baker, D. & Donnelly, P.G. (1986) 'Neighbourhood criminals and outsiders in two communities indications that criminal localism varies', *Sociology and Social Research*, 71(1), 58–65.
Baldwin, J. & Bottoms, A.E. (1976) *The Urban Criminal* (London: Tavistock Publications).
Banton, M. (1964) *The Policeman in the Community* (London: Tavistock).
Barr, R. & Pease, K. (1990) 'Crime placement, displacement, and deflection', in Tonry, M. & Morris, N. (eds), *Crime and Justice: A Review of Research. Vol. 12* (Chicago, IL: University of Chicago Press).
Barton, L.C. & Barton, H. (2011) 'Challenges, issues and change: What's the future for UK policing in the twenty-first century?' *International Journal of Public Sector Management*, 24(20), 146–156.
Bayley, D.H. (1994) *Police for the Future* (Oxford: Oxford University Press).
Bayley, D.H. (2010) 'Foreword', in Kuhns, J.B. & Knutsson, J. (eds), *Police Use of Force: A Global Perspective* (Santa Barbara: Praeger).
Bayley, D.H. (2011) 'Et tu brute: Are police agencies managed better or worse than universities?' *Police Practice and Research*, 12(4), 313–316.
BBC News (2004) At a glance Soham report 22.6.2005, http://news.bbc.co.uk/1/hi/uk/3829125.stm (date accessed 14.1.13).
BBC on line news (2006) MI5 tracking 30 UK Terror Plots, http://news.bbc.co.uk/1/hi/uk/6134516.stm (date accessed 08.2.09).
Beck, U. (1992) *The Risk Society* (Cambridge: Polity Press).
Bell, C. (2013) Inside the Coalition's Controversial 'Nudge Unit', *The Telegraph*, 11.2.13. http://www.telegraph.co.uk/news/politics/9853384/Inside-the-Coalitions-controversial-Nudge-Unit.html (date accessed 14.2.13).
Belur, J. (2010) 'Police "Encounters" in Mumbai, India', in Kuhns, J.B. & Knutsson, J. *Police Use of Force: A Global Perspective* (Santa Barbara: Praeger).
Bennis, W. & Townsend, R. (1995) *Reinventing Leadership* (Piatkus: London).
Berry, J. (2009) Reducing Bureaucracy in Policing (interim report), http://webarchive.nationalarchives.gov.uk/20100418065544/http:/police.homeoffice.gov.uk/publications/police-reform/reducing-bureaucracy-policing2835.pdf?view=Binary (date accessed 12.11.12).
Berry, J. (2009) Reducing Bureaucracy in Policing (final report) https://www.gov.uk/government/publications/reducing-bureaucracy-in-policing (date accessed 18.10.12).
Berry, J. (2010) *Criminal Justice Units and Case Building: Reducing Bureaucracy in Policing* (London: Home Office).
Berry, G., Briggs, P., Erol, R. & van Staden, L. (2011) 'The Effectiveness of Partnership Working in a Crime and Disorder Context' Home Office Research Report 52 (London: Home Office).
Bittner, E. (1970) *The Functions of the Police in Modern Society* (Washington DC: US Government Printing Office).

Bittner, E. (1974) 'Florence Nightingale in pursuit of Willie Sutton: A theory of the police', in Jacob, H. (ed.), *Potential for Reform* (Beverley Hills: Sage).

Bittner, E. (1990) *Aspects of Police Work* (Boston: Northeastern University Press).

Blair, I. (2005) 'What kind of police service do we want?' *The Dimbleby Lecture*, BBC1, 16th November.

Blalock, G., Kadiyali, V. & Simon, D.H. (2007) 'The impact of post 9/11 airport security measures on the demand for air travel', *Journal of Law and Economics*, 50(4), 731–755.

Bolling, K., Clemans, S., Grant, C. & Smith, P. (2003) *British Crime Survey of England & Wales 2002–03*, http://www.esds.ac.uk/doc/5059/mrdoc/pdf/5059userguide.pdf (date accessed 6.11.12).

Bolling, K., Grant, C. & Sinclair, P. (2007) *British Crime Survey of England and Wales 2006/07*. Online report. http://www.esds.ac.uk/doc/5755/mrdoc/pdf/5755techreport_vol2.

Boorom, M.L., Goolsby, J. & Ramsey, R.P. (1998) 'Relational communication traits and their effect on adaptiveness and sales performance'. *Journal of the Academy of Marketing Science*, 26(1), 16–30.

Bottoms, A. (2012) 'Developing socio-spatial criminology', in Maguire, M., Morgan, R., & Reiner, R. (eds), *The Oxford Handbook of Criminology*. (Oxford: Oxford University Press).

Bowers, K. & Johnson, S. (2003) 'Measuring the geographical displacement and diffusion of benefit effects of crime prevention activity'. *Journal of Quantitative Criminology*, 19(3), 275–301.

Bowling, B. (1999) 'The rise and fall of New York murder: Zero tolerance or crack's decline?' *British Journal of Criminology*, 39(4), 531–554.

Bradford, B. (2011) *Police Numbers and Crime Rates – A Rapid Evidence Review* (London: HMIC).

Bradford, B., Jackson, J. & Stanko, J. (2009) 'Contact and confidence: Revisiting the impact of public encounters with the police', *Policing & Society: An International Journal of Research and Policy*, 19(10), 20–46.

Braga, A. & Baston, N. (2012) 'Boston Safe Street Team Initiative', *Presentation given to the Problem Oriented Policing Conference*, Providence, RI.

Brantingham, P.J. & Brantingham, P.L. (eds) (1991) *Environmental Criminology* (Prospect Heights, OH: Waveland).

Brantingham, P.L. & Brantingham, P.J. (1993) 'Environment, routine and situation: toward a pattern theory of crime', in Clarke, R.V. & Felson, M. (eds), *Routine Activity and Rational Choice: Advances in Criminological Theory*, Vol. 5. (New Brunswick, NJ: Transaction Press).

Broeders, A.P.A. (2007) 'Principles of forensic identification science', in Newburn, T., Williamson, T., and Wright, A. (eds), *Handbook of Criminal Investigation* (Cullompton: Willan).

Brown, A. & Wildavsky, A.B. (1984) 'What should evaluation mean to implementation', in Pressman, J.L. & Wildavsky, A.B. (eds), *Implementation: How Great Expectations in Washington Are Dashed in Oakland* (Berkeley: University of California Press).

Brown, G. (2008) Security and Liberty, http://www.labour.org.uk/gordon_brown_security_liberty (date accessed 06.10.12).

Bruinsma, G. & Bernasco, W. (2004) 'Criminal groups and transnational illegal markets', *Crime, Law and Social Change*, 41, 79–94.

Bullock, K., Clarke, R.V. & Tilley, N. (2010) *Situational Prevention of Organised Crimes* (Collumpton: Willan Publishing).

Bullock, K., Erol, R. & Tilley, N. (2006) *Problem Oriented Policing and Partnerships: Implementing an Evidence Based Approach to Crime Reduction* (Cullompton: Willan Publishing).

Burke, J. (2004) *Al-Qaeda: The True Story of Radical Islam* (London: Tauris).

Burkhart, B.R. (1980) 'Conceptual issues in the development of police selection procedures', *Professional Psychology*, 11(1), 121–129.

Burman, M., Lovett, L. & Kelly, L. (2009) *Different systems, similar outcomes? Tracking attrition in reported rape cases in 11 countries*. www.sccjr.ac.uk/documents/scotland_2.pdf (date accessed 14.11.12).

Burnes, B. (2000) *Managing Change*, 3rd edn (London: Pitman).

Burrows, J., Hopkins, M. Robinson, A. Speed, M. and Tilley, N. (2005) *Understanding the attrition process in volume crime investigation*. Home Office Research Study 295. London: Home Office.

Buttle, J.W. (2010) 'Officer safety and public safety: Training the police to use Force in the UK', in Kuhns, J.B. & Knutsson, J. (eds), *Police Use of Force: A Global Perspective* (Santa Barbara: Praeger).

Cain, M. (1973) *Society and the Policeman's Role* (London: Routledge and Kegan Paul).

Canter, D., Alison, L.J., Alison, E. & Wentink, N. (2004) 'The organized/disorganized typologies of serial murder: Myth or model?' *Psychology, Public Policy and Law*, 10, 7–36.

Cantle, T. (2001) *Community Cohesion: A Report of the Independent Review Team.* (London: Home Office).

Capone, D. & Nichols, W.J. (1975) 'Crime and distance: An analysis of offender behaviour in space', *Proceedings of the Association of American Geographers*, 7, 45–49.

Carle, G. (2008) 'Overstating our fears' *The Washington Post.* 13 July, 2008. http://articles.washingtonpost.com/2008-07-13/opinions/36820920_1_al-qaeda-qaeda-jihadist (date accessed 9.1.13).

Carson, D. (2005) 'Models of investigation', in Newburn, T., Williamson, T. & Wright, A. (eds), *Handbook of Investigation* (Cullompton: Willan Publishing).

Castells, M. (1996) *The Information Age (i). The Rise of the Network Society* (Oxford: Blackwell).

Castells, M. (1998) *The Information Age (iii). End of Millennium* (Oxford: Blackwell).

Caulkin, S. (2011) *A Summary of Policing in Austerity*, a Vanguard event, http://www.systemsthinking.co.uk/docs/Policing%20in%20Austerity%20final.pdf (date accessed 12.2.13).

Caulkin, S. (2012) *Doing the Right Thing: The Learning So Far.* http://www.systemsthinking.co.uk/docs/Police_art_Jul11.pdf (date accessed 4.3.13).

Chainey, S.P. (2008) 'Identifying priority neighbourhoods: Using the vulnerable localities index' *Policing: A Journal of Policy and Practice*, 2(2), 196–209.

Chainey, S. (2012) 'Improving the explanatory content of analysis products using hypothesis testing', *Policing*, 6(2), 108–121.

Chalfin, A. & McCrary, J. (2012) *The Effect of Police on Crime: New Evidence from US cities, 1960–2010*, Law and Economics Workshop, Berkeley Program in Law and Economics, UC Berkeley.

Chan, J. (1997) *Changing Police Cultures* (Cambridge: Cambridge University Press).

Chappel, A.T. (2007) 'Community policing: Is field training the missing link?' *Policing: An International Journal of Police Strategies and Management*, 30(3), 498–517.

Chesterman, S (2011) *Operation Bridge: Peer review into the response of Cumbria Constabulary following the actions of Derrick Bird on 2nd June 2010*, ACPO Lead – Armed Policing Working Group, http://www.cumbria.police.uk/Admin/uploads/attachment/files/News_Files/Inquest/Running_Orders/ACC_Chestermans_report.pdf (date accessed 4.5.12).

Chibnall, S. (1977) *Law and Order News* (London: Tavistock).

CJS online (2012) The aims and objectives of the Criminal Justice System. www.cjsonline.gov.uk (date accessed 7.3.13).

Clarke, R.V.G. (1997) *Situational Crime Prevention: Successful Case Studies* (Monsey, New York: Criminal Justice Press).

Clarke, R.V. (1999) 'Hot Products: Understanding, Anticipating and Reducing the Demand for Stolen Goods', *Police Research Series Paper 112* (London: Home Office).

Clarke, R.V.G. (2004) 'Technology, criminology and crime science', *European Journal on Criminology, Policy and Research*, 10, 55–63.

Clarke & Eck (2003) *Crime Analysis for Problem Solvers: In 60 Small Steps* (Washington: US Department of Justice).

Clarke, R.V. & Hough, J.M. (1984) 'Crime and Police Effectiveness', *Home Office Study No.79* (London: HMSO).

Clarke, R. & Newman, G. (2006) *Outsmarting the Terrorists* (New York: Praeger Security International).

Clifford, B.R. & Hollin, C.R. (1981) 'Effects of the type of incident and the number of perpetrators on eye witness testimony', *Journal of Applied Psychology*, 66, 364–370.

Cohen, L.E. & Felson, M. (1979) 'Social Change and Crime Rate Trends: A Routine Activity Approach', *American Sociological Review*, 44, 588–608.

Cohen, S. (1972) *Folk Devils and Moral Panics*, 3rd edn (London: Routledge).

Cohen, S. (1985) *Visions of Social Control* (Cambridge: Polity Press).

Colman, A.M. & Gorman, P.L. (1982) 'Conservatism, Dogmatism, and Authoritarianism in Police Officers', *Sociology*, 16, 1–11.

Communities and Local Government Committee (2010) *Preventing Violent Extremism* (London: HMSO), http://www.publications.parliament.uk/pa/cm200910/cmselect/cmcomloc/65/65.pdf (date accessed 11.1.13).

Communities and Local Government (2012) *Government Response to the Future of Local Audit Consultation* (London: Department for Communities and Local Government).

Connors, E., Lundregan, T., Miller, N. & McEwen, T. (1996) Convicted by Juries, Exonerated by Science: Case Studies in the Use of DNA (Washington: US Department of Justice).

Cook, P.M. (1977) 'Empirical Survey of Police Attitudes', *Police Review*, 85, 1042–1045.

Cope, N. (2004) 'Intelligence led policing or policing led intelligence: Integrating volume crime analysis into policing', *British Journal of Criminology*, 44, 188–203.

Cordesman, A.H. (2005) *The Challenge of Biological Weapons* (Washington, DC: Center for Strategic and International Studies).
Cornish, D. & Clarke, R.V. (1986) *The Reasoning Criminal: Rational Choice Perspectives on Offending* (New York: Springer-Verlag).
Cornish, D. & Clarke, R.V. (2003) 'Opportunity, Precipitators and Criminal Decisions', in *Theory for Practice in Situational Crime Prevention*, Crime Prevention Studies, Vol. 16 (Monsey, NY: Criminal Justice Press).
Corsaro, W.A. & Eder, D. (1990) 'Children's Peer Cultures', *Annual Review of Sociology*, 16, 197–220.
Coupe, T. & Griffiths, M. (1996) 'Solving Residential Burglary', *Crime Detection and Prevention Series 77* (London: Home Office).
Covey, S. (2004) The 7 habits of highly effective people (London: FranklinCovey).
CPS (2012) *Narrowing the Justice Gap*. www.cps.gov.uk/ publications/prosecution/ justicegap.html (date accessed 2.10.12).
Crawford, A. (1997) *The Local Governance of Crime* (Oxford: Oxford University Press).
Crawford, A. (1998) *Crime Prevention and Community Safety: Politics, Policies and Practices* (Essex: Addison Wesley Longman Limited).
Crego, J. (2008) 'The Journey', in Alison, L. & Crego, J. (eds), *Policing Critical Incidents: Leadership and Critical Incident Management* (Cullompton: Willan).
Crime and Disorder Act (1998) Available from: http://www.legislation.gov.uk/ ukpga/1998/37/contents (date accessed 2.5.11).
Critchley, T.A. (1973) The Idea of Policing in Britain: Success or Failure? Chapter in Alderson, J. & Stead, P.J. (eds) *The Police We Deserve* (London: Wolfe).
Daily Mail (2010) Stop and Search UK. http://www.dailymail.co.uk/news/article-1266332/A-Briton-interrogated-police-20-seconds-90-arent-arrested.html (date accessed 13.9.12).
Daily Telegraph (2011) Police use of terrorism stop and search powers drops 90%. http://www.telegraph.co.uk/news/uknews/terrorism-in-the-uk/8824203/ Police-use-of-terrorism-stop-and-search-powers-drops-90-per-cent.html (date accessed 13.12.12).
Dalton, J., Elias, M. & Wandersman, A. (2007) *Community Psychology: Linking Individuals and Communities*, 2nd edn (Belmont, CA: Wadsworth).
Daly, K. & Bouhours, B. (2010) 'Rape and Attrition in the Legal Process: A Comparative Analysis of 5 Countries', *Crime and Justice: An Annual Review of Research*, 39, 485–565.
Davies, M., Croall, H. & Tyrer, J. (2005) *Criminal Justice: An Introduction to the Criminal Justice System in England & Wales*, 3rd edn (Harlow: Pearson Education).
Davies, N. (2003) Fiddling the figures, *Guardian* 11th July, available online http://www.guardian.co.uk/uk/2003/jul/11/ukcrime.prisonsandprobation1 (date accessed 16.8.12).
DCL News Editorial (2003) *Revealed: Qantas Airlines Mechanics' wicked sense of humor*. http://www.dclab.com/asides/qantas_mechanics_humor.asp (date accessed 8.2.13).
Degani, A. & Wiener, E.L. (1993) Cockpit checklists: Concepts, design, and use. Human Factors, 35(2), 345–359.
della Porta, D. & Reiter, H. (2006) 'The Policing of transnational protest: A conclusion', in della Porter, D., Peterson, A. & Reiter, H. (eds), *The Policing of Transnational Protest* (Aldershot: Ashgate).

DeLisi M. & Scherer, A. (2006) 'Multiple Homicide Offenders: Offense Characteristics, Social Correlates and Criminal Careers', *Criminal Justice and Behaviour*, 33(3), 367–391.

Dennis, N. (ed.) (1997) *Zero Tolerance Policing a Free Society*. (London: IEA Health and Welfare Unit).

Department for Communities & Local Government (2010) Preventing Violent Extremism: 6th Report of session (London: TSO).

De Rugy, V. (2010) 'The Economics of Homeland Security', in Friedman, B.H., Harper, J. & Preble, C.A. (eds), *Terrorizing Ourselves: Why US Counterterrorism Policy Is Failing and How to Fix It* (Washington DC: Cato Institute).

de Vries, E.N., Prins, H.A., Crolla, R.M.P.H., den Outer, A.J., van Andel, G., van Helden, S. (2010) 'Effect of a Comprehensive Surgical Safety System on Patient Outcomes,' *New England Journal of Medicine* 363(20): 1928–37.

Dobby, J., Anscombe, J. & Tuffin, R. (2004) *Police Leadership: Expectations and Impact. Home Office Online Report 20/04* (London: Research Development and Statistics Office).

Downes, D. & Morgan, R. (1994) 'Hostages to Fortune? The Politics of Law and Order in Post War Britain', in Maguire, M., Morgan, R. & Reiner, R. (eds), *The Oxford Handbook of Criminology*, 1st edn (Oxford: Oxford University Press).

Drew, J.M. (2012) 'Approaches to Improving Organizational Effectiveness: The Impact of Attraction, Selection and Leadership Practices in Policing', in Prenzler, T. (ed.) *Policing and Security in Practice* (New York: Palgrave Macmillan).

Drucker, P.F. (2002) *The Effective Executive: The Definitive Guide to Getting the Right Things Done.* (New York: Harper Collins).

Duborg, R. & Pritchard, S. (2007) *Organised Crime: Revenues, Economic and Social Costs and Criminal Assets Available for Seizure* (London: Home Office).

Duffy, B., Wake, R., Burrows, T. & Bremner, P. (2007) *Closing the Gaps – Crime and Public Perceptions*, http//ipsos-mori.com/_assets/reports/closing-the gaps.pdf (date accessed 12.5.09).

Durlak, J.A. & DuPre, E.P. (2008) 'Implementation matters: A review of research on the influence of implementation on program outcomes and the factors affecting implementation', *American Journal of Community Psychology*, 41, 689–708.

Eck, J. (1983) Solving Crime: A Study of the Investigation of Burglary and Robbery (Washington, D.C.: Police Executive Research Forum).

Eck, J (2003) Police Problems: The Complexity of Problem Theory, Research and Evaluation, *Crime Prevention Studies*, 15, 79–113.

Eck, J.E. & Maguire, E.R. (2000) 'Have Changes in Policing Reduced Violent Crime: An Assessment of the Evidence.' in Blumstein, A. & Wallman, J. (eds), *The Crime Drop in America* (Cambridge: University Press).

Eck, J.E. & Spelman, W. (1987) *Problem Solving: Problem Oriented Policing in Newport News* (Washington, DC: Police Executive Research Forum).

Ekblom, P. (1995) 'Less Crime by Design', *Annals of the American Academy of Political and Social Science*, 539, 114–129.

Ekblom, P. (2002) 'From the Source to the Mainstream is Uphill: The Challenge of Transferring Knowledge of Crime Prevention Through Replication, Innovation and Anticipation.' In: N. Tilley (ed.) Analysis for Crime Prevention, Crime

Prevention Studies 13: 131–203 (Monsey, N.Y.: Criminal Justice Press/Devon, UK: Willan Publishing).

Ekblom, P. (2003) 'Organised Crime and the Conjunction of Criminal Opportunity Framework', in Edwards, A. & Gill, P. (eds), *Transnational Organised Crime: Perspectives on Global Security* (London: Routledge).

Ekblom, P. (2005) 'How to Police the Future: Scanning for Scientific and Technological Innovations which Generate Potential Threats and Opportunities in Crime, Policing and Crime Reduction', in M. Smith and N. Tilley (eds), Crime Science: *New Approaches to Preventing and Detecting Crime* (Cullompton: Willan).

Ekblom, P. (2012) *Crime Prevention, Security and Community Safety Using the 5Is Framework* (Basingstoke, UK: Palgrave Macmillan).

Elmsley, C. (1991) *The English Police: A Political and Social History*, 2nd edn (London: Longman).

Engel, R.S. & Calnon, J.M. (2004) 'Examining the influence of drivers' characteristics during traffic stops with police: Results from a national survey', *Justice Quarterly*, 21(1), 49–90.

Europol (2011) Te-Sat 2011: EU Terrorism situation and trend report. Retrieved from https://www.europol.europa.eu/sites/default/files/publications/te-sat2011_0.pdf (date accessed 7.7.13).

European Sourcebook of Crime and Criminal Justice Statistics (2010) Den Haag: WODC, www.europeannsourcebook.org/ (date accessed 17.3.13).

Evans, J. & Kebbell, M. (2012) 'Integrating Intelligence into Policing practice', in Prenzler, T. (ed.), *Policing and Security in Practice* (New York: Palgrave Macmillan).

Eurostat (2009) *Crime Statistics. European Commission Online Report.* Epp.eurostat.ec.europa.eu/statistics (date accessed 21.1.13).

Evening Standard (2012) 'Third of people arrested by Met in London are foreigners – 8.10.12. http://www.standard.co.uk/news/crime/a-third-of-people-arrested-in-london-are-foreigners-8202113.html (date accessed 10.10.12).

Eyre, M., Alison, L., Crego, J. & McLean, C. (2008) 'Decision Inertia: The Impact of Organisations on Critical Incident Decision Making', in Alison, L. & Crego, J. (eds), *Policing Critical Incidents: Leadership and Critical Incident Management* (Cullompton: Willan Publishing).

Falkenberg, S., Gaines, L.K. & Corner, G. (1991) 'An examination of the constructs underlying police performance appraisals', *Journal of Criminal Justice*, 19(4), 351–360.

Farrell, G. & Clark, K. (2004) *What does the world spend on criminal justice?* HEUNI Paper 20. Helsinki, Finland: Helsinki European United Nations Institute for Crime Prevention and Control.

Farrell, G., Tilley, N., Tseloni, A. & Mailley, J. (2008) 'The Crime Drop and the Security Hypothesis', *British Society of Criminology* Newsletter, No. 62.

Felson, M. (2002) *Crime and Everyday Life*, 3rd edn (Thousand Oaks, CA: Sage).

Felson, M. & Clarke, R. (1999) *Opportunity Makes the Thief: Practical Theory for Crime Prevention.* Police Research Series Paper 98 (London: Home Office).

Fetterman, D.M. (1996) 'Empowerment Evaluation: An Introduction to Theory and Practice', in Fetterman, D.M., Kaftarian, S.F. & Wandersman, A. (eds), *Empowerment Evaluation: Knowledge and Tools for Self-assessment and Accountability* (Thousand Oaks, CA: Sage).

Finch, E. & Fafinski, S. (2012) *Criminology Skills* (Oxford: Oxford University Press).

Finckenauer, J.O. (2005) Problems of definition: what is organized crime? *Trends Organized Crime* 8(3):63–83.

Fisher, A.C. (2012) *The Power of Three*, Unpublished D. Prof. thesis submitted to London Metropolitan University.

Fiti, R., Perry, D., Giraud, W. & Ayres, M. (2008) *Motoring Offences and Breath Test Statistics, England and Wales 2006* (London: Ministry of Justice).

Fitzgerald, G.E. (1989) *Report of the Commission of Inquiry into Possible Illegal Activities and Associated Police Misconduct* (Brisbane, Australia: Government Printer).

Fixen, D.L., Naoom, S.F., Blasé, K.A., Friedman, R.M. & Wallace, F. (2005) *Implementation Research: A Synthesis of the Literature* (Tampa, FL: University of South Florida, The National Implementation Research Network).

Flanagan, Sir, R. (2008) *Review of Policing: The Final Report* (London: HMSO).

Fleming, J. (2009) Performance Management in Wakefield, A. & Fleming, J. (eds) *The Sage Dictionary of Policing*, pp. 224–226 (London: Sage).

Focault, M. (1977) *Discipline and Punish: The Birth of the Prison* (London: Allen Lane).

Francis, R. (QC) (2013) *Report of the Mid Staffordshire NHS Foundation Trust Public inquiry*, http://www.midstaffspublicinquiry.com (date accessed 1.4.13).

Frankel, P. (2001) *An Ordinary Atrocity: Sharpeville and Its Massacre* (New Haven: Yale University Press).

Freeman, R.E. (1984) *Strategic management: A stakeholder approach*, Boston: Pitman.

Frigenti, E. & Comninos, D. (2006) *The Practice of Project Management: A Guide to the Business Focused Approach* (London: Kogan).

Fyffe, J.J. (1999) 'Good Policing', in Stojkovic, S., Klofas, J. & Kalinich, D. (eds), *The Administration and Management of Criminal Justice Organisations*, 3rd edn (Prospect Heights, IL: Wareland Press).

Garland, D. (2001) *The Culture of Control: Crime and Social Order in Contemporary Society* (Oxford: Oxford University Press).

Garner, R., Ferdinand, P. & Lawson, S. (2012) *Introduction to Politics* (Oxford: Oxford University Press).

Gawande, A. (2010) *The Checklist Manifesto: How to Get Things Right* (London, UK: Profile Books).

Geiselman, R.E., Fisher, R.P., Firstenberg, I., Hutton, L.A., Sullivan, S., Avetissian, I. & Prosk, A. (1984) 'Enhancement of eyewitness memory: An empirical evaluation of the cognitive interview', *Journal of Police Science and Administration*, 12, 74–80.

Ghaffur, T. (2007) *The Nexus Between Terrorism, Organised Crime and Communities in the UK*. Presentation prepared for discussion across MPS.

Gilham, P. & Marx, G. (2000) 'Complexity and irony in policing and protesting: The World Trade Organization in Seattle', *Social Justice*, 27(2), 212–236.

Gill, M., Hart, J., Livingstone, K. & Stevens, J. (1996) 'The Crime Allocation System: Police Investigations into Burglary and Auto Crime', *Home Office Police Research Series No.16* (London: HMSO).

Gilmour, S. (2008) 'Understanding organized crime: A local perspective', *Policing*, 2(1), 18–27.

Giuliani, R. CNN 22.7.05. http:/articles.cnn.com/2005-07-22/us/giuliani_1_giuliani_suicide_bombers_london.

Glebbeek, M.L. (2010) 'ManoDura: Fighting Crime, Violence and Insecurity with an Iron Fist in Central America', in Kuhns, J.B. & Knutsson, J. (eds) *Police Use of Force: A Global Perspective* (Santa Barbara: Praeger).

Golding, B. & Savage, S.P. (2008) 'Leadership and Performance Management', in Newburn, T. (ed.), *Handbook of Policing* (Devon: Willan Publishing).

Goldstein, H. (1979) Improving Policing: A Problem-Oriented Approach, *Crime & Delinquency*, 25(2), 236–258.

Goldstein, H. (1990) *Problem Oriented Policing* (New York: McGraw-Hill).

Goldstein, H. (2005) An interview with Herman Goldstein, www.popcenter.org/learning/goldstein_interview/ (date accessed 12.9.12).

Goldstein, H. (2012) *An Audience with Herman Goldstein*, breakfast presentation at International POP Conference, Providence, R.I.

Graham, K.M. & Homer, R. (2008) *Raising the Bar: Preventing Aggression in and Around Bars, Pubs, and Clubs* (Cullompton: Willan Publishing).

Grabosky, P. (1988) Efficiency and effectiveness in Australian policing, Trends and issues in Crime and Criminal Justice, No. 16, Australian Institute of Criminology, Canberra.

Grant, C., Harvey, A., Bolling, K. & Clemens, S. (2005) *The British Crime Survey of England & Wales (2004/05)*, http://www.esds.ac.uk/doc/5347/mrdoc/pdf/5347userguide1.pdf (date accessed 14.10.12).

Gresswell, A. & Hollin, C. (1994) 'Multiple murder: A review', *The British Journal of Criminology*, 34(1).

Grieve, J. (2008) 'Critical Incidents', *Dictionary of Policing* (Cullompton: Willan).

Grieve, J. (2008) 'Understanding Critical Event Learning and Leadership: Hydra/10kV Immersive Learning, Debriefing and Other Tools' in Alison, L. & Crego, J. (eds), *Policing Critical Incidents: Leadership and Critical Incident Management* (Cullompton: Willan).

The Guardian (2012) *Police recorded 8,500 corruption allegations in 3 years*, http://www.guardian.co.uk/politics/2012/may/24/police-watchdog-corruption-complaints (date accessed 12.3.13).

Guerette, R.T. & Bowers, K.J. (2009) 'Assessing the extent of crime displacement and diffusion of benefits: A review of situational crime prevention evaluations', *Criminology*, 47(4), 1331–1368.

Hales, J., Nevill, C. Pudney, S. & Tipping, S. (2009) *Longitudinal Analysis of Offending, Crime & Justice Survey 2003–06* (London: Home Office).

Hansard (4 June 2007) *Written answers*. Column 108W. http://www.publications.parliament.uk/pa/cm200607/cmhansrd/cm070604/text/ 70604w0027.htm.

Harfield, C. & Harfield, K. (2008) *Intelligence: Investigation, Community and Partnership* (Oxford: Oxford University Press).

Hartfield, P. (2009) Nightlife and Crime; Social Order and Governance in International Perspective, Oxford: Oxford University Press.

Hempel, A., Meloy, R. & Richards, T. (1999) 'Offender and offense characteristics of a nonrandom sample of mass murderers', *Journal of American Academy of Psychiatry and Law* 27(2), 213–225.

Henry, V.E. (2003) *The Compstat Paradigm: Management Accountability in Policing, Business and the Public Sector* (Flushing, NY: Looseleaf Law Publications, Inc).

HMIC (1997) *Policing with Intelligence, Criminal Intelligence: A thematic inspection of good practice* (HMIC: London).

HMIC (2000a) Securing and maintaining public confidence. Retrieved from www.hmic.gov.uk (date accessed 2.8.12).

HMIC (2000b) On the Record. Thematic inspection report on Police Crime Recording, the PNC, & Phoenix Intelligence System. Retrieved from www.hmic.gov.uk (date accessed 14.9.12).

HMIC (2004) *Modernising the Police Service: A Thematic Inspection of Workforce Modernisation – The Role, Management and Deployment of Police Staff in the Police Service of England and Wales* (London: HMIC).

HMIC (2006) *Closing the Gap: A Review of the 'Fitness for Purpose' of the Current Structure of Policing in England and Wales.* http://crime reduction.homeoffice.gov.uk/policing (date accessed 30.3.09).

HMIC (2009a) *Developing the Policing Pledge: Early Findings* (London: Central Office of Information).

HMIC (2009b) *Getting Together: A Better Deal for the Public through Joint Working* (London: HMIC).

HMIC (2009c) *Adapting to Protest: Review of the Policing of Public Protest* (London: HMIC).

HMIC (2010a) Valuing the Police: Policing in an age of austerity. Retrieved from www.hmic.gov.uk (date accessed 9.9.12).

HMIC (2010b) Police governance in austerity, Retrieved from www.hmic.gov.uk (date accessed 9.9.12).

HMIC (2011) *Policing Public Order* (London: HMIC).

HMIC (2012a) *Taking Time for Crime* (London: HMIC). Retrieved from www.hmic.gov.uk (date accessed 14.12.12).

HMIC (2012b) Improvements needed to the systems and processes of police crime and incident reports, Retrieved from http://www.hmic.gov.uk/news/releases-2012/0032012-improvements-needed-police-crime-and-incidents-reports/ (date accessed 12.11.12).

HM Prison (2008) Perrie Lectures – 'Foreign nationals in prison and detention', www.hmprisonservice.gov.uk/prisonservicejournal/index.asp (date accessed 9.12.09).

Higgins, M.K. (2010) 'Systematic Police Violence in Brazil', in Kuhns, J.B. & Knutsson, J. (eds), *Police Use of Force: A Global perspective* (Santa Barbara: Praeger).

Hirschfield, A.F.G., Bowers, K.J. & Brown, P.J.B (1995) 'Exploring relations between crime and disadvantage on merseyside', *European Journal on Criminal Policy and Research*, 3(3), 93–112.

Hoare, J. (2009) 'Extent and Trends', in Walker, A. Flatley, J. Kershaw, C. & Moon, D. (eds), *Crime in England and Wales 2008/09, Volume 1: Findings from the British Crime Survey and Police Recorded Crime.* Home Office Statistical Bulletin 11/09 volume 1 (London: Home Office).

Hoffman, B. (2006) Inside Terrorism, New York: Columbia University Press.

Hogan, R. & Kurtines, W. (1975) 'Personalogical correlates of police effectiveness', *The Journal of Psychology*, 91, 289–295.

Holgersson, S. & Knutsson, J. (2011) 'Dialogue Policing: A Means for Less Crowd violence?' in Madensen, T.D. & Knutsson, J. (eds), *Preventing Crowd Violence* (Colorado: Lynne Rienner Publishers).

Home Office (1983) *Manpower, Effectiveness, and Efficiency in the Police Service,* Circular 114/83 (London: HMSO).

Home Office (1990) *Partnership and Crime Prevention,* Home Office circular 44/1990 (London: HMSO).

Home Office (1993) *Police Reform: A Police Service for the Twenty-First Century* (London: HMSO).
Home Office (2004) *Building Communities, Beating Crime – A Better Police Service for the 21st Century* (London: HMSO).
Home Office (2007) *Delivering Safer Communities: A Guide to Effective Partnership Working, Police and Crime Standards Directorate (PCSD)* (London: Home Office).
Home Office (2011) *Local to Global: Reducing the Risk from Organized Crime*, www.homeoffice.gov.uk/publications/crime/organised-crime-strategy (date accessed 14.2.13).
Homel, P. (2006) 'Joining up the Pieces: What Central Agencies need to do to Support Effective Local Crime Prevention', in Knutsson, J. & Clarke, R. (eds), *Putting Theory to Work: Implementing Situational Prevention and Problem-Oriented Policing*, Crime Prevention Studies, 20 (Monsey, NY: Criminal Justice Press).
Hope, T. (1985) *Implementing Crime Prevention Measures*, p. 39 (London: Home Office).
Hope, T. & Murphy, D. (1983) 'The problems of implementing crime prevention: The experience of a demonstration project', *The Howard Journal of Criminal Justice*, 22, 38–50.
Hough, J. & Roberts, J.V. (2005) 'Just How Punitive Is the Public?' *Criminal Justice Matters*, 60, 10–11.
Hough, M. (2006) 'Not Seeing the Wood for the Trees: Mistaking Tactics for Strategy in Crime Reduction Initiatives', in Knutsson, J. & Clarke, R. (eds), *Putting Theory to Work: Implementing Situational Prevention and Problem-Oriented Policing*. Crime Prevention Studies, 20 (Monsey, NY: Criminal Justice Press).
Huff, R., Rattner, A. & Sagarin, E. (1996) *Convicted but Innocent: Wrongful Conviction and Public Policy* (Thousand Oaks, CA: Sage).
Innes, M. (1999) 'An iron fist in an iron glove? The zero tolerance policing debate', *Howard Journal*, 38, 397–410.
Innes, M. (2011) 'Public Perceptions', in Chaplin, R., Flatly, J. & Smith, K. (eds), *Crime in England & Wales 2010/11: Findings from the British Crime Survey and Police Recorded Crime* (London: Home Office).
Innes, M. & Fielding, N. (2002) 'From community to communicative policing: Signal crimes and the problem of police reassurance', *Sociological Research online*, 7(2), http://www.socresonline.org.uk/7/2/Innes.html (date accessed 11.8.12).
Innes, M. & Thiele, D. (2008) 'Policing Terror', in Newburn, T. (ed.) *Handbook of Policing*, 2nd edn (Cullompton: Willan Publishing).
IPCC (2011) *Police Complaints: Statistics for England & Wales 2010/11*. IPCC Research & Stats Service series paper 22.
IPCC (2012) *Annual Report and Statement of Accounts 2011/12* (London: HMSO).
Ipsos Mori (2013) Politicians trusted less than estate agents and bankers and journalists. http://www.ipsos-mori.com/researchpublications/researcharchive/3133/Politicians-trusted-less-than-estate-agents-bankers-and-journalists.aspx (date accessed 28.3.12).
Irvine, B. & Dunningham, C. (1993) *Human Factors in the Quality Control of CID Investigations*. Royal Commission on Criminal Justice, Research Study 21 (London: HMSO).
Jick, T.D. (1979) 'Mixing qualitative and quantitative methods: Triangulation in action', *Administrative Science Quarterly*, 24(4), Qualitative Methodology, 602–611.

Johnson, G., Scholes, K. & Whittington, R. (2008) *Exploring Corporate Strategy*, 8th edn (Harlow: Pearson).

Johnston, L. (1992) The Re-birth of Private Policing, London: Routledge.

Joint Consultative Committee (1990) 'Operational Policing Review' as cited by Wright, A. 'Managing the Future: An Academic's View', in Leishman, F., Loveday, B. & Savage, S. (eds), *Core Issues in Policing* (Essex: Longman).

Jones, E.E. (1979) 'The Rocky Road from Acts to Dispositions', *American Psychologist*, 34, 107–117.

Jones, T. & Newburn, T. (2007) *Policy Transfer and Criminal Justice* (Maidenhead: Open University Press).

Kahneman, D. & Tverskey, A. (1973) 'On the Psychology of Prediction', *Psychological Review*, 80, 237–251.

Kantner, R.M., Stein, B.M. & Jick, T.D. (1992) *The Challenge of Organizational Change* (New York: Free Press).

Karmen, A. (2004) 'Zero Tolerance in New York City: Hard Questions for a get Tough Policy', in Hopkins Burke, R. (ed.) *Hard Cop, Soft Cop: Dilemmas and Debates in Contemporary Policing* (Cullompton: Willan Publishing).

Kebbel, M.R. & Wagstaff, G.F. (1999) *Face Value? Evaluating the Accuracy of Eyewitness Information*. Police Research Series: Paper 102. Available www.homeoffice.gov.uk/rds/prgpdfs/fprs102.pdf (date accessed 12.6.08).

Kennedy, D.M. (2008) Deterrence and Crime Prevention: Reconsidering the Prospect of Sanction (London: Routledge).

Keeney, B. & Heide, K.M. (1995) 'Serial murder: A more accurate and inclusive definition' *International Journal of Offender Therapy and Comparative Criminology*, (39)4, 299–306.

Kelling, G.L., Pate, T. & Dieckman, D. (1974) *The Kansas City Preventative Patrol Experiment* (Washington, DC: Police Foundation).

Keren, G. & Tiegen, K. (2004) 'Yet Another Look at the Heuristics and Biases Approach', in Koehler, D. & Harvey, N. (eds), *Blackwell Handbook of Judgement and Decision Making* (Oxford: Blackwell Publishing).

Kets de Vries M.F.R. (1994) 'The leadership mystique', *Academy of Management Executive*, 8(3), 73–89.

Kirby, A. (2007) 'The London Bombers as Self Starters: A Case Study in Indigenous Radicalization and the Emergence of Autonomous Cliques', *Studies in Conflict and Terrorism*, 30, 415–428.

Kirby, S. & Nailer, L. (2013) 'Reducing the offending of a UK organized crime group, using the principles of Situational Crime Prevention and crime disruption – a three year case study', Trends in Organized Crime, 10.1007/s12117-013-9195-3.

Kirby, S. & Penna, S. (2010) 'Policing Mobile Criminality: Towards a Situational Crime Prevention Approach to Organised Crime', in Bullock, K. Clarke, R.V. & Tilley, N. (eds), *Situational Prevention of Organised Crime* (Cullompton: Willan Publishing), pp. 193–212.

Kirby, S. & Penna, S. (2011) 'Policing mobile criminality: Implications for UK police forces', *Policing: An International Journal of Police Strategies and Management*, 34(2), 182–197.

Kirby, S. & Turner, G. (2007) 'The use of ANPR in major crime investigation', *Journal of Homicide and Major Incident Investigation* (Wyboston: NPIA).

Kirton, M.J. (1989) 'Adaptors and Innovators: Styles of Creativity and Problem Solving', London: Routledge, cited by Burnes, B. 3rd edn (2000) *Managing Change.* (London: Pitman).

Kleemans, E.R. & de Poot, C.J. (2008) 'Criminal careers in organized crime and social opportunity structure', *European Journal of Criminology*, 5, 69–98.

Kleemans, E.R., Soudijin, M.R.J. & Weenink, A.W. (2010) 'Situational Crime Prevention and Cross Border Crime', in Bullock, K. Clarke, R.V. & Tilley. N. (eds), *Situational Crime Prevention of Organised Crimes* (Cullompton: Willan Publishing).

Kleinig, J. (1996) *The Ethics of Policing* (Cambridge: Cambridge University Press).

Kotter, J.P. (1990) *What Leaders Really Do* (Boston: Harvard Business School Press).

Kotter, J.P. (2007) 'Leading Change: Why Transformation Efforts Fail', *Harvard Business Review*, January, 96–103.

Kreitner, R., Kinicki, A. & Buelens, M. (2002) *Organisational Behaviour*, 2nd edn (London: McGraw Hill).

Kuhns, J.B. & Knutsson, J. (2010) *Police Use of Force: A Global Perspective* (Santa Barbara: Praeger).

Lab, S.P. (2010) *Crime Prevention; Approaches Practices and Evaluations*, 7th edn (New Providence: LexisNexis Group).

Lanagan, P.A., Greenfeld, L.A., Smith, S.K., Durose, M.R. & Levin, D.J. (2003) *Police and the Public: Findings from the 1999 National Survey* (Washington, DC: Bureau of Justice Statistics, NJ184957).

Lancashire Constabulary (2006) When an industry's practices kill: Turning the tide, Operation Seaquest, available from http://wwwpopcenter.org/conference/?presentationsX2006 (date accessed 18.4.09).

Langworthy, R. (1999) 'Measuring What Matters: A Police Research Institute', in Langworthy, R. (ed.) *Measuring What Matters: Proceedings from the Police Research Institute Meeting* (Washington, DC: NIJ).

Laqueur, W. (1987) *The Age of Terrorism* (Boston MA: Little Brown & Co).

Laqueur, W. (1996) *Post Modern Terrorism: New Rules for an Old Game* (Foreign Affairs).

Latino, R.J. (2008) Contributors to human error and how to lower rates of committing error, Briefings on Patient Safety, retrieved from http://www.reliability.com/healthcare/articleshcp/feb_08_Contributors%20to%20Human%20Error%20and%20How%20to%20Lower%20Rates%20of%20Committing%20Error.pdf (date accessed 7.7.13).

Laycock G. (2005) 'Deciding What to Do', in Tilley, N. (ed.) *Handbook of Crime Prevention and Community Safety* (Cullompton: Willan Publishing).

Laycock, G. (2012) 'Happy birthday?' *Policing*, 6(2), 101–107.

Lea, J. (2002) *Crime and Modernity: Continuities in Left Realist Criminology* (London: Sage).

Legrand, T. & Bronitt, S. (2012) 'Policing to a Different Beat: Measuring Police Performance', in Prenzler, T. (ed.) *Policing and Security in Practice* (New York: Palgrave Macmillan).

Leishman, F. & Mason, P. (2003) *Policing and the Media: Facts, Fictions, & Factions* (Cullompton: Willan).

Lentz, Susan A. & Chaires, Robert H. (2007) 'The invention of peel's principles: A study of policing "textbook" history', *Journal of Criminal Justice*, 35(1), 69–79.

Levi, M. & Maguire, M. (2004) 'Reducing and preventing organized crime: An evidence based critique', *Crime, Law and Social Change*, 41(5), 397–469.

Levinson, W. & Chameton, N. (1999) 'Communication between surgeons and patients in routine office visits', *Surgery* 125(2), 127–134.

Levinson, W., Roter, D.L., Mullooly, J.P. & Frankel, R.M. (1997) 'Physician-patient communication: The relationship with malpractice claims among primary care physicians and surgeons', *The Journal of the American Medical Association*, 277(7), 553–559.

Levitt, Steven D. (1997) 'Using electoral cycles in police hiring to estimate the effect of police on crime', *American Economic Review*, 87(3), 270–290.

Liker, J. (2003) *The Toyota Way: 14 Management Principles from the World's Greatest Manufacturer* (New York: McGraw-Hill).

Loader, I. (2000) 'Plural policing and democratic governance', *Social and Legal Studies*, 9(3), 323–345.

Lock, D. (2001) *The Essentials of Project Management*, 2nd edn (Aldershot: Gower).

Loftus, B. (2010) 'Police occupational culture: Classic themes, altered times', *Policing and Society*, 20(1), 1–22.

London Evening Standard (2009) (21.4.09) G20 police were too violent, www.standard.co.uk/news/920-police-were-too-violent6715012.html (date accessed 14.10.12).

London Evening Standard (2012) Notting Hill Carnival, Body Armour Gang held, 28 August 2012), http://www.standard.co.uk/news/crime/notting-hill-carnival-body-armour-gang-held-on-way-to-festival-one-man-remains-critical-8083875.html (date accessed 22.1.13).

Lum, C., Koper, C.S. & Telep, C.W. (2011) 'The evidence-based policing matrix', *Journal of Experimental Criminology*, 7, 3–26.

MacCoun, R.J. (2005) 'Voice, Control and Belonging: The Double-Edged Sword of Procedural Fairness', *Annual Review of Law and Social Science*, 1, 171–201.

Machin, S. & Marie, O. (2011) 'Crime and police resources: The street crime initiative', *Journal of the European Economic Association*, 9(4), 678–701.

Mack, A. (2008) 'Dying to Lose: Explaining the Decline in Global Terrorism', in Human Security Brief, Vancouver, BC: School for International Studies, Simon Fraser University. www.hsrgroup.org/.../HSB2007/2007HumanSecurityBrief-FullText.pdf (date accessed 15.9.12).

Madensen, T.D. & Eck, J.E. (2011) 'Crowd-Related Crime: An Environmental Criminological Perspective', in Madensen, T.D. & Knutsson, J. (eds), *Preventing Crowd Violence* (Colorado: Lynne Rienner Publishers).

Madensen, T.D. & Knutsson, J. (eds) (2011) *Preventing Crowd Violence* (Colorado: Lynne Rienner Publishers).

Maguire, M. (2003) 'Criminal Investigation and Crime Control', in Newburn, T. (ed.) *Handbook of Policing* (Cullompton: Willan).

Maguire, E.R. (2010) A Journey through the world of Police use of Force, in Kuhns, J.B. & Knutsson, J. (eds) *Police use of Force: A global perspective*, Santa Barbara: Praeger.

Maguire, M. (2012) 'Criminal Statistics and the Construction of Crime', in Maguire, M., Morgan, R. & Reiner, R. (eds), *The Oxford Handbook of Criminology* (Oxford: Oxford University Press).

Malouf, J.M. & Schutte, N.S. (1986) 'Using biographical information to hire the best new police officers: Research findings', *Journal of Police Science and Administration*, 14(3), 175–177.

Marshall, A. (2013) Presentation given to the ACPO National Conference for Learning and Development, Preston UK on 14.3.13.

Martinson, R. (1974) 'What Works? Questions and Answers about Prison Reform', *Public Interest*, 35, 22–54.

Mastrofski, S. (1981) 'Surveying clients to assess police performance', *Evaluation Review*, 5(3), 397–408.

Mastrofski, S. (1988) 'Police agency accreditation: A skeptical view', *Policing: An International Journal of Police Strategies & Management*, 21, 202–205.

Mastrofski, S.D. & Willis, J.J. (2010) 'Police organization, continuity, and change into the 21st century', *Crime & Justice*, 39(1), 55–144.

Matrix Knowledge Group (2007) *The Illicit Drug Trade in the United Kingdom*, Home Office Online Report 20/07 (London: Home Office).

Mawby, R.C. (2008) 'Zero Tolerance Policing' in T. Newburn and P. Neyroud (eds) *Dictionary of Policing, Cullompton,* (Cullompton: Willan Publishing).

Mawby, R.C. & Wright, A. (2008) 'The Police Organisation', in Newburn, T. (ed.) *The Handbook of Policing*, 2nd edn (Cullompton: Willan Publishing), pp. 224–252.

Mawby, R.I. (1999) *Policing Across the World: Issues for the 21st Century* (London: Routledge).

May, Rt Hon. T. (2010a) Speech to the ACPO Conference, http://www.homeoffice.gov.uk/media-centre/speeches/theresa-may-sp-NPC (date accessed 4.9.12).

May, Rt Hon. T. (2010b) Speech to the Police Federation, http://www.homeoffice.gov.uk/media-centre/speeches/theresa-may-police-fed?version=1 (date accessed 02.06.12).

May, Rt.Hon. T. (2011) Review of the existing counter-radicalisation strategy known as Prevent. Home Secretary statement to House of Commons. Retrieved from https://www.gov.uk/government/speeches/review-of-the-existing-counter-radicalisation-strategy-known-as-prevent. (date accessed 7.7.13).

May, Rt.Hon. T. (2012) Police Superintendents' Association Conference: Home Secretary's speech. www.gov.uk/government/speeches/police-superintendents-association-conference-home-secretarys-speech.

Maylor, H. (2010) *Project Management*, 4th edn (Harlow: Pearson Education Ltd).

McChesney, C., Covey, S. & Huling, J. (2012) *The 4 Disciplines of Execution* (London: Simon & Schuster).

McLaughlin, E. (2007) *The New Policing* (London: Sage).

Mclean, F. & Hillier, J. (2011) *An Observational Study of Response and Neighbourhood Officers* (London: NPIA).

Meloy, J.R., Hempel, A.G., Gray, B.T., Mohandie, K., Shiva, A. & Richards, T.C. (2004) A comparative analysis of North American adolescent and adult mass murderers, Behavioural Sciences and the Law, 22, 291–309.

Meo N., Alexander H. & Mendick R. (2011) Norway Killings: The Laughing Gunman who shot 85 Young Victims, One by One, *The Telegraph* online, http://www.telegraph.co.uk/news/worldnews/europe/norway/8657475/Norway-killings-The-laughing-gunman-who-shot-85-young-victims-one-by-one.html (date accessed 18.12.11).

Ministry of Justice (2012) *Prison Population Projection 2012–2018 in England & Wales*, http://www.justice.gov.uk/statistics/prisons-and-pop (date accessed 12.3.13).

Mirrlees-Black, C., Budd, T., Partridge, S. & Mayhew, P. (1998) The 1998 British Crime Survey: England & Wales. Home Office online report 21/98, www.

nationalarchives.gov.uk/ERORecords/HO/421/2P2/RDS/PDFS/HOSB2198.PDF (date accessed 5.7.13).

Moffat, S. & Fitzgerald, J. (2006) 'The Relationship between Petrol Theft and Petrol Prices', *Crime & Justice Bulletin* 101, 1–6.

Monahan, T. & Palmer, N.A. (2009) *The Emerging Politics of DHS Fusion Centres*, Security Dialogue, 40, 617–636.

Monbiot, G. (2012) Yes lead poisoning could really be a cause of violent crime, http://www.guardian.co.uk/commentisfree/2013/jan/07/violent-crime-lead-poisoning-british-export (date accessed 20.12.13).

Moore, M.H. (1990) 'Police Leadership: The Impossible Dream?' in Hargrove & Glidewell, J. (eds), *Impossible Jobs in Public Management* (Kansas: University Press).

Moore, M.H. & Braga, A.A. (2003) 'Measuring and Improving police performance: The lessons of compstat and its progeny', *Policing: An International Journal of Police Strategies and Management*, 26(3), 439–453.

Moss, K. (2009) Security and Liberty: Restriction by Stealth, Basingstoke: Palgrave MacMillan.

Moynah, M. & Worsley, R. (2000) *Tomorrow* (London: A & C Black Publishers Ltd).

Mueller, J. & Stewart, M.G. (2011) *Terror, Security and Money: Balancing the Risks, Benefits and Costs of Homeland Security* (New York: Oxford University Press).

Mullins, S., Alison, L. & Crego, J. (2008) 'Towards a Taxonomy of Police Decision Making in Murder Enquiries', in Alison, L. & Crego, J. (eds), *Policing Critical Incidents: Leadership and Critical Incident Management* (Cullompton: Willan).

Murray, J. (2005) 'Policing terrorism: A threat to community policing or just a shift in priorities?' *Police Practice and Research*, 6(4), 347–361.

Myhill, A. & Beak, K. (2008) *Public Confidence in the Police* (London: NPIA).

Myhill, A. & Quinton, P. (2011) *It's a Fair Cop? Police Legitimacy, Public Cooperation and Crime Reduction: An Interpretive Evidence Commentary* (Wyboston: NPIA).

Nas, J. (2012) Interview conducted on the 13.11.12 (Utrecht, NL).

National Research Council (NRC) (2004) 'Fairness and Effectiveness in Policing. The Evidence Committee to Review Research on Police Policy and Practices', in Skogan, W. & Frydl, K. (eds), *Committee on Law and Justice, Division of Behavioural and Social Sciences and Education* (Washington DC: The National Academies Press).

National Commission on Terrorist attacks in US report (2004) Retrieved from http://www.9-11commission.gov (date accessed 7.7.13).

National Research Council of the National Academies (2010) *Review of the Department of Homeland Security's Approach to Risk Analysis* (Washington, DC: National Academies Press).

NCIS (2000) *The National Intelligence Model* (London: National Criminal Intelligence Service).

NCIS (2005) UK Threat Assessment Report (para 1.1) (London: HMSO).

NCPE (2005) *Professionalising Investigation Programme Information Pack* (Wyboston: NCPE).

Newman, O. (1972) *Defensible Space: Crime Prevention through Urban Design* (New York: Collier).

Newburn, T. (2007) *Criminology* (Cullompton: Willan).

Newburn, T. & Reiner, R. (2007) 'Policing and the Police', in Maguire, M., Morgan, R. & Reiner, R. (eds), *The Oxford Handbook of Criminology*, 4th edn (Oxford: Oxford University Press).

Neyroud, P. & Beckley, A. (2001) *Policing, Ethics and Human Rights* (Cullompton: Willan).

Nicol, C., Innes, M., Gee, D. & Feist, A. (2004) *Reviewing Murder Investigations: An Analysis of Progress Reviews from Six Police Forces* (London: Home Office).

Nisbett, R.E. & Ross, L. (1980) *Human Inference: Strategies and Shortcomings of Social Judgement* (Englewood Cliffs, NJ: Prentice Hall).

Noaks, L. & Wincup, E. (2009) *Criminological Research: Understanding Qualitative Methods*, 2nd edn (London: Sage Publishing).

Northouse, P. (2007) *Leadership: Theory and Practice*, 4th edn (London: Sage).

NPIA (2007) *Critical Incident Management*, http://www.npia.police.uk/en/docs/Critical_Incident_Management_PA_2007.pdf (date accessed 4.5.12).

Obeng, E. (1996) *All Change: The Project Leader's Secret Handbook* (Financial Times: Prentice Hall).

O'Connor, Sir D. (2012) *Valedictory lecture – "The importance of a plan to win"*, Presented at the Policy Exchange, 11 September 2012.

Ormerod, D. & Sturman, J. (2005) 'Working with the Courts: Advice for Expert Witnesses', in Alsion, L. (ed.) *The Forensic Psychologists Casebook: Psychological Profiling and Criminal Investigation* (Cullompton: Willan Publishing).

PA Consulting (2001) 'Diary of a Police Officer', *Home Office Police Research Series Paper 149* (London: Home Office).

Palmer, S.H. (1988) *Police and Protest in England and Ireland 1780–1850* (USA: Cambridge University Press).

Pantazis, C. & Pemberton, S. (2009) 'From the "old" to the "new" suspect community: Examining the impacts of recent UK counter-terrorist legislation', *The British Journal of Criminology*, 49(5), 646–666.

Pantazis, C. & Pemberton, S. (2011) 'Re-stating the Case for the Suspect Community: a reply to Greer'. *British Journal of Criminology*.

Paoli, L. (2002) 'The paradoxes of organized crime', *Crime, Law and Social Change*, 37(1), 51–97.

Pareto, (2012) Vilfredo in Britannica, http://www.britannica.com/EBchecked/topic/443519/Vilfredo-Pareto (date accessed 23.3.12).

Parmar, A. (2011) 'Stop search in London: Counter terrorist or counter productive?' *Policing & Society*, 21(4), 369–382.

Patton, M.Q. (2002) Qualitative Research and Evaluation Methods, Thousand Oaks: Sage.

Pawson, R. & Tilley, N. (1997) *Realistic Evaluation* (London: Sage).

Pearson, G. (1983) *Hooligan: A History of Respectable Fears* (Basingstoke: Macmillan).

Pease, K. (2009) Foreword in Moss, K. Security and Liberty: Restriction by Stealth, Basingstoke: Palgrave MacMillan.

Pekkanen, P. & Niemi, P. (2012) 'Process performance improvement in justice organizations – Pitfalls of performance measurement', *International Journal of Production Economics*, http://dx.doi.org/10.1016/j.ijpe.2012.08.009.

Penna, S. & Kirby, S. (2012) Bridge Over the River Crime: Mobility and the Policing of Organised Crime. Mobilities, advanced access: DOI:10.1080/17450101.2012.705508. pp. 1–19.

Peters, T. & Waterman, R. (1982) *In Search of Excellence* (New York: Harper and Row).

Petersilia, J., Abrahamsen, A. & Wilson, J.Q. (1987) *Police Performance and Case Attrition* (Washington: National Institute of Justice).
Porter, S., Yuille, J.C. & Lehman, D. (1999) 'The Nature of Real, Implanted, and Fabricated Memories for Emotional Childhood Events: Implications for the Recovered Memory Debate', *Law and Human Behavior*, 23, 517–538.
Posen, I. (1995) *Review of Police Core and Ancillary Tasks* (London: HMSO).
Povey, D. Mulchandani, R., Hand, T. & Panesar, L.K. (2011) *Police Powers and Procedures in England and Wales 2009/10* (London: Home Office).
Prenzler, T. (ed.) (2012) *Policing and Security in Practice: Challenges and Achievements* (Basingstoke: Palgrave Macmillan).
Presage Group (2012) *Human Error*, http://presagegroup.com/human-error/ (date accessed 26.9.12).
Preti, A. (2008) 'School shooting as a culturally enforced way of expressing suicidal hostile intentions', *The Journal of the American Academy of Psychiatry and The Law*, 36, 544–550.
Prime, J., White, S., Liriano, S. & Patel, K. (2001) Criminal Careers of Those Born Between 1953 and 1978. London: Home Office.
Punch, M. & Taylor, T. (1973) 'The Police: A Social Service', *New Society*, 17(554), 358–361.
Ratcliffe, J. (2008) *Intelligence-Led Policing* (Cullompton: Willan Publishing).
Rawley, A. & Caddy, B. (2007) *Damilola Taylor: An Independent Review of Forensic Examination of Evidence by the Forensic Service* (London: Home Office).
Rawlings, P. (2002) *Policing: A Short History* (Cullompton: Willan).
Read, T. & Tilley, N. (2000) 'Not Rocket Science? Problem Solving and Crime Reduction', *Crime Reduction Series Paper 6* (London: Home Office Research, Development and Statistics Directorate).
Reason, J. (1990) *Human Error* (New York: Cambridge University Press).
Redekop, V. & Pare, S. (2010) *Beyond Control: A Mutual Respect Approach to Protest Crowd–Police Relations* (London: Bloomsbury Academic).
Reece-Smith, R. & Kirby, S. (2013) 'Exploring the VLI, for identifying priority neighbourhoods, in the context of multi-agency community safety initiatives', *Policing*, 7(1), 42–52.
Reicher, S. (2011) 'From Crisis to Opportunity: New Crowd Psychology and Public Order Policing Principles', in Madensen, T. & Knutsson (eds), *Preventing Crowd Violence* (London: Lynne Rienner).
Reiner, R. (1992) *The Politics of the Police*, New Jersey: Prentice Hall.
Reiner, R. (2000) *The Politics of the Police*, 3rd edn (Oxford: Oxford University Press).
Reisig, M. (2007) 'Procedural justice and community policing: What shapes residents' willingness to participate in crime prevention programs?' *Policing: A Journal of Policy and Practice*, 1(3), 356–369.
Reisig, M. & Lloyd, C. (2009) 'Procedural justice, police legitimacy, and helping the police fight crime', *Police Quarterly*, 12(1), 42–62.
Reith, C. (1956) *A New Study of Police History* (Great Britain: Cunningham and Sons).
Repetto, T. (1976) 'Crime Prevention and the Displacement Phenomenon', *Crime & Delinquency*, 22, 166–177.
Reza, B. & Magill, C. (2006) *Section 95 and the Criminal Justice Act 1991. Race and the Criminal Justice System: An Overview to the Complete Statistics 2004–2005*, Criminal Justice System Race Unit.

Richardson, L. (2006) *What Terrorists Want: Understanding the Terrorist Threat* (London: John Murray).
Riots Communities and Victims Panel (2012) *After the Riots* (London: RCVP).
ROSPA (2012) How many people are killed on Britain's roads? http://www.rospa.com/faqs/detail.aspx?faq=296.
Roberts, L.D. & Indermaur, D.W. (2009) 'What Australians Think About Crime and Justice: Results from the 2007 Australian Survey of Social Attitudes', *Research and Public Policy Series* (Canberra: Australian Institute of Criminology).
Robinson, C.D., Scaglion, R. & Olivero, J.M. (1994) 'Police in Contradiction: The Evolution of The Police Function in Society', Westport, Connecticut: Greenwood Press, as cited in Johnson, L. *Policing in Britain: Risk, Security and Governance* (London: Longman).
Romaniuk, P. (2010) *Multilateral Counter-Terrorism: The Global Politics of Cooperation and Contestation* (New York, NY: Routledge).
Roosevelt, T (1894) 'Citizenship in a Republic', Speech at the Sorbonne, Paris, April 23, 1910 cited by the Theodore Roosevelt Association, http://www.theodoreroosevelt.org/life/quotes.htm (date accessed 13.7.12).
Rosenbaum, D.P. (1986) *Community Crime Prevention: Does It work?* (Beverley Hills, CA: Sage Publications).
Rosenbaum, D.P., Lewis, D.A. & Grant, J.A. (1986) 'Neighbourhood-Based Crime Prevention: Assessing the Efficacy of Community Organizing in Chicago', in Rosenbaum, D. (ed.) *Community Crime Prevention: Does It work?* (London: Sage).
Rowe, M. (2008) *Introduction to Policing* (London: Sage).
Sageman, M. (2008) *Leaderless Jihad* (Philadelphia: University of Pennsylvania Press).
Salfati, C. G., Petee, T. & Field, J. L. (2006, November) *Serial and spree homicide: Different crimes or all serial crimes?* Presentation at American Society of Criminology Conference, Los Angeles, USA.
Sampson, R., Raudenbush, S., & Earls, F. (1997) 'Neighborhoods and violent crime: A multilevel study of collective efficacy', *Science, 277*, 918–924.
Sampson, R.J. (2004) 'Neighbourhood and Community: Collective Efficacy and Community Safety', *New Economy*, 11, 106–113.
Sampson, R.J. (2006) Collective Efficacy Theory: Lessons learnt and directions for future inquiry, in Cullen, F.T., Write, J.P., & Bevins, K.R. (eds) Taking stock: The status of criminological theory, 15, 149–186, New Brunswick, NJ: Transaction Publishers.
Sampson, R.J. & Byron Groves, W. (1989) 'Community structure and crime: Testing social disorganization theory', *American Journal of Sociology*, 94, 774–802.
Sampson, R.J. & Raudenbush, S.W. (1999) 'Systematic social observation of public spaces: A new look at disorder and crime', *American Journal of Sociology*, 105, 603–651.
Sanders, B.A. (2008) 'Using personality traits to predict police officer performance', *International Journal of Police Strategies and Management*, 31(1), 129–147.
Sandler, T., Arce, D.G. & Enders, W. (2008) *Transnational Terrorism*, Paper presented to the Copenhagen Concensus Center initiative. www.copenhagenconsensus.com (date accessed 8.9.12).
Sarre, R. (1991) 'Community Policing: Success or Failure? Exploring Different Models of Evaluation' in Sandra McKillop and Julia Vernon (eds) *Proceedings of*

The Community and the Police Conference (Australian Institute of Criminology Conference Proceedings No. 5), pp. 75–82 (Canberra: AIC).

Savage, S.P. (2007) *Police Reform: Forces for Change* (Oxford: Oxford University Press).

Savolainen, J. (2005) 'Think nationally, act locally: The municipal-level effects of the national crime prevention program in Finland', *European Journal on Criminal Policy and Research*, 11, 175–191.

Sced, M. (2004) *Public Satisfaction with Police Contact – Part 1, Police Initiated Contacts*. Australian Centre for Policing Research.

Schafer, J.A. & Mastrofski, S.D. (2005) 'Police leniency in traffic enforcement encounters: exploratory findings from observations and interviews', *Journal of Criminal Justice*, 33(3), 225–238.

Scheider & Thurman, Q. (2002) 'Funding Community Policing to Reduce Crime: Have COPS Grants Made a Difference?' *Criminology and Public Policy*, 2, 7–32.

Schein, E. (1992) *Organisational Culture and Leadership*, 2nd edn (San Francisco: Jossey-Bass).

Schutt, R. (2006) *Investigating the Social World: The Process and Practice of Research*, 5th edn (Thousand Oaks, CA: Sage).

Scott, M.S. & Kirby, S. (2012) *Implementing POP: Leading, Structuring, and Managing a Problem-Oriented Police Agency* (Washington: US Department of Justice).

Scott, M.S. (2007) 'Shifting and Sharing Police Responsibility to Address Public Safety Problems', in Tilley, N. (ed.), *Handbook of Crime Prevention and Community Safety* (Cullompton: Willan Publishing).

Scott, M.S. (2010) Evaluating the effectiveness of problem-oriented policing, *Criminology & Public policy*, 9(1), 135–139.

Seddon, J. (2008) *Systems Thinking in the Public Sector* (Axminster: Triarchy Press).

Seng, J.S. (1998) 'Praxis as a conceptual framework for participatory research in nursing', *Advance Nurse Science*, 20(4), 37–48.

Shane, J.M. (2010) 'Organizational stressors and police performance', *Journal of Criminal Justice*, 38, 807–818.

Shapiro, J. (1982) 'Evaluation as theory testing: An example from head start', *Situational Evaluation and Policy Analysis*, 7(1), 341–353.

Shapland, J. & Vagg, J. (1988) *Policing by the Public* (London: Tavistock).

Shappell, S. & Wiegmann, D. (2000) *The Human Factors Analysis and Classification System (HFACS)* (Report No. DOT/FAA/AM-00/7), Washington DC: Federal Aviation Administration.

Shappell, S. & Wiegmann, D. (2001) 'Applying reason: The Human Factors Analysis and Classification System (HFACS)', *Human Factors and Aerospace Safety*, 1(1), 59–86.

Shappell, S. & Wiegmann, D. (2004) HFACS Analysis of Military and Civilian Aviation Accidents: A North American Comparison, Paper presented for ISASI. Asasi.org/papers/2004/Shappell%20et%2Oal_HFACS_ISASI04.pdf (date accessed 2.9.12).

Sharf, D. & Binder, A. (1983) 'The Badge and the Bullet: Police Use of Deadly Force' cited by Buttle, J.W. 'Officer Safety and Public Safety: Training the Police to Use Force in the UK', in Kuhns, J.B. & Knutsson, J. (2010) *Police Use of Force: A Global Perspective* (Santa Barbara: Praeger).

Shaw, C. & McKay, M. (1942) *Juvenile Delinquency and Urban Areas* (Chicago: University of Chicago Press).

Sheehan, M.A. (2008) *Crush the Cell: How to Defeat Terrorism without Terrorizing Ourselves* (New York: Crown).

Sherman, L.W. (1998) *Ideas in American Policing: Evidence-Based Policing* (Washington: Police Foundation).

Sherman, L.W. (1995) 'The Police', in Wilson, J.Q. & Petersilia, J. (eds), *Crime* (Oakland, CA: ICS Press).

Sherman, L.W. (1997) 'Policing for Crime Prevention', in Sherman, L.W. Gottfredson, D., MacKenzie, D., Eck, J., Reuter, P. & Bushway, S. (eds), *Preventing Crime: What Works, What Doesn't, What's Promising* (Washington DC: National Institute of Justice, US Department of Justice).

Sherman, L.W., Farrington, D.P., Welsh, B.C., & MacKenzie, D.L. (eds) (2002) *Evidence-Based Crime Prevention* (New York: Routledge).

Sherman, L.W. Gottfredson, D., MacKenzie, D., Eck, J., Reuter, P. & Bushway, S. (eds), (2007) *Preventing crime: What works, what doesn't, what's promising* (Washington DC: National Institute of Justice, US Department of Justice).

Sherman, L.W. & Weisburd, D. (1995) 'General Deterrent Effects of Police Patrol in Crime 'Hot Spots': A Randomized, Controlled Trial', *Justice Quarterly*, 12, 623–648.

Sherman, L.W., Farrington, D.P., Welsh, B. and MacKenzie, D. (2002) (eds), Evidence-Based Crime Prevention (Routledge: London).

Sidebottom, A., Belur, J., Bowers, K., Tompson, L. & Johnson, S.D. (2011) 'Theft in price volatile markets: On the relationship between copper price and copper theft', *Journal of Research in Crime and Delinquency*, 48(3), 396–418.

Sidebottom, A., Tilley, N. & Eck, J. (2012) 'Towards checklists to reduce common sources of problem-solving failure', *Policing*, 6 (2), 194–209.

Silke, A. (2004) 'The Road Less Travelled: Recent Trends in Terrorism Research', in Silke, A. (ed.) *Research on Terrorism Trends, Achievements and Failures* (London: Frank Cass).

Silvestri, M. (2007) 'Doing police leadership: Enter the new smart macho', *Policing and Society*, 17(1), 38–58.

Simmons, J. & Dodd, T. (eds) (2003) *Crime in England and Wales 2002/03*, Home Office Statistical Bulletin 07/03 (London: Home Office).

Simms, P. (2010) *Rapist Policeman Who Attacked 30 Women During Five-Year Reign Is Finally Behind Bars*, http://www.dailymail.co.uk/news/article-1332707/Rapist-PC-Stephen-Mitchell-jailed-attacking-30-women-5-years.html (date accessed 6.2.13).

Skogan, W. (2006) 'The Promise of Community Policing', in Weisburd, D. & Braga, A.A. (eds), *Police Innovation: Contrasting Perspectives* (Cambridge: Cambridge University Press).

Skogan, W. & Hartnett, S. (1997) *Community Policing, Chicago Style* (New York: Oxford University Press).

Skogan, W.G. (1998) Community Policing in Chicago, in Alpert, G.P. & Piquero, A. (eds) *Community Policing: Contemporary Readings*, Prospect Heights, IL: Waveland Press.

Skogan, W.G. (2005) 'Citizen satisfaction with police encounters' *Police Quarterly*, 8(3), 298–301.

Skogan, W.G. & Frydl, K. (2004) Fairness and effectiveness in policing: The evidence, Washington, DC: The National Academies Press.

Skolnick, J. (1996) *Justice without Trial* (New York: Wiley).

Sloan, S. (1978) The anatomy of Non-territorial terrorism: An analytical essay, Gaithersburg: International Association of Chiefs of Police.

Sloan, J.H., Kellermann, A.L., Reay, D., Ferris, J.A., Koepsell, T.D., Rivara, F.P., Rice, C., Gray, L., and LoGerfo, J. (1988) Handgun regulations, crime, assaults, and homicide. NEJM, 319(19), 1256–1262.

Sluka, J. (1989) Hearts and Minds, Water and Fish: Support for the IRA and INLA in a Northern Ireland Ghetto (Connecticut: JAI Press).

Small Arms Survey (2011) *Small Arms Survey: States of Security*, http://www.smal larms survey.org/publications/bytypre/yearbook/small-arms-survey-2011.html (date accessed 02.8.12).

Smelser, N. (2007) *The Faces of Terrorism: Social and Psychological Dimensions* (Princeton, NJ: Princeton University Press).

Smith, D.C. (1980) Paragons, Pariahs, and Pirates: A Spectrum-Based Theory of Enterprise, Crime & Delinquency, 26(3), 358–386.

Smith, Dame J. (2003) *The Shipman Inquiry, Second Report: The Police Investigation of March 1988* (London: HMSO).

SOCA (2006) *The United Kingdom Threat Assessment of Serious Organised Crime 2006/07* (London: Serious Organised Crime Agency).

Southgate, P. (1983) *Police-Public Encounters*, H.O. Research Study, 90 (London: HMSO).

Sparrow, M.K. (2008) *The Character of Harms* (Cambridge: Cambridge University Press).

Stelfox, P. (2009) *Criminal Investigation: An Introduction to Principles and Practice* (Cullompton: Willan Publishing).

Stott, C. (2011) 'Crowd Dynamics and Public Order Policing', in Madensen, Y. & Knutsson, J. (eds), *Preventing Crowd Violence* (Colorado: Lynne Rienner Publishers).

Sunstein, C.R. (2005) *Laws of Fear: Beyond the Precautionary Principle* (New York: Cambridge University Press).

Taylor, B., Koper, C. & Woods, D. (2010) 'A Randomized controlled trial of different policing strategies at hot spots of violent crime', *Journal of Experimental Criminology*, 7(2), 149–181.

Taylor, C. (2007) *Unreasonable Force* (Glasgow: Unbound Press).

Terrill, W. & Paoline, E.A. III (2010) 'Non-lethal Force by Police in the United States: The Various Lenses through Which Appropriateness Is Examined', in Kuhns, J.B. & Knutsson, J. (eds), *Police Use of Force: A Global Perspective* (Santa Barbara: Praeger).

Thaler, R. & Sunstein, C.R. (2008) Nudge: Improving decisions about health, wealth, and happiness (New Haven: Yale University Press).

The Telegraph (2012) Police Officer Simon Harwood cleared of killing Ian Tomlinson, http://www.telegraph.co.uk/news/uknews/9412232/Police-officer-Simon-Harwood-cleared-of-killing-Ian-Tomlinson.html (date accessed 20.2.13).

Thompson, E.P. (1964) *The Making of the English Working Class* (London. Gollancz).

Thomson, J.A. (2007) '*DHS AWOL?: Tough Questions about Homeland Security Have Gone Missing*' (Spring 2007) 31, RAND Review, 30.

Tilley, N. (1993a) *After Kirkholt: Theory, Method and Results of Replication Evaluations*, Crime Reduction Unit Paper 47 (London: Home Office).

Tilley, N. (2003) 'Community Policing, Problem Oriented Policing and Intelligence Led Policing', in T. Newburn (ed.), *Handbook of Policing* (Cullompton: Willan Publishing).

Tilley, N. (2006) 'Knowing and Doing: Guidance and Good Practice in Crime Prevention', in Knutsson, J. & Clarke, R. (eds), *Putting Theory to Work: Implementing Situational Prevention and Problem-Oriented Policing*. Crime Prevention Studies, 20 (Monsey, NY: Criminal Justice Press).

Tilley, N. (2008) 'Modern Approaches to Policing: Community, Problem-Oriented and Intelligence Led', in Newburn, T. (ed.) *The Handbook of Policing*, 2nd edn (Devon: Willan Publishing).

Tilley, N. (2009) *Crime Prevention* (Cullompton: Willan Publishing).

Tilley, N. (2010) 'Whither problem-oriented policing', *Criminology & Public Policy*, 9(1), 183–195.

Tilley, N. & Laycock, G. (2002) *Working Out What to Do; Evidence Based Crime Reduction*, Crime Reduction Series Paper 11 (London: Home Office).

Tilley, N., Robinson, A. & Burrows, J. (2007) 'The Investigation of High-Volume Crime', in Newburn, T., Williamson, T. & Wright, A. (eds), *Handbook of Criminal Investigation* (Cullompton: Willan Publishing).

Tilley, N., Smith, J., Finer, S., Erol, R., Charles, C. & Dobby, J. (2004) 'Problem-Solving Street Crime: Practical Lessons from the Street Crime Initiative'. Home Office Research Report, http://www.homeoffice.gov.uk/rds/streetcrime_04.html (date accessed 10.8.12).

Tong, S., Bryant, R.P., & Horvath, M.A.H. (2009) *Understanding Criminal Investigation* (Chichester: John Wiley & Sons Ltd).

Topp, B.W. & Kardash, C.A. (1986) 'Personality, achievement, and attrition: Validation in a multiple-jurisdiction police academy', *Journal of Police Science and Administration*, 14(3), 234–241.

Traynor, I. (2011) *Liege attack: police find body at Belgian gunmans flat as city mourns victims*, http://www.guardian.co.uk/world/2011/dec/14/liege-attack-police-body-victims (date accessed 4.4.13).

Treverton, G.F. (2009) *Intelligence for an Age of Terror* (New York: Cambridge University Press).

Tuffin, R., Morris, J. & Poole, A. (2006) *An Evaluation of the Impact of the National Reassurance Policing Programme*, Home Office Research Study 296. (London: Home Office).

Tverskey, A. & Kahneman, D. (1974) 'Judgment under Uncertainty: Heuristics and Biases', *Science*, 185, 1124–1131.

Tyler, T.R. (1990) *Why People Obey the Law* (New Haven: Yale University Press).

Tyler, T.R. (2004) 'Enhancing Police Legitimacy', *Annals of the American Academy of Political & Social Science*, 593, 84–99.

Tyler, T.R. & Fagan, J. (2008) 'Legitimacy and Cooperation: Why do People Help the Police Fight Crime in their Communities?' *Ohio State Journal of Criminal Law*, 6, 231–275.

Tyler, T.R. & Huo, Y.J. (2002) *Trust in the Law: Encouraging Public Co-operation with the Police and Courts* (New York: Russell Sage Foundation).

Tyler, T.R., Schulhofer, S. & Huq, A.Z. (2010) Legitimacy and deterrence effects in counterterrorism policing: A study of Muslim Americans, *Law & Society Review*, 44(2), 365–402.

United Nations (2004) *United Nations Convention against Transnational Organised Crime and the Protocols Thereto* (Vienna: United Nations Office on Drug and Crime).

United Nations Convention Against Transnational Organized Crime (2000), Excerpt published in Trends in Organized Crime 6(2), 48–49.

United Nations Office on Drugs and Crime (UNODC) (2007) Cocaine trafficking in Western Africa: Situation report. Vienna: UN Office on Drugs and Crime.

UNODC (2011) *The Globalization of Crime*, www.unodc.org/documents/data-andanalysis/tocta/TOCTA_Report_2010_low_res.pdf.

Urry, J. (2007) *Mobilities* (Cambridge: Polity Press).

Van der Heijden, T. (1996) 'Measuring Organized Crime in Western Europe', in Milan, P. (ed.), *Policing in Central and Eastern Europe: Comparing First Hand Knowledge with Experience from the West* (Slovenia: College of Police and Security Studies).

Van Dijk, J.J.M., Van Kesteren, J. & Smit, P. (2007) *Criminal Victimisation in International Perspective: Key Findings from the 2004–2005 ICVS and EU ICS.* WODC Report 257 (The Hague: Boom Jurisische uitgevers).

Van Dijk, J. (1994) 'Understanding Crime Rates: On Interactions between Rational Choices of Victims and Offenders', *British Journal of Criminology*, 34, 105–121.

Van Dijk, J. (2012) *Closing the Doors*. Stockholm Prizewinners lecture. http://www.criminologysymposium.com/download/18.4dfe0028139b9a0cf4080001575/TUE13,+van+Dijk+Jan.pdf (date accessed 28.2.13).

Vick, C. (2000) Aspects of police leadership, Police research and management, Summer 2000, pp. 3–14.

van Koppen, M.V., de Poot, C.J., Kleemans, E.R. & Nieuwbeerta, P. (2010) 'Criminal Trajectories in Organized Crime', *British Journal of Criminology*, 50, 102–123.

Von Lampe, K. (2002) 'Organized Crime Research in Perspective', in van Duyne, P., von Lampe, K. & Passas, N. (eds), *Upperworld and Underworld in Cross-Border Crime* (Nijmegen: Wolf Legal Publishers).

Von Lampe, K. (2011) 'The application of the framework of situational crime prevention to "organized crime"', *Criminology & Criminal Justice*, 11(2), 145–163.

Von Lampe, K. (2012) *Definitions of Organized Crime*, www.organizedcrime. de/organizedcrime definitions.htm (date accessed 12.5.12).

Waddington, P.A.J. (1999) 'Police (canteen) subculture: An appreciation', *British Journal of Criminology*, 39(2), 286–308.

Wake, R., Simpson, C., Homes A. & Ballantyne, J. (2007) *Public Perceptions of the Police Complaints System*, IPPC Research and Statistics Series: Paper 6.

Walters, R. (1996) 'The "dream" of multi-agency crime prevention: Pitfalls in policy and practice', in Homel, R. (ed.) *The Policy and Practice of Situational Crime Prevention. Crime Prevention Studies, 5* (Monsey, NY: Criminal Justice Press).

Wandersman, A. (2009) 'Four Keys to Success (Theory, Implementation, Evaluation and Resources/System Support): High Hopes and Challenges in Participation', *American Journal of Community Psychology*, 43(1–2), 3–21.

Wandersman, A., Goodman, R.M. & Bullerfoss, F.D. (2005) 'Understanding Coalitions and How They Operate', in Minkler, M. (ed.), *Community Organizing and Community Building for Health* (New Brunswick, NJ: Rutgers University Press).

Warner & Pierce (1993) 'Reexamining social disorganization theory using calls to the police as a measure of crime', *Criminology*, 31(4), 493–517.

Weatheritt, M. (1986) *Innovations in Policing,* (Beckenham: Crook Helm Ltd).

Weisburd, D. & A. Braga (eds) (2006) *Police Innovation: Contrasting Perspectives* (Cambridge: Cambridge University Press).

Weisburd, D., Mastrofski, S.D. McNally, A.M. Greenspan, R. & Willis, J. (2003) 'Reforming to preserve: Compstat and strategic problem solving', *Criminology and Public Policy*, 2(3), 421–456.

Weisburd, D., McElroy, J. & Handyman, P. (1988) 'Challenges to Supervision in Community Policing: Observing on a Pilot Project', *American Journal of Police*, 7, 29–50.

Weisburd, D., Telup, C.W., Hinkle, J.C., & Eck, J.E. (2010) 'Is problem oriented policing effective in reducing crime and disorder? Findings from a Campbell Systematic Review', *Criminology & Public Policy*, 9(1), 139–172.

Wells, G. & Olson, E. (2003) *Eyewitness Testimony*, Annual Review of Psychology, 54, pp. 277–95, doi: 10.1146/annurev.psych.54.101601.145028.

Wells, W. (2007) 'Type of contact and evaluations of police officers: The effects of procedural justice across three types of police-citizen contacts', *Journal of Criminal Justice*, 35(6), 612–621.

Westmarland, L. (2013) *Police Integrity Feedback Report*, Open University http://www3.open.ac.uk/media/fullstory.aspx?id=24990 (date accessed 2.4.13).

Whitfield, K., Alison, L. & Crego, J (2008) 'Command, Control and Support in Critical Incidents', in Alison, L. & Crego, J. (eds), *Policing Critical Incidents: Leadership and Critical Incident Management* (Cullompton: Willan).

Wiegmann, D. & Shappell, S. (2003) *A Human Error Approach to Aviation Accident Analysis: The Human Factors Analysis and Classification System* (Aldershot, Great Britain: Ashgate Publishing Company).

Wiktorowicz, Q. (2005), *Radical Islam Rising: Muslim Extremism in the West*, Lanham: Rowman and Littlefield.

Wiles, P. & Costello, A. (2000) *The 'Road to Nowhere': The Evidence for Travelling Criminals*, Home Office Research Study 207 (London: Home Office).

Willis, J.J. & Mastrofski, S.D. (2012) 'Compstat and the new penology: A paradigm shift in policing?' *British Journal of Criminology*, 52(1), 73–92.

Willis, J.J., Mastrofski, S.D., & Weisburd, D. (2004) CompStat and bureaucracy: A case study of challenges and opportunities for change. *Justice Quarterly*, 21 (3), 463–496.

Wilson, J.Q. (1968) *Varieties of Police Behaviour* (Cambridge, MA: Harvard University Press).

Wilson, L. & Stevens, A. (2008) *Understanding Drugs Markets and How to Influence Them* (Oxford: The Beckley Foundation Drug Policy Programme).

Wolfgang, M., Figlio, R.M. & Sellin, T. (1972) *Delinquency in a Birth Cohort* (Chicago: University of Chicago Press).Woodworth, M. & Porter, S. (1999) 'Historical Foundations and Current Applications of Criminal Profiling in Violent Crime Investigations', *Expert Advice*, 7, 241–264.

Wright, A. (2002) *Policing: An Introduction to Concepts and Practice* (Cullompton: Willan Publishing).

Wright, A. (2006) *Organized Crime* (Cullompton: Willan).

Wright, A. (2007) 'Ethics and Corruption', in Newburn, T., Williamson, T. & Wright, A. (eds) *Handbook of Criminal Investigation* (Cullompton: Willan).

Wright, S. (2008) *Milly: The Litany of Police Mistakes which let her Murderer Escape*, Mail on Line 26.2.08, http://www.dailymail.co.uk/news/article-518673/Milly-The-litany-police-mistakes-let-murderer-escape-justice.html (date accessed 16.2.13).

Young, J. (1997) 'Left Realist Criminology: Radical in Its Analysis, Realist in Its Policy', in Maguire, M., Morgan, R. & Reiner, R. (eds), *The Oxford Handbook of Criminology*, 2nd edn (Oxford: Oxford University Press).

Young, J. (2003) 'Winning the Fight Against Crime? New Labour, Populism and Lost Opportunities', in Young, J. & Matthews, R. (eds), *The New Politics of Crime and Punishment* (Cullompton: Willan Publishing).

Young, J. (2007) *The Vertigo of Late Modernity* (London: Sage).

Yu, O. & Zhang, L. (1999) 'Under recording of crime by police in China: A case study', *Policing; International Journal of Police Strategies and Management*, 22(3), 252–263.

Zedner, L. (2006) 'Opportunity Makes the Thief-Taker: The Influence of Economic Analysis on Crime Control', in Newburn, T. & Rock, P. (eds), *The Politics of Crime Control* (Oxford: Clarendon Press).

Index

Printed and bound by CPI Group (UK) Ltd, Croydon, CR0 4YY

The manufacturer's authorised representative in the EU is Springer Nature Customer Service Centre GmbH, Europaplatz 3, 69115 Heidelberg, Germany. If you have any concerns regarding our products, please contact ProductSafety@springernature.com

Printed and bound by CPI Group (UK) Ltd, Croydon, CR0 4YY
14/10/2026
02233132-0005